REALISING PARTICIPATION

 CENTRE FOR HEALTH
RESEARCH
AND EVALUATION

The Centre for Health Research and Evaluation was set up within the School of Health Studies in November 1993. There are presently five full-time equivalent research staff working at the Centre.

The main aims of the Centre are to:
- Provide a focus for interdisciplinary research and scholarship in the School of Health Studies;
- Provide independent research and consultancy services in health and social care services research and evaluation;
- Develop research partnerships within health and social care purchasers and providers;
- Act as a resource for non-medical health services research and evaluation;
- Support the development of evidence-based health care;
- Provide training in health studies research design and methodology and data analysis;
- Support a doctoral programme in nursing and health services research.

Under its Director, Dr Tom Chapman, the Centre has been successful in generating external funding for research and consultancy projects. The current focus of the Centre's research interests revolves around intermediate care services; those services aimed at or meeting the needs of people who are physically stable but who could improve the quality of their lives, increasing their ability to live independently through timely intensive therapeutic intervention. These services can be provided in a range of settings spanning the continuum from hospital to home.

Centre for Health Research and Evaluation
School of Health Studies, Edge Hill
Accredited by the University of Lancaster

Realising Participation

Elderly people as active users of health and social care

KATHRYN ROBERTS
TOM CHAPMAN

Routledge
Taylor & Francis Group

LONDON AND NEW YORK

First published 2001 by Ashgate Publishing

Reissued 2018 by Routledge
2 Park Square, Milton Park, Abingdon, Oxon OX14 4RN
711 Third Avenue, New York, NY 10017, USA

Routledge is an imprint of the Taylor & Francis Group, an informa business

Publisher's Note
The publisher has gone to great lengths to ensure the quality of this reprint but points out that some imperfections in the original copies may be apparent.

Disclaimer
The publisher has made every effort to trace copyright holders and welcomes correspondence from those they have been unable to contact.

A Library of Congress record exists under LC control number: 2001095877

ISBN 13: 978-1-138-70313-1 (hbk)
ISBN 13: 978-1-138-63104-5 (pbk)
ISBN 13: 978-1-315-20336-2 (ebk)

Contents

List of Figures

List of Tables

ix

Preface

This study is one of a series of reports into the organisation and delivery of health and social care carried out by researchers at the *Centre for Health Research and Evaluation* based at Edge Hill, a university sector college in West Lancashire.

The first research report, published by Avebury in 1995, was one of the first large scale health and social care audits carried out in the UK exploring the needs of elderly people (Chapman and Johnson, 1995). The study was funded by the North West Regional Health Authority and was an attempt to sample, under the Department of Health's 'Local Voices Initiative', the views of the public, health and social care professionals, and local service users on aspect of health and social care.

The population sampled (n=760) was an almost exact match of the age profile of the England and Wales population, by age and sex, and enabled the study to become a useful planning and purchasing tool for health authorities and local authorities nation-wide.

It became clear during this study that an interesting dynamic was at work within the population sampled (people aged 65 and over). Many were content to simply avail themselves of local services, seemingly accepting what was provided, or what was not provided, without much question. A vocal minority, however, adopted a more participative and critical attitude. They sought to behave as 'consumers' who believed that they had 'rights', and were exercised to use them.

The present study explored the interesting dynamic of 'consumerism' or 'public participation' in health and social care. It is primarily concerned to establish some empirical evidence to affirm or disconfirm that a major shift in public involvement in welfare is indeed taking place, reflecting the very considerable rhetoric woven into a new millennium.

Abstract

This study investigated the utilisation of health and social care services by a sample of people aged 70 years and above on discharge from inpatient care and in the short period afterwards. We were concerned to explore how *active* users were during this process with reference to the principles of *participation, representation, access, choice, information* and *redress*. Two essential elements explored were the extent to which real opportunities were being provided for users to play an active role and their ability and willingness to assume such a role.

It was hypothesised in this study that elderly people (defined as 70 years and over) are the most 'critical' age group for testing whether the rhetoric of consumerism and public participation is indeed a powerful force in determining and shaping the delivery and uptake of health and social care. It is argued that if the realisation of participation can be demonstrated within this age group, assumed to be least likely to manifest shifts in values and norms, then it can feasibly be extrapolated to the wider population.

Both qualitative and quantitative methodologies were utilised in order to provide sufficient breadth and depth to the investigation. Questionnaire and semi-structured interview data was collected from samples of service users (n=260 and n=30 respectively) regarding *experience* and *behaviour* in assuming an active role whilst their *attitude* towards doing so was only available from interview data. Semi-structured interviews were employed with health and social care professionals (n=21) to ascertain both *experience* and *views* regarding service users assuming an active role.

This study revealed substantial evidence of a user-oriented approach to the delivery of welfare. It also demonstrated however that a number of areas remain in which it does not appear practicable to give priority to the wishes of service user or for them to play an active role in their care. Some of the principles explored appeared both more straightforward to implement in practice and more readily embraced by service users than others. On defining sub-groups of the sample of service users for experience and behaviour, general social inequality in terms of gender and socio-economic grouping was reflected. It was also revealed how respondents with limited social support and a negative self-reported health status were least able and willing to assume an active role.

Acknowledgements

On any research project of this scale a debt is owed to literally hundreds of people for helping to build up a picture of how things are. We are sincerely grateful to the many ex-patients and health and social care professionals who allocated time to help us with our inquiries.

Our special thanks to Jenifer Ormrod who helped with manuscript production.

1 Introduction

Rationale

The far-reaching changes to the delivery of welfare underpinned by the rhetoric and underlying philosophy of successive Conservative administrations between 1979 and 1997, and the New Labour government from May 1997, provide the rationale for this research. Policy implemented prior to 1997 introduced private sector mechanisms and values into the welfare services and indeed the wider public sector (McCarthy, 1989; Farnham and Horton, 1993; Kirkpatrick and Lucio, 1995) with the twin aims of reducing the role of the state and increasing efficiency. Emphasis was given to the introduction of competition into the provision of services along with other market-oriented principles with the ostensible aims of improving quality and 'getting closer to the service user'. In terms of welfare provision, this was particularly apparent in the post-1989 period when, prominent amongst the rhetoric, were references to how the position of the service user would be enhanced (for example, Department of Health, 1989a; Department of Health, 1989b; Department of Health, 1991; NHS Management Executive, 1992; Department of Health, 1994b). This was both in terms of service provision becoming more responsive to users and in the provision of opportunities for service users to assume an active role. It is against this policy framework (analysed in Chapter 3) that the present study took place.

Whilst the new Labour government aims to eliminate market-oriented bureaucracy in the provision of welfare, the principles that services should be responsive and accessible to those who seek to use them remain of paramount importance (Department of Health, 1997a; NHS Executive, 1997; The Labour Party, 1997).

Indeed, it is very evident in official policy documents published since New Labour assumed power in May 1997 that patient empowerment and patient participation have become important principles designed, amongst others, to foster a radical change in the relationship between service users and health and social care professionals. Following the publication of the NHS National Plan (July 2000) Julian Neuberger, the Chief Executive of the King's Fund, claimed that 'For the first time in its 52 year history, patients have been put at the heart of the NHS . . . The NHS now has a clear statement of values for the 21st Century to reinforce its 1948 founding values. By bringing patients into all parts of the NHS, the National Plan should ensure that they have a much greater say in how the service is run, and in how care is provided' (King's Fund press release, 27 July 2000).

In December 2000 The Health and Social Care Bill reinforced the message that 'patients are a the heart of a modern NHS'. For the first time, the NHS has a duty to consult with and involve the public on the planning and delivery of local health services, with mechanisms placing patients and public in the driving seat.

This study took place between 1996 and 1998. It's findings provide evidence of the extent to which one segment of the public are ready to respond to the government's invitation to place themselves in the driving seat. It is also a critical test of the extent to which the Conservative 'reforms' in the 1990's which claimed to introduce 'consumerism' into welfare have changed perceptions and practices on the part of both the providers and usersof services. The study is a search for hard evidence.

Scope of Investigation

This research investigates the utilisation of health and social care services by a defined sector of the population, with particular reference to how *active* users are in this process. The concept of *participation* which is central to this investigation; is a fairly wide-ranging term that can incorporate a number of activities (see Chapter 2). A number of associated concepts are also explored.

The criteria upon which this study is based are *participation, representation, access, choice, information* and *redress*. These are derived from the work of Potter (1988), Barnes, Prior and Thomas (1990) and Deakin and Wright (1990). In relation to the public sector, these authors respectively perceive these criteria as necessary to shift the balance of power towards users (as relating to user control) and as necessary for the position of the user to be fully recognised and strengthened. The criteria were all addressed in official policy documents and guidance issued throughout the 1989-1997 period (see Chapter 3). These criteria are used in the empirical part of this study to analyse how far services are oriented towards users and the extent to which users are able and willing to assume an active role in the process of using health and social care.

The service users selected are a sample of people aged 70 years and above on discharge from inpatient care. The particular age group is defined as a 'critical case' (see below and Chapter 4) for this exploration of service utilisation and participation. The discharge process and the short period after is selected for investigation due to the possibility of (elderly) service users utilising both health and social care. Policy documentation during the period studied referred quite separately to the provision of care provided by the NHS and that provided by Local Authority Social Services but due to the increasingly indistinct boundaries between 'health care' and 'social care' it was necessary to consider both sectors. In addition, the possibility of respondents using care from both sectors would provide an element of comparison.

There is a diverse range of literature analysing and evaluating the reforms to the welfare state during this period, particularly focusing on specific initiatives and their implementation. This literature is drawn upon as appropriate in both formulating the analytical background to the study and in discussing the findings. The present study however is more in-depth and focused than any of this previous work as it explores a range of criteria relating to the use of both *health* and *social* care by the *individual* service user during and in the short period after hospital discharge. In addition, it seeks to explore both the *experience* and *behaviour* of elderly service users during this period from the perspective of both users themselves and also service providers.

Aims

Within the broad aim of exploring service utilisation and participation during and in the short period after hospital discharge among a sample of people aged 70 years and above, the specific aims of this research are:

1.   to explore the experience and behaviour of elderly users of health and social care services with regard to criteria indicating user influence or control (namely, *participation, representation, access, choice, information* and *redress*);

    1.1   to compare the experience of elderly service users with regard to stipulated policies for service delivery;

    1.2   to explore the ability and willingness of service users to assume an active role in the use of health and social care;

2.   to determine the experience of health and social care professionals (managers and front-line workers) regarding the introduction of user-oriented services, including the ability and willingness of elderly service users to assume an active role;

3.   to explore perceived barriers to the introduction of user-oriented health and social care services from the experience of elderly service users and health and social care professionals.

A 'Critical' Case

It is hypothesised here that elderly people (defined as 70 years and over) are the most 'critical' age group for testing whether user-oriented policies have a real and consequential role in the delivery of welfare. It is argued that elderly people are least likely to expect to 'make a difference' in their own care. They belong to a generation conditioned to being the passive recipients of decisions made on their behalf within the public services (Chapman and Johnson, 1995).

The idea of a 'critical case' was first used by Goldthorpe *et al.* (1971) in their study considering the *embourgeoisement* of the working class. They concentrated their resources on a single-case study – a *critical case* – and researched a population whose characteristics appeared *most* conducive to the shifts in values and norms being studied. This was to allow a relatively intense inquiry to take place. The rationale was to provide an opportunity to either study the phenomenon first hand or to confirm in as decisive a manner as possible doubts about its existence. If the process under study was not found to be in evidence, assumptions could then be made as to it being unlikely to occur anywhere else in society.

This study works on the opposite assumption in that the population group being studied is presumed the *least* likely to assume an active role; that is, the *least* likely group amongst which to witness the phenomena under investigation. The analysis in Chapter 4 of the social and economic circumstances of the elderly population of the United Kingdom provides a further rationale for this assumption. On this basis, if evidence is apparent of users in this age group assuming an active role, it can feasibly be extrapolated to the wider population.

Whilst the population studied are considered as a group for the purposes of sampling, every effort is taken to demonstrate the diversity of the elderly population included in this research. The analysis and discussion of the findings use various demographic, social and economic characteristics namely, gender, age group, household composition, socio-economic grouping and self-reported health status to demonstrate the heterogeneous nature of the sample. Whilst this limits the ability to draw definite conclusions, it ensures that the analysis is thorough and that no unfounded generalisations are made.

Structure of the Study

Following this *Introduction*, Chapter 2 traces the origins of 'participation' by users of public services up to 1979 to provide a historical context. It considers various definitions of 'participation', arguing this to be the most central and prominent of the six criteria explored by this study, in addition to considering ways in which increasing participation may be beneficial or advantageous. A basic overview of mechanisms for political participation is provided to acknowledge some of the most widespread general mechanisms in existence by which people can play a role in the policy process. The rest of Chapter 2 is then devoted to exploring ways in which users of public services have, since the 1960s, increasingly played an active role. This has been as a result of the changing nature and context of welfare delivery in addition to demands made by (groups of) users themselves and the implementation of official policy.

Chapter 3 is an exploration of policy documentation and guidance issued by the Department of Health under the Conservative administrations between 1979 and 1997, with an emphasis on the post-1989 period. Expressed intentions to make the delivery of health and social care user-oriented and to encourage users to play an active role in aspects of their care are presented with particular reference to the six criteria outlined above. Specific guidance relating to the hospital discharge process is also examined in order to provide a focused context for the empirical study.

Chapter 4 is a review and summary of the literature relating to the social and economic position of elderly people in the United Kingdom insofar as it is relevant to this study. Such literature, coupled with statistics relating to demographic change and use of welfare services, show the prominence of the age group under study and strengthens the case for applying the 'critical case' concept to this particular sample. Incorporated within this is a review of empirical studies exploring similar issues as those considered by this study. This serves to highlight how the present study builds on existing work but also demonstrates how it is more comprehensive.

The methodology employed in the data collection phase of this study is discussed in Chapter 5, demonstrating the rationale for the research approach in terms of meeting the aims of the study and the contribution made to the validity and reliability of the findings. Ethical considerations are given particular prominence in this chapter with specific reference to the age group under study. Details of the method of analysis employed are also included in Chapter 5. The 'Findings' are reported in Chapter 6.

Chapters 7 and 8 comprise a discussion and interpretation of the findings of the empirical study in terms of the key themes to emerge. These themes incorporate the relationship between users and providers of care and the divide between health and social care along with differences in user experience and behaviour associated with various inter-related socio-economic and health-related variables. These chapters also provide links to existing research and theory and to the analytical background in Chapters 2 to 4. Chapter 9 contains a summary and evaluation of the research undertaken, together with a conclusion and a reconsideration of the aims of the study along with areas for further study stemming from this research.

For ease of reading and continuity, each chapter begins with an 'introduction' and ends with a 'summary' to locate it within the wider progression of the argument.

2 User Participation in the Welfare State

Introduction

The evolution of the welfare state in the United Kingdom between 1942 and 1948 marked a major shift from individual responsibility for welfare via private, informal or charitable provision to a more comprehensive publicly funded and publicly provided system. In terms of health and personal social care, resources would in the main, be distributed on the basis of professionally assessed need – 'enlightened paternalism' (Klein, 1984). As such, there would be little opportunity for service users to play an active role in decisions about their use of statutory care although there was still to be a role for private, informal and voluntary provision.

From the standpoint of official discourse, the provision of health and personal social care in the 1990s is quite different. Contemporary welfare provision advocates an active role for service users regarding their care in addition to the provision of services being more responsive to those who seek to use them. This quite dramatic policy shift can be directly traced to the ideology of Conservative governments in power between 1979 and 1997 (see Chapter 3). Indeed it was during this period that service provision oriented towards users and an active role for service users were explicitly promoted in policy initiatives. However, preceding this significant change in government rhetoric, widespread examples of users seeking to play a role in the formulation and implementation of public services policy can in fact be traced from the 1960s through various social and political movements (Pateman, 1970; Croft and Beresford, 1990). There were also examples of government legislation during the 1960s and 1970s which aimed to increase the role and influence of users in how public services were run (Boaden et al., 1982; Deakin and Wright, 1990).

This chapter analyses the origins of user participation in the public services, specifically, the provision of health and personal social care.

'Participation' is an important concept in the investigation of whether users play an active role when utilising public services. Other concepts however are also relevant. The criteria of *participation, representation, access, choice, information* and *redress* are explored as important concepts in assessing whether users are assuming an active role and indeed as being indicative of any shifts in power or influence between providers and users. They have been identified as necessary to shift the balance of power towards users (Potter, 1988), as some of the *'generally accepted criteria'* relating to user control (Barnes, Prior and Thomas, 1990: 134) and as necessary for the position of the user to be fully recognised and strengthened (Deakin and Wright, 1990).

This discussion of user participation in public services provides a very broad context for the specific policies of the Conservative governments between 1979 and 1997; the analysis of which forms the basis of the next chapter. This chapter begins by exploring the concept of 'participation' and defining it as the central theme in users of welfare services playing an active role. The analysis then focuses around the role of public service users at various stages in the formulation and implementation of policy including an overview of mechanisms for political participation and an exploration of the origins of increasing participation by users of public services. Chapter 3 then provides a focused framework of policy developments between 1979 and 1997, particularly those post – 1989, which specifically aimed to promote user orientation and an active role for service users in the delivery of health and social care. It is within this framework that the empirical study takes place.

The Concept of Participation

'Participation' is quintessentially the central concept in any discussion of the extent to which users of health and social care are active in aspects of their care. The other concepts of *representation, access, choice, information and redress* are necessary to facilitate and indeed support the 'participation' of service users. Definitions of these concepts as used in this study and indeed the inter relationships between them and to participation are explored later in this chapter. Because of the centrality of participation, it is necessary to clarify what is meant by the term in this context and what activities or beliefs can be expected to fall within its meaning. The difficulties in doing so, but also the reasons why further exposition is required, are suggested by Croft and Beresford (1992) who begin their article on the politics of participation by claiming participation to be *'one of those contentious words ... which can seem to mean everything and nothing'* (p.20).

Drawing upon examples from the United States, Sherry Arnstein (1969) produced a typology of levels of 'citizen participation' in the form of a ladder, in an attempt to heighten understanding of the concept. She believes citizen participation to be a *'categorical term for citizen power'* (p.216) or the redistribution of power towards the 'have-nots' but concedes that participation may not ultimately affect the distribution of power. In her typology she identifies eight levels, which are grouped into three broad themes: degrees of citizen power, degrees of tokenism and non-participation. 'Citizen power' at the highest level involves citizen control, then delegated power and partnership; 'degrees of tokenism' are placation, consultation and informing whilst 'non-participation' is simply therapy or at the lowest level, manipulation. Rather than an attempt at defining citizen participation, Arnstein can be argued to be seeking to demonstrate the many ways in which citizens' relationships with the 'power holders' can be interpreted as dimensions of 'participation'. Importantly, she demonstrates that participation does not exist on only one level.

Richardson (1983), in a comprehensive review of issues, analyses the meaning of the term 'participation' and offers a discussion on what it could encompass. She believes it to mean *'taking part in some activity with other people'* (p.8), that is, doing something instead of doing nothing, but immediately questions the level of involvement or even influence that this implies and stresses that the 'activity' needs to be specified. In addition, she then considers whether it is necessary for anyone else to be involved, concluding that for her purposes it is. Participation is next contrasted to apathy and is extended to incorporate being concerned about issues whether or not any action is subsequently taken (p.9). In terms of social policy issues, more specifically, she believes that people participate when they engage in activities relating to the provision of social services by central or local government. This is defined as encompassing a role in the processes of policy formulation and execution, usually entered into in order to influence their course (p.10). More specifically, in an earlier article she had defined participation as:

> ... an activity undertaken by one or more individuals previously excluded from the decision making process in conjunction with one or more individuals who were previously the sole activists in that process (Richardson, 1979: 228).

Richardson (1983) then goes on to distinguish between direct and indirect forms of participation. That is, methods of 'taking part' by the public which involve personal interaction with official spokesmen or government officials compared to methods which do not involve such personal interaction. The latter form of 'participation' would involve interaction solely with peers.

Earlier, Boaden *et al.* (1982) had explored the concept of public participation in services provided by local government. In this context, they discuss how 'participation' can be defined as *'forming part of something'* or *'taking part with others, in some action or other'* (pp.11-12) concluding that the latter is the more accurate definition in relation to local service provision. Plainly, even this definition is open to interpretation. 'Taking part' might involve shifting the balance of power towards individuals or groups in the community or may be interpreted in terms of *'the right of people to make representations, to express one's views, or to be given a hearing on matters which affect them'* (p.12).

A more precise and individualised definition of 'participation' is offered by McEwen *et al.* (1983) with specific reference to the delivery of health care. They use the term to mean:

> ... the process whereby a person can function on his or her own behalf in the maintenance and promotion of health, the prevention of disease, the detection, treatment and care of illness and the restoration of health or where recovery is not possible, adaptation to continuing disability (p.1).

Going beyond an individual's role in their own care, McEwen et al. also deem 'participation' to include activities performed on behalf of others in relation to the above areas and in the planning, management and evaluation of health care provision.

McEwen *et al.* (1983) then go on to specify the main broad activities which are subsumed under 'participation', as they define it. Firstly, an *active* as opposed to the traditional passive role of an individual in all aspects of their own health care; secondly, *'deprofessionalisation'* whereby tasks which normally fall within the professional remit are taken on by the individual and thirdly, *'democratisation'* or a desire to assume responsibility for decision making regarding wider aspects of social policy and health care provision (p.2).

Bates (1983), in a review of the position of the health care user in Australia, the United States and Great Britain, believes that participation for health service users refers to purposeful activities in which members of the public take part in relation to government. She then distinguishes public *action* from public *involvement* as more specific components of participation per se, defining the former as *'action initiated by the public and controlled by them for purposes they determine'* and the latter as mechanisms *'initiated and controlled by governments to gain support for decisions already made, or to develop discussion and consultation on issues still to be decided'* (p.15). The former includes the activities of public interest groups, local action groups, self-help groups and voluntary service groups whilst the latter includes activities such as public meetings, consultation, discussion documents and attitudinal surveys.

Brownlea (1987) is more specific defining 'participation' as:

> ... getting involved or being allowed to become involved in a decision-making process or the delivery of a service ... or even simply to become one of a number of people consulted on an issue or matter (p.605).

Three major issues arise from the foregoing analysis which are relevant in clarifying the use of the term in this study: whether participation is *direct* or *indirect*, whether users participate on an individual or collective basis and whether they participate at the level of determining broad welfare policy or simply in relation to their own care. For the purposes of this study, the focus is on individuals playing an active role in issues relating to their own personal care on discharge from hospital and in the short period afterwards; that is, *direct* participation or interaction with service providers or decision makers on an *individual* basis for their personal benefit. This position is compatible with both Richardson's and Boaden *et al.*'s definitions of 'taking part' and Brownlea's definition of 'being involved', yet is less extensive than Richardson's view of 'being concerned', without necessarily taking any action. Additionally, the definition to be utilised here is not as comprehensive as that given by McEwen *et al.*

Arnstein and Boaden *et al.* gave shifting the balance of power towards individuals or groups in the community as a possible outcome of 'participation' although Arnstein questions the extent to which this is a realistic aim. Potter (1988) cites *access, choice, information, redress* and *representation* as the five key factors necessary to shift the balance of power in favour of users. Both Barnes, Prior and Thomas (1990) and Deakin and Wright (1990) use the criteria of *access, choice, information, representation, participation* and *redress* as relating to increasing user control or strengthening the position of the service user. Similarly, the National Consumer Council (1986), in relation to local authority services, have also given *access, choice, information, redress* and *representation* as fundamental to increasing user influence and power. Extending the analysis to incorporate the private sector, the *rights* of users of goods and services have been given as those of *access, choice, information* and to *complain* (Buskirk and Rothe, 1970).

Participation as a wide ranging term, demonstrated by the above analysis, is taken here to be the major issue in service users assuming an active role. The other indicators of an active role for service users – *representation, access, choice, information* and *redress* – explored by this study are mainly interpreted as components of participation. Again, the definitions of such terms are open to interpretation. As with participation, these principles are all interpreted here in terms of an individual assuming an active role, or being provided with opportunities to do so, in relation to their own care during the process of hospital discharge and in the short period afterwards.

For the purposes of this study, *representation* is defined as the participation in the decision making process of informal third parties who can be assumed to be acting in the best interests of the final service user (for example, family, friend or neighbour). As such, the analysis of participation above may be adapted to incorporate roles for such third parties as well as the individual service user. The definitions of Potter (1988), Deakin and Wright (1990), Barnes, Prior and Thomas (1990) and the National Consumer Council (1986) are largely compatible with this usage but also encompass representation (both formal and informal) in the wider process of policy making at both local and national level. Potter defines representation as ensuring that the views of users are '*adequately represented to decision makers at all points in the system where decisions are taken concerning their interests*' (p.154). Barnes, Prior and Thomas group representation and participation together, broadly defining the terms as enabling the users' views to be heard and discuss the role of family members and advocates whilst Deakin and Wright pose:

> Are there effective means by which representatives of the whole citizen body and users of the service can take an appropriate share of responsibility for the service by participating in discussion and decision making on policy and practice? (p.12).

The National Consumer Council similarly perceive representation to be facilitated by the existence of channels to communicate users and public views.

Definitions of access provided by these authors were useful for informing the application of the term in this study. Barnes, Prior and Thomas provide a fairly general discussion in terms of 'obtaining' Local Authority Social Services acknowledging that eligibility criteria must exist and that (potential) users need to negotiate with gatekeeper(s). Deakin and Wright and the National Consumer Council both consider the availability and equity of service provision as issues of access, that is, whether services are available and easy to use for everyone who wishes or needs to use them. Potter on the other hand believes that explicit criteria for the allocation of public services must exist to enable (potential) users to gain access as, only in this way, can decisions be understood and challenged. Going beyond an individual's role in their own personal care, Potter also considers *accessibility* in terms of more 'open', that is less bureaucratic, authorities and organisations.

Access is explored in this study as the extent to which users are in receipt of all services they feel they require and the ease with which (potential) service users feel able to obtain services that they wish for or feel they need. This is linked closely to participating in that active participation by service users or their representatives may secure access to statutory services. However service users and their representatives must first gain access to the decision making process in order to assume an active role therein.

Choice in the use of services is perhaps self-explanatory and the term is used in this study to explore the extent to which service users were able to exercise choice(s) over the services they were to receive. This included whether to receive services, and which ones, and how and when the care would be provided. As such it is a component of participation in that it is assumed that choices that were offered, or were otherwise expressed by service users, would be apparent during the process of participation in the decision making process.

Potter discusses how individuals having the power to choose (and an appropriate range of options to choose from) may ultimately encourage service provision that is sensitive to user needs and preferences.   The availability of a range of options is further implied by Deakin and Wright who discuss the availability of 'free choice' to public service users. Limited resources, as a feature of public service provision, are acknowledged by these authors as restricting choice and Barnes, Prior and Thomas define choice in terms of users' rights to services once need is established but how demand may still exceed resources.

Information is also closely linked to *choice* in that it is assumed that ·the former is required in order to exercise the latter.   Indeed information is given by Potter as necessary to enable individuals to make choices about the services they wish to obtain and to gain maximum benefit from their use. Similarly, the National Consumer Council gives the value of information as aiding both awareness and use of services. Information is also necessary in making (potential) service users aware of their rights to services and the eligibility criteria enforced (Potter, 1988; Barnes, Prior and Thomas, 1990), a factor explored above as necessary for users to attempt to gain access.   As such, information is also fundamental in facilitating the *participation* and *representation* of service users in the decision making process (Brearley, 1990; Hogg, 1990) both at an individual level and in the wider process of how public services are run (Potter, 1988).   To enable (potential) service users and their representatives to play a fully active role therefore information is required about the availability, organisation and performance of a public service (Deakin and Wright, 1990) including the responsibilities of service users, the decision making process, about why decisions are taken and what those decisions are (Potter, 1988).

Information is explored by this study as any written or verbal information, advice or explanation that may have been provided to, or sought out by, service users during the process of hospital discharge and in the short period afterwards. Again, this is focused on the individual user as playing an active role in their own use of health and social care and as such is not as wide-ranging as some of the above definitions.

The complaints procedure is used in this study to analyse mechanisms for redress, that is, both users' knowledge of how to make a complaint if dissatisfied and whether or not they would do so. This is in line with, yet more comprehensive than, the authors upon which this study draws. Potter, the National Consumer Council, Deakin and Wright and

Barnes, Prior and Thomas simply define *redress* as the existence of a grievance procedure. Potter defines the importance of redress as an *'obvious need'* (p.153) for mechanisms for individuals to settle their grievances, the National Consumer Council see it as the existence of channels to pursue complaints whilst Deakin and Wright believe such channels need to be *'readily accessible'* (p.12) and Barnes, Prior and Thomas believe there needs to exist *'proper procedures for complaints and redress'* (p. 143). Hogg (1990) includes 'audit' along with complaints and redress as factors in empowering health service users. She identifies the need for procedures which enable users to express grievances and have them fully investigated; procedures for monitoring standards and disciplining staff and an allowance for compensation to patients as required (p.161). This is more comprehensive than the definition employed by this study which was designed to explore the existence of procedures for investigating dissatisfaction. As such, it is interpreted as a further way in which users may play an active role regarding their own personal care.

All criteria were explored in this study for both evidence of services being oriented towards users, in the provision of opportunities to assume an active role, and for evidence of ways in which users were willing and able to both take and create opportunities to assume such a role. That is, the concern is with the *implementation* of health and social care policy. It is clear from some of the above definitions however that the terms can also be interpreted in relation to the *formulation* of public policy and as enabling users to play a role in the policy process.

The Case 'For' Participation

Returning to participation as the key theme, it seems pertinent to raise the question of what may be achieved by increasing the participation of users in their care and in the wider policy process. An almost unquestioned assumption appears to be that it is a positive measure which will inevitably result in a higher quality of care or that at least the quality of care, other factors being equal, will not decline.

Arguments for participation can be made on a range of moral, practical, philosophical or political grounds. Put at its simplest, participation should be advanced since those who are affected by decisions have the right to be involved in their devising. That is, it is consistent with human and civil rights (Croft and Beresford, 1992). An extension of this viewpoint is that participation (or at least representation) in specific aspects of public service provision reflects the wider ethos of democracy (explored below).

Other arguments for participation can be advanced in terms of improving the provision of services and playing a developmental role in those who become involved. It is believed that service provision will be enhanced as it will be more responsive to (potential) users and there will be increased mutual understanding between users and providers (Richardson, 1983; Clayton, 1988). In terms of health care, this may in turn lead to increased patient responsibility and commitment to services and hence better utilisation (Richardson, 1979; McEwen *et al.*, 1983) and ultimately to enhanced satisfaction with services (Richardson, 1983). These reasons may also be the basis for Croft and Beresford's assertion that participation '*makes for more efficient and cost-effective services*' (1992: 36), a claim for which they provide neither explanation nor analysis.

The developmental role that increased participation can play is perhaps the most well documented (Brearley, 1990). That is, the ways in which the process of participating can develop people's capacities, capabilities and personalities (Hadley and Hatch, 1981; Clayton, 1988). This can be in terms of increased dignity, self-respect, personal involvement, autonomy and control (Held, 1987), along with the expressive benefits it provides such as opportunities to choose, to be heard, to discuss, to criticise and protest (Richardson, 1983).   In addition, participation may encourage people's independence and self-determination (Croft and Beresford, 1992).

All of the above may similarly be cited as reasons why users themselves may wish to participate. The most likely reasons are probably the provision of services which are more responsive to their needs or, less specifically, an enhancement of the quality of services. On an *individual* basis, the level with which this study is mainly concerned, service users may wish to influence or perhaps understand the decisions that are taken in regard to them and their likely outcomes. These are all potential benefits to users of participating. However, 'costs' may also be incurred, for example, the 'investment' required in time, knowledge, social skills and self-confidence (Klein, 1984; Croft and Beresford, 1990).

The Case 'Against' Participation

Less positive outcomes of a more active role for public service users have also been documented. These include the conflict of interest that may arise in the user-provider relationship along with claims that by the involvement of more people, delays and therefore costs are inevitably incurred. Other potential disadvantages relate to *collective* as opposed to *individual* participation. These include the fact that some groups of users are more forceful, articulate, willing or capable of playing an active role than others. The possibility must exist therefore of these users promoting and defending their own interests at the expense of those who are less able or willing to play a role, leading to inequalities in provision. A similar situation may ensue should representatives be sought to put forward the views of service users (Croft and Beresford, 1990); that is, they are likely to be drawn from the sectors of the population who are most articulate and already advantaged by the system of welfare provision. It would be questionable therefore as to how far they represented the majority view or how far they wished to further their own interests (Brownlea, 1987).

A further argument is that encouraging participation may be construed as tokenism or even as social control or manipulation of service users by providers (Richardson, 1979; Hill and Bramley, 1986; Brownlea, 1987; Clayton, 1988). That is, the interests of providers are placed before those of service users and a pretence of participation is used to give legitimacy and support for decisions and to those in authority to justify claims of participation and accountability (Richardson, 1983). This is suggested by the definition of *public involvement* given by Bates (1983) of activities to gain support for decisions already taken and by Arnstein's *degrees of tokenism*. An example of this is stated, in a seemingly patronising tone, by Griffiths (who had been influential on reforms to the delivery of health and community care throughout the 1980s):

> ... when people are consulted ... whilst their wishes may not be met, they are assured that their point of view has been ... taken into account and they will accordingly more readily respect management's right to take the decision (Griffiths, 1990: no page number).

Alternatively, only those views which support the equilibrium or the values and interests of decision makers may be encouraged or taken into account. The objective of legitimising the process rather than securing real public participation can similarly be levelled against the wider electoral system. Indeed, before the discussion shifts to ways in which participation has evolved as an important concept in the formulation and implementation of welfare policy, it is useful to provide a brief overview of relevant mechanisms for 'political' participation.

Political Participation

At a basic level the idea of public participation in the political arena in the United Kingdom is certainly not new. Whilst this is obviously a complex area, a brief overview of ways in which individuals can play a role in the policy process is sufficient here to demonstrate fairly widespread, long-standing mechanisms for public participation. It also demonstrates how some sectors of the population are more willing and able to play an active role than others.

Political participation can be analysed as the activities of members of society in the selection of rulers and decision makers and in directly or indirectly influencing public policy (Verba *et al.*, 1978; Dowse and Hughes, 1986; Parry *et al.*, 1992; Rush, 1992). That is, it is concerned with action by citizens which is aimed at influencing decisions which are ultimately taken by public representatives. Analysis of the various stages of the policy process is therefore useful to consider the relative influence of different groups and organisations in decision making (Ham and Hill, 1993).

Suffice to say, policy is a difficult concept to define (see Ham and Hill, 1993; Jenkins, 1993; Colebatch, 1998). The interest in this section however is not the content or outcome of policy making but rather the decision making process and in particular the individuals or groups involved at each stage. The policy process in the UK can be analysed according to a number of stages yet these can only serve as a model as activities are not always undertaken in such a logical, ordered fashion nor in such a simplified manner. Essentially, policy decisions are made, implemented and evaluated in a cycle. Within this broad process however are more specific stages which involve initiation, information, consideration, decision, implementation, evaluation and termination (Jenkins, 1993) or agenda setting, policy formulation, policy adoption, policy implementation and policy evaluation (Colebatch, 1998).

It is suggested that this model of the policy process can be viewed alongside Milbrath's (1965) hierarchy of political participation which ranges from non-involvement through contacting public officials and attending meetings to the holding of public or party office. That is, as the policy process advances and becomes more precise, public access becomes increasingly restricted. As such, the higher the level of activity in Milbrath's hierarchy, the lower the level of participation, as measured by the number of citizens engaged in the activity (Rush, 1992).

Milbrath (1965) places voting and exposing oneself to political stimuli as the lowest levels of actual participation. In the UK the majority of the population aged 18 years and over are eligible to vote in electing representatives, at both national and local level, to act on their behalf in determining and implementing policy (Rush, 1981). Such is the nature of representative democracy. General political participation of this sort has been classed as an example of 'indirect' participation (Richardson, 1983, see earlier definition), or even as 'non-participatory' representative democracy (Hadley and Hatch, 1981), whilst Navarro (1986) believes that representative democracy converts the process of participation from *active* to *passive* as power is delegated to elected representatives. This still however appears compatible with the definition of participation given by Boaden *et al.* (1982) of the right of people to 'make representations'.

Electoral participation can be classed as 'indirect' for a number of reasons. Firstly, the policy makers are distant from the electorate and so do not come directly into contact with them; participation is through the ballot box. As such elected representatives cannot hope, or attempt, to know and promote the exact interests of all the people they represent (Bates, 1983). Secondly, the electorate are unlikely to be given opportunities to participate in specific issues and the election of representatives takes place on the basis of their broad ideological stance over a range of issues. Electoral participation relates to the participation of individuals solely at the level at which agendas are set, the initial stage of the policy process defined above. The electorate are informed of broad policy proposals in this way (Rush, 1992) and can elect their representatives accordingly. The political parties, via manifestos, are the principal agenda setters. There is also a role for pressure groups, business interests, the media and so on who may highlight and provide evidence or analysis of issues or problems to attempt to gain them a place on the political agenda.

A further characteristic of public participation via elections, which could be classed as a limitation, is that it is a defined opportunity which occurs only periodically as opposed to other forms of participation which may be ongoing or regular. Hill and Bramley (1986) argue that due to the increasingly complex nature of society, a periodic right to make representation is insufficient and that other methods of 'participation' at community or service-specific level are necessary. Some examples of such methods are explored later in this chapter.

Political participation is also a means of *collective* or *community*, as opposed to individual, participation. However, whilst all those eligible to participate in the electoral process have equal rights to do so, some are more willing to take part than others as well as being perceived to be more advantaged than others by doing so. This must be related to the discussion earlier that some sections of the population are both more likely to participate and more likely to stand as representatives than others. For example, non-voting has been found to be more commonly associated with the youngest and eldest sections of the electorate and with the less educated and with manual and unskilled workers (Jones *et al*., 1978; Dowse and Hughes, 1986; Parry *et al*., 1992; Rush, 1992). The generally low turnout at general elections, but particularly at local elections, illustrates that political participation is not a universally embraced role (Pateman, 1970; Parry *et al*., 1992). However it has been shown to be the most embraced political activity and that other activities such as contacting MPs and campaigning are assumed by less than a quarter of the population (Parry and Moyser, 1990). Dowse and Hughes (1986) conclude that, whilst central to democracy, electoral participation ultimately has little direct influence on policy making.

Pateman (1970) gives a very basic summary of the workings of democracy, from the works of Dahl, Berelson, Sartori and Eckstein, which is largely based on the idea of competition between leaders (elites) for the votes of the people. She believes that 'participation' for the majority of the population is participation in the choice of decision-makers and that its function is solely a protective one, that is, protection from the arbitrary decisions of elected leaders. The centrality of direct participation to democracy is disputed (for example, Dahl, 1956; Pateman, 1970; Schumpter, 1976) on the grounds that the *competition* for votes is the vital feature of democracy (also, Hadley and Hatch, 1981). As such, democracy is classed as a *representative* rather than a *participative* institution.

More direct ways in which citizens can become active within the system of representative democracy include joining political parties or pressure or interest groups, standing for election themselves and campaigning on behalf of candidates or issues. Such activities can facilitate participants' influence in agenda setting but also contribute to their influence in the *formulation* of policy, that is, ways in which alternatives are considered and chosen to realise the policy objectives. Activities which may influence policy formulation relate to the mid levels of Milbrath's hierarchy. Rush (1992), who uses a similar hierarchy, classes playing an active role in various types of political or quasi political organisations, including political parties and pressure groups, as falling within the middle range of participation.

Pressure or interest groups can be loosely grouped with political parties in that they both seek to promote or defend particular ideas, situations, persons or groups of persons by trying to stimulate and channel political participation in the formulation of policy. The interests of pressure groups tend to be more limited and specific compared to political parties as they are concerned with single issues or a narrow range of interests (Rush, 1992). Political parties on the other hand must have interests and attitudes over a broader spectrum of issues and seek to exercise power rather than just influence it. Pressure groups are discussed along with other social movements as a 'challenge from below' later in this chapter.

Once decisions are made and policy is adopted, the process moves to the stage of *implementation*, whereby the objectives of the policy decisions may be realised (Hogwood and Gunn, 1984). In practice however it may be difficult to distinguish between policy making and policy implementation (Ham and Hill, 1993; Colebatch, 1998) as policy may need to be adapted to make implementation feasible and the various groups who influence the formulation of policy may also seek to influence its implementation. Indeed implementation can be seen as a further stage of negotiation between policy makers and people in organisations who share an interest in its outcome, for example, industry, local government and groups representing the intended service user (Colebatch, 1998) or between service providers and individual service users.

Evaluation of policy is the next stage of the process; that is, consideration of the extent to which the objectives have been achieved by the changes introduced. Evaluation becomes difficult if it is accepted that policy is still being made during the process of implementation. Indeed, evaluation by interested groups and organisations, can be seen as a continuation of the policy process in that modifications may be made to accommodate any such evaluations. Again, it may be pressure groups (representing both providers and users) and voluntary organisations who play a role.

It is the level at which policy is implemented with which this study is mainly concerned. Indeed the *implementation* of the policy of successive Conservative governments between 1979 and 1997 (see Chapter 3) is the focus. However changing circumstances in the provision of care since the founding of the welfare state but prior to this period (yet continuing post-1979) are now argued to have implications for users assuming an active role at this level.

The Changing Nature of Welfare Professionalism

Broad welfare policy is formulated nationally and indirect participation for the majority of service users at this level will be through the system of representative democracy. For the vast majority of members of the general public there will be no direct participation with official spokespersons to influence overall welfare policy. Intermediate levels at which lay people may play a more active role include representation via Community Health Councils, voluntary bodies, self help groups or pressure groups as shown above. However it is mainly at the level of personalised care provided to them as individuals that is, at the stage of policy *implementation*, that opportunities for directly assuming an active role in relation to their own care are likely to arise.

The delivery of services within the two areas of provision with which this thesis is concerned, that is, the NHS and Personal Social Services have traditionally been dominated by service providers. When the services were introduced in 1948, resources were allocated to individuals in the form of services on the basis of professionally determined need. Such a paternalistic system contrasts with subsequent notions of users assuming an active role in their care. The level of professionalism, the nature of the service and of the clientele, as determinants of the level of (potential) participation, have all seen significant change since 1948 and are now explored. The differences between 'health' and 'social' care provision regarding these factors are also explored.

Until the 1970s, the medical profession was portrayed as clinically autonomous, politically and medically dominant and almost beyond control (Klein, 1983; Hart, 1985; Elston, 1991). Such a portrayal was largely the result of the classification of medicine as a science, whereby knowledge is held to be certain and absolute, along with a continuing emphasis on health care as curative by focusing on disease and the individual (Levitt, 1984; Hart, 1985; Turner, 1987; Watkins, 1987; Ham, 1993). As a result, lay contact with the medical profession would be periodic and individuals would acquire little knowledge. This can be seen to legitimise the expert: non-expert dichotomy and the associated implications for control and dominance in the medical encounter (Navarro, 1986). That is, the denial of power to users in the allocation of resources (Ham, 1992) and the passivity and acceptance of patients and lack of user participation (Hogg, 1990; Calnan and Gabe, 1991).

The individual as the focus of disease and the ability of only the expert to diagnose and cure can be seen as central to the activities to be assumed by patient and doctor in enacting the sick role (Parsons, 1951). That is, both have duties to fulfil in restoring the patient to 'normal' functioning and able to resume their role within society. The role for the patient is essentially submissive in that s/he is required to seek and act upon medical advice. It is suggested here that, relative to other occupations, the authority of the doctor is high as sick people are obliged, in the interests of society, to seek medical advice (Johnson, 1972).

In an important contribution to the debate about how a 'profession' is defined, Millerson (1964), cites a number of key traits of an occupation which would lead it to be classed as a profession. These include the possession of skills based on theoretical knowledge, specialised training and education, competence, organisation, adherence to a professional code of conduct and altruistic service. These all relate to institutionalised control of occupational activity. In terms of the professional-client relationship, Johnson (1972) believes an important element to be 'mystification' and that dependence upon the skills of professionals reduces the common areas of knowledge and experience which creates social distance and may heighten the professional's prestige and autonomy (Turner, 1987). Turner also believes that a requirement to *interpret* this knowledge is fundamental to maintaining this distance as a 'systematic body of knowledge' suggests the potential for routinisation and deskilling. It is the ability to interpret knowledge therefore that allows the medical profession to retain authority over their clients and for example nurses, social workers and other professions supplementary to medicine.

The analysis by Turner suggests that the definition of a profession by Millerson is too broad for the purposes here and further that the distinction between the medical profession and 'subordinates' is an important one. It can be suggested that there may not be the same power difference between users and other welfare professionals as there is between doctors and users thereby implying a greater potential for user participation in the former relationship. The highly professionalised nature of health care has led it to be classed as '*the prototype of a service in which public participation is low*' (Maxwell and Weaver, 1984: 12).

Academic challenges to this professional dominance soon became apparent. From the late 1960s sociological critiques of medical power and monopoly over the definition and treatment of illness in both its physical and mental dimensions began to emerge (Freidson, 1970; McKeown, 1976; Navarro, 1976; Johnson, 1977). In addition, the Patients Movement actively asserted the independence and rights of users (Watkins, 1987) and began to question both the legitimacy of professionals in determining needs and also the dominance they exerted in decision making (Ehrenreich, 1978). This can be seen alongside a decline in unquestioning trust in doctors (Haug and Lavin, 1983) and in the context of increasing lay knowledge about medicine, declining deference to experts in society (Watkins, 1987) and changing patterns of morbidity and dependence which changed expectations about the doctor-patient relationship (Elston, 1991).

Changing patterns of morbidity demonstrate how advances in the treatment of communicable and acute illness have served to highlight the emergence of a variety of more chronic conditions (Ashton and Seymour, 1988; Ham, 1992; Wells, 1992; Moon, 1995). It is posited that this is likely to affect the role of users both in relation to their own care and in their interaction with the medical profession. That is, individuals will have greater experience of their condition, may be more knowledgeable about it and therefore may assume a greater role in managing it and so interact on more equal terms with professionals (Brearley, 1990). Similarly with health promotion and the prevention of ill health, both of which are being increasingly encouraged.

The three areas of *self medication* given by McEwen *et al.* (1983: 51) are health promotion, additional care in chronic conditions and treatment of trivial conditions. Health promotion is classed as a situation pertaining more to the 'education of equals' or a partnership and one in which the professional plays a key role in supporting or enabling rather than controlling the user (Williams, J., 1993). This is possible to the extent that knowledge is construed as socially constructed rather than absolute. It also entails a shift from individualised definitions of illness and an increasing focus on behavioural and environmental causes of ill health (Levitt, 1984; McCarthy, 1992). Health promotion and illness prevention both assume the active participation of service users and along with the increase in chronic conditions highlight a move away from a science-based curative role for doctors. This can also be interpreted as an awareness of the limitations of medical treatment (Hart, 1985).

The prevalence of chronic conditions and the emphasis on health promotion and illness prevention also have implications for the level of contact between user and provider and the relative power held by each, defined by the level of knowledge brought to the encounter. Importantly, it may lead to lay people interacting with professionals when in a stable health state, unlike when experiencing an acute episode of illness. Collectively, these trends have coincided with and contributed to a gradual shift away from institutional or hospital based treatment towards the primary and community sectors of care. This trend which began in the 1970s was to continue and accelerate throughout the 1980s and 1990s and is explored further in Chapter 3.

In the case of the Personal Social Services, there appears a paradox in terms of professional dominance. The 'social' care provided by Personal Social Services can be defined as that which is provided in practice '*when people experience problems to which their existing care networks (if any) are unable to respond*' (Barnes *et al.*, 1990: 105) or to '*people in adversity*' (National Institute of Social Work, 1982: 199). The emphasis tends to be on practical and emotional help and support. It would appear that there would be less of an imbalance of 'professional' or 'specialised' knowledge between service users and providers than exists in the area of medicine and health (Hill and Bramley, 1986). The role of the social worker is based more on interpersonal skills which are 'intuitive' (England, 1986) and are not derived from a body of 'expert' or theoretical knowledge. A further contrast with health care is that social care is more likely to be provided on a continuing basis by virtue of the probable higher levels of dependency of those seeking care. Both factors suggest a greater potential for an active user role in the use of social care compared to health care. Yet (potential) users generally refer themselves to the NHS (at least to the first point of contact) whereas referrals to a social worker generally go through a third party and may even be counter to users' wishes. In addition social care is largely means tested rather than universal and, from the definitions above, appears to have a 'last resort' quality, suggesting that users of such care are likely to be the least privileged, most dependent and least participant members of society (Barnes *et al.*, 1990; Croft and Beresford, 1990).

The increasing prevalence of chronic and disabling conditions, the ageing of the population (see Table 1, Chapter 3) and the trend towards primary and community based care all suggest increasing and ongoing contact between social care professionals, including social workers, and users. Whilst this suggests increased opportunities for participation by users, the nature of the clientele may counter the extent to which these opportunities are taken.

As with health care, a critique of social work provision emerged during the 1960s and 1970s. Despite the 'intuitive' practice of social work, the state-based, theoretically grounded professional status and power of social work came under attack from both within the profession itself and from social work clients during this time (Bailey and Brake, 1975; Brake and Bailey, 1980). 'Radical' social work entailed a critique of the perceived emerging bureaucratic professionalism and control exercised by social workers (Langan and Lee, 1989) and the remoteness of the service from users was believed to increase with the types of social work and areas of expertise. Proponents argued instead for personal relationships to be nurtured between client and worker and for a commitment to participatory styles of decision making, to include the client. As with critiques of health care provision, the individual as the focus of social problems was a main point of attack upon social work provision. Whilst it was arguably a significant development at the time, the radical social work movement went into decline in the late 1970s along with the wider political left.

The traditional dominance of professionals in the provision of welfare therefore showed signs of changing as a result of shifting philosophical and social values regarding the extent to which people, on the one hand, had a right to play a role in services that were provided to them and, on the other, were able to do so. Challenges to professional dominance and demands from user groups demonstrate how certain users were both making and taking opportunities to play a more active role in aspects of their care. This was to continue throughout the 1970s and further examples are given below. Contrasting to the above analysis, which focuses on the implementation of policy to the individual service user, examples throughout the rest of the chapter relate to the participation of individuals or groups throughout various stages of the policy process.

The Challenge from Below

Pateman (1970) begins her book by asserting that during the final years of the 1960s, the word 'participation' became part of the popular political vocabulary. She cites students in higher education as an example of a group who sought to heighten their participation in decisions affecting them. Boaden *et al.* (1982) begin in their preface in a similar way by classing 'participation' as becoming a 'vogue word' in the mid-1960s. They express this in relation to the system of representative government and how pressure came from those who wished for greater participation in decisions about public policy. Klein and Lewis (1976) state how calls for participation in the public sector were 'fashionable' during this period. The numerous 'social movements' which evolved during the period, seeking to increase the participation and influence of members in decisions in which they had a vested interest, were in addition to existing pressure or interest groups. Such activities can be classed as examples of *public action* (Bates, 1983), that is, participatory action initiated by the public as opposed to the government. Whilst the diversity of groups in terms of size, activity and so on permit few generalisations to be made, the aims of 'user movements' can be given generally as aiming to influence various stages of the policy process in relation to their own interests.

The limitations in the system of representative democracy outlined earlier, particularly the fact that only broad and imprecise issues are represented, and only on a periodic basis, can be argued as reasons for the growth of movements representing specific interests, including pressure groups. In addition, as analysed above, electoral participation allows very limited influence on the formulation or implementation of public policy.

In terms of service provision, the increasing size, bureaucracy and therefore remoteness of the welfare state and the increasingly complex and varied needs of (potential) service users can be identified as major factors in encouraging moves to enhance user participation (Jones *et al.*, 1978; Boaden *et al.*, 1982; Richardson, 1983). Indeed, inequalities in the provision of welfare (Oliver, 1990, writing as a proponent of the disability movement; Williams, F., 1993) and the fact of services being unavailable at the time of need (Bates, 1983) have been identified as major influences on the development of social movements in the 1960s and 1970s. Lack of choice and information were also factors in the development of the user movement in health (Hogg, 1990). Moves towards greater user participation in public services during this period can also be interpreted as a further challenge to professional dominance (Klein, 1983; Giddens, 1984; Calnan and Gabe, 1991).

It is suggested here that it is the individuals or groups in society who gain least from the process of representative democracy and feel disillusioned with existing systems of public service provision who are the most likely to initiate, belong to or otherwise support such movements (including pressure groups). That is, disadvantaged or oppressed groups – the 'generally disenfranchised' (Touraine, 1981). Ward and Mullender (1993) believe the choice for oppressed sectors of society is between adopting the values of the oppressor or of fighting back. The latter option has been taken by those involved in social movements; the gay and lesbian, black, women's and disability movements can be interpreted as arising from feelings of exclusion, oppression and marginalisation (Croft and Beresford, 1992).

A crucial distinction between playing an active role in social movements (including pressure groups) and participating via the ballot box is that the former can be classed as 'active' with the latter classed as 'reactive'. That is, social movements can be seen as seeking to bring about change in circumstances which they define whilst voting can simply amount to a choice between pre-determined alternatives. This distinction is perhaps over simplistic as the former must also be reactive in that action probably arises from dissatisfaction with current provision or with actual or proposed changes in provision. The fundamental difference being that they are also active in the sense that they create opportunities for participating. Returning to the model of the policy process, social movements and pressure groups can be argued to seek to play a role in agenda setting and also in influencing the formulation and adoption of policies as well as the implementation and evaluation of such policies. As such, activities may range throughout the hierarchy of political participation given by Milbrath (1965) rather than remaining at the lower levels.

The social movements of the 1960s and 1970s emerged in addition to existing pressure or interest groups many of which have a very long history and are well-established. A distinction between the two however is that, although many pursue interests over a range of issues, pressure groups tend to concentrate on a more narrowly defined range of interests than the newer social movements. In addition the latter have the aim of allowing people to speak for themselves in an attempt to gain more say and control over their lives compared to the former which may provide more opportunities for representation than participation. The newer social movements represent a desire to enhance and become involved in *participatory* politics. As such, their activities can be seen as political activity within civil society, that is, not in the conventional realm of democracy (Oliver, 1990). This is contrasted to political activity within the state which comprises traditional party politics and pressure group activities. That is:

> These social movements are 'new' in the sense that they are not grounded in traditional forms of political participation through the party system or single-issue pressure group activity targeted at political decision makers (Oliver, 1990: 113).

The social movements which evolved in the 1960s and 1970s went beyond seeking representation or 'having a voice' in the policy process as they were concerned with how their members were treated and regarded within wider society and issues such as quality of life, equality, individual self-realisation and human rights (Habermas, 1981). Indeed rather than seeking to represent their peers, members of such groups sought to encourage the broader participation of their peers as an element in the underlying struggles for genuine participatory democracy, social equality and justice, which had arisen out of industrialisation (Touraine, 1981). This can be related to the *developmental* benefits that increasing participation may bring (see earlier discussion). As such they can be viewed as:

> Agents of liberty, equality, social justice ... or even as appeals to modernity or to the liberation of new forces in a world of traditions, prejudices and privileges (Touraine, 1981: 29).

Characteristics of 'new' social movements include a pragmatic, rather than a strictly ideological, orientation for example in seeking to expand members' participation in decision making; their grievances are linked with beliefs and values relating to belonging to a differentiated social group and can often involve personal and intimate aspects of life (Johnston *et al.*, 1994).

A prominent example of a social movement during the 1960s and 1970s and which was a prime force in the rise of other user movements was the women's movement. This was very diverse and manifest in a variety of forms as women became very vocal in their criticism of both the quality and the quantity of services available to them through the welfare state. This was mainly against male dominance and bias in medicine (Ruzek, 1986; Stacey, 1988; Doyal, 1994) but also against male-dominated social security, housing, education, pensions and personal social services (Williams, F., 1993). Subordinate social groups, particularly women, were believed to be overlooked and marginalised and inequalities were reproduced in a '*patriarchal and racially structured capitalism*' (Williams, F., 1993: 82). In the United States the women's movement saw the establishing of services by women emphasizing self-help and minimising professional distinctions (Ruzek, 1986). In the United Kingdom, action by women largely constituted campaigns to influence policies affecting services provided to women, for example, to control their own reproduction (Ruzek, 1986; Watkins, 1987); to be informed of procedures and the risks and benefits involved; to demedicalise childbirth and for services to be provided to meet the specific needs of women such as antenatal clinics (Calnan and Gabe, 1991) and women's refuges (Williams, F., 1993). A notable example was that of women exercising choice by going to maternity units which offered the service they wanted, even if they had to travel (Hogg, 1990). Other activities aimed to raise consciousness of women's issues and provide education and information.

Further critiques of welfare state provision and demands for more responsive and equitable services came from ethnic groups and disabled groups. These movements all influenced each other and, ultimately, the introduction of anti-discrimination legislation.

The new social movements were in addition to *self help groups* of which there is a huge variety, ranging over many medical, social or behavioural conditions. The majority of self-help groups were formed in the early 1970s (Richardson and Goodman, 1983). The issues or 'problems' dealt with in this way tend to be long term or have a significant effect on the life of an individual or family members. Similar to pressure or interest groups, the diversity in size, causes and activities engaged in, make it difficult to produce any kind of definition or generalisations.

A major reason for the forming of self-help groups given by Kelleher (1994) was as a challenge to professionalism. That is, questioning the status of 'expert' knowledge, asserting the value of lay knowledge and thereby implicitly criticising existing care provision and its failure to provide necessary help and support (Brownlea, 1987). Kelleher (1994) explores some common elements that run through the activities of self help groups and concludes that they place a value on experiential knowledge – '*the expertise of sufferers*' (McEwen *et al.*, 1983: 112) – thus challenging the authority of professionals to define what it is to have a particular condition and how it should be managed. Mutual assistance and the exchange of advice and information are therefore central activities (Hatch, 1984) with the underlying themes of participation, self-reliance and reciprocity. This would be particularly applicable or feasible in the case of chronic or disabling conditions for which there is no cure or conditions which are of a continuing or delicate nature (McEwen *et al.*, 1983). Other authors however have stressed how friendship and common understanding are the major objectives of self help or 'mutual aid' groups (Richardson and Goodman, 1983). Richardson and Goodman also stress how eliciting high member participation and emphasising independence are important objectives of such groups, which appears compatible with the notion of 'challenging' professionalism.

Kelleher believes that self help groups can be defined as a new social movement to the extent that they offer individuals a means of reconstructing their identities and they play a part in reinvigorating the public sphere. Whilst self-help groups have not effected any major political change the extent to which this was an aim of their activities must be questioned. The changes which they aim to achieve may be in terms of the quality of life of the members. This is a way in which self-help movements can be contrasted to pressure or interest groups which do aim for influence in the policy process. As McEwen *et al.* (1983) point out however some pressure groups can also fulfil the role of a self-help group whilst pressure group activities have been given as an option open to self-help groups (Richardson and Goodman, 1983). This demonstrates how there may also be a role for such groups in various stages of the policy process in addition to the main purpose of providing practical help and support.

The crucial factor is that new social movements and self help groups were created as organisations *of* rather than organisations *for* various groups of people. This can be contrasted to many voluntary organisations and pressure groups which are not entirely composed of users or 'sufferers'. As such, new social movements and self help groups were concerned with people speaking and acting for themselves and must be seen as an important element in attempts to 'empower' service users whether or not they ultimately seek to influence policy.   Voluntary organisations and pressure groups also have more explicit functions in terms of attempting to influence the policy process.

Participation, representation, access, choice and *information*, as aspects of 'user control', can all be seen to be explicitly promoted by the above examples of users seeking to play a more active role in their care. Whilst *redress* is not specifically addressed, the questioning of existing service provision and seeking alternatives demonstrate the willingness of some users to express their dissatisfaction.

Top Down Initiatives

The empirical component of this thesis is mainly shaped by the policies and legislation introduced by the Conservative government post-1979 with reference to the provision of health and social care. This is analysed in the following chapter. It has been suggested however that the initial pressure for greater user involvement in public services came from the political Left (Deakin and Wright, 1990). A number of examples of state initiatives prior to 1979, aimed at increasing public participation in the policy process, are now explored. These can be classed as examples of *public involvement* (Bates, 1983), that is, initiated by government and took place alongside the user movements detailed above.

The Labour government which assumed power in 1964 under Wilson advocated public participation in the formulation and implementation of public policy out of a desire to improve the responsiveness of services in the face of increasing levels of bureaucracy. They forwarded the idea of 'open government' and placed emphasis on publishing policy proposals and allowing access to information (Boaden *et al.*, 1982). A demonstration of this was the introduction of consultation documents – Green Papers – on policy proposals which ostensibly offer the electorate as a whole the chance to discuss proposed changes.

When the Labour party returned to power in 1974 they sought to make statutory status available to neighbourhood councils and grant them formal rights of consultation with local authorities over planning matters. This move was opposed by voluntary organisations on the grounds that existing groups within the neighbourhood would allow a greater degree of flexibility and would be non-party political (Boaden *et al.*, 1982). Also, self-help and user groups, analysed above, were favoured by individuals for the more specific and direct participation opportunities they could offer. There were however some notable government reports prior to this time which promoted the participation of users in the implementation of public services policy. The most significant were the Seebohm Report (1968) 'Report of the Committee on Local Authority and Allied Personal Services' (later the Local Authority Social Services Act, 1970) and the Skeffington Report (1969) 'People and Planning: Report of the Committee on Public Participation in Planning'. These related to personal social services and land planning use respectively.

The Seebohm Report endorsed public participation as a goal for the new larger local authority Social Services departments and included measures to promote the role of the user in running services (Deakin and Wright, 1990). The main recommendation was to encourage user representation on Social Services committees and sub-committees (Jones *et al.*, 1978) with the general aim of developing understanding and co-operation in decision making and implementation. The report however contained few practical guidelines for the achievement of greater participation and no formalised participatory structure was incorporated into the 1970 Social Services Act.

Environmental issues produced a number of opportunities for lay participation. Rapid and large scale changes had been taking place in the urban environment during the late 1960s which, together with a growing demand from the public to be heard on planning matters affecting their property, saw the movement for public participation in land use planning gain momentum (Hampton, 1990). The Town and Country Planning Acts of 1968 and 1971 and the Skeffington Report of 1969 required the public to be consulted on planning proposals and given the right of appeal yet the word 'participation' was not used in the legislation (Hampton, 1990). It appears that the main emphasis in these documents was with ensuring adequate publicity of proposed developments, perhaps a factor which led to the assertion that Skeffington appeared to confuse participation with public relations (Jones *et al.*, 1978). Similarly, the 1969 Housing Act recognised a need to organise public participation in policy making but only a requirement to publish information was specified. Whilst these developments in planning have been identified as *'the first large scale government intervention in 'participation"* (Croft and Beresford, 1992: 28) they failed to mark the beginnings of widespread participation in the public sector policy process.

The reorganisation of the NHS which took place in 1974 was the first in its twenty-six year life. The main outcome of this reorganisation was to increase bureaucracy and top-down control via the centralisation of the service which distanced policy making from service users. However, two notable moves in terms of this study were the appointment of a Health Service Commissioner to investigate grievances and the establishment of Community Health Councils (CHCs) to represent the voice of the service user. The Labour government wished to increase the role of the public in the supervision of local health services (Hadley and Hatch, 1981). The Commissioner's role however appears fairly limited in that only grievances from individuals, as opposed to groups, of a non-clinical nature which had already been through the normal complaints procedure would be investigated. Community Health Councils on the other hand were formed to represent the people's voice on all issues relating to the NHS and their establishment served to demonstrate the acceptance of the need for such an outlet (Boaden *et al.*, 1982). Whilst they have certain rights in relation to health authorities and local services, the relationship established with health authorities can be important in determining the scope and effectiveness of CHC activity.

It was also during the early 1970s that a number of Patient Participation Groups were established by '*enthusiastic GPs*' (McEwen *et al.*, 1983: 90). These had the aim of gaining feedback from patients, of improving communication between staff and patients with the ultimate aim of improving services, in particular, increasing their responsiveness to service users. They comprised a group of patients, as representatives of the practice population, who would meet periodically with practice staff (Wood, 1984). Whilst little is documented about what they achieved, perhaps the important point again is that they were established at all; that is, an additional forum was created for feedback regarding the NHS, this time about a specific aspect of service. The most obvious difficulty with such forums must be ensuring the representative nature of the groups. The possibility also exists that professional members may dominate the group's activities or that the groups may be used to gain approval for decisions already taken.

A further notable movement which created opportunities for public participation was the series of Community Development Projects at the end of the 1960s. This involved collective rather than individual action with the explicit objective of involving people in the regeneration of their local infrastructure (Higgins, 1983) for example housing and employment regeneration and the development of voluntary work in the community. Whilst such schemes may also involve community workers and associated professionals, the main concerns were with bringing about change through the participation of local people (Croft and Beresford, 1992). These projects were largely unsuccessful due to the low level of resources they were granted and the complex problems they were expected to deal with (Boaden *et al.*, 1982) for example poverty which is rooted in the structure of society. The projects were state initiated and so can be argued as a further example of an attempt at social control whilst giving the illusion of participation.

Throughout the 1970s a number of schemes were established by local authorities to encourage the participation of tenants in the management of housing (Richardson, 1979). A variety of mechanisms were advocated to involve tenants with councillors and officers in discussions about both day-to-day and long-term decisions about their housing. Such involvement was subsequently a statutory requirement of the 1980 Housing Act.

The above examples of legislation addressed many of the aspects of user control with which this study is concerned, namely, *participation, representation, access, choice, information* and *redress*. This demonstrates how, by the mid 1970s, the importance of encouraging public service users to play a role in the policy process had been acknowledged.

Summary

This chapter has demonstrated that participation by public service users in the policy process is not a recent concept and has traced the origins of public participation from the 1960s when it gained in prominence. It has demonstrated how all the aspects of 'user control' to be addressed by this study (*participation, representation, access, choice, information* and *redress*) had been addressed to some degree in the delivery of public services during the 1960s and 1970s. It has also demonstrated that not all sectors of the population have become involved to the same extent either in taking up opportunities presented by officials (for example, voting) or in making opportunities (for example, joining political parties, forming or joining pressure groups, social movements or self-help groups). The empirical component of this study is carried out using elderly people (70 years and over) suggesting that they are the least likely to either take or make opportunities to assume an active role in their use of health and social care although the heterogeneity of the elderly population is acknowledged. This is explored further in Chapter 4.

Chapter 3 now provides an analysis of explicit legislation introduced post-1979 in relation to the implementation of health and social care policy. This policy ostensibly aimed to both increase the responsiveness of services to those who seek to use them and provide opportunities for users to play an active role in the use of services.

3 The Policy Concept

Introduction

Chapter 2 has illustrated how the concept of user participation has become increasingly prominent in the development of a number of areas of public services policy since the 1960s. Demands for a greater role for service users stemmed from perceptions about the unresponsive and inequitable nature of service delivery and decision making along with changing expectations about welfare and came from both service users and official policy makers.

This chapter analyses the programme for health and social care of successive Conservative administrations between 1979 and 1997 and specifically those initiatives which explicitly aimed to promote an active role for service users at the stage of policy implementation. Key to many of these initiatives was the introduction of market principles in order to achieve certain objectives. New Right ideology permeated substantial areas of policy during this period, key principles of which include efficiency, choice and individualism (Green, 1987; King, 1987; Flynn, 1990) all of which are theoretically fostered by the use of market principles in allocating scarce resources. Fundamentally, the analysis in this chapter provides a rhetorical backcloth against which to explore actual practice, tested by the empirical phase of this study.

The culmination of welfare policy throughout the period also heralded a shift from care in the acute hospital sector to the community and from the secondary to the primary sector. This is one of the reasons for the choice of hospital discharge as the process for investigation. Other reasons include that hospital discharge is a critical time in the use of care services for (elderly) people and that continuing care may cross the health – social care divide.

Elderly people have been presented in the media as one of the groups most affected by changes in the delivery of health and social care (for example, The Guardian, 29/3/95 'Grim Time for Greyheads'; The Independent, 15/10/96 'Hospital puts ban on elderly patients'; The

Observer, 14/9/97 'Thrown off the ward and into the wild'). This is largely due to the rising numbers of people aged 70 years and over and their high level of use of welfare services. Elderly people have been chosen as the subjects of this study for these and other reasons explored in greater depth in Chapter 4.

This chapter analyses welfare policy and the ideological forces that shaped it during this period. This provides a context for the specific policy guidance relating to elderly people on discharge from hospital, which itself provides the defined focus for the present study. The criteria to be explored as indicative of a strengthening of the position of the service user in relation to public services as defined by Potter (1988), Barnes, Prior and Thomas (1990) and Deakin and Wright (1990) of *participation, representation, access, choice, information* and *redress* (see Chapter 2) are particularly highlighted. Evidence for these principles is explored in the empirical phase of this study. Finally, a summary of the political rhetoric is given and the potential implications for an active role for service users are briefly addressed.

Conservative Ideology and the Public Sector

The Conservative Party Manifesto on which the party, led by Margaret Thatcher, fought and won the 1979 general election, stated the belief that enlarging the role of the state and reducing the role of the individual was detrimental to the economic future of Great Britain. It was asserted that these two trends had crippled enterprise on which a prosperous economy must depend (Conservative Party, 1979). As such, throughout the 1980s and 1990s a major macro objective within the public sphere was economic efficiency, to be achieved by a return to *laissez faire* ideology, deregulation and removal of the 'dependency culture' by reducing the role of the state. The underlying aims were to create a dynamic enterprise culture and a free market economy (Hambleton *et al.*, 1989; Farnham and Horton, 1993; Allsop, 1995).

Other arguments for reducing the role of the state were that state provided services were fundamentally flawed as they were not sufficiently responsive to user preferences, provided no choice and were not adequately accountable (Deakin and Wright, 1990; Young, 1991). Lessons from the private sector including free market principles and competition were promoted as the key to achieving efficient public services which were responsive to users (Pierre, 1995). Accordingly, during the period of Conservative governance, responsibility for the provision of public services and welfare shifted from mainly monopolistic state provision to 'welfare pluralism' or a 'mixed economy' consisting of private, public, voluntary and informal providers (Marsh and Rhodes, 1992; Pinker, 1992; Farnham and Horton, 1993). Advocates of market mechanisms in the delivery of welfare saw the benefits as five fold: choice, flexibility, a reduction in bureaucracy, competition and a reduction in public expenditure (Parker, 1993).

Collectively, these trends have been referred to as 'rolling back the frontiers of the state' (King, 1987; Hudson, 1992; Thomson, 1992) or 'privatisation' of which, needless to state, there are many definitions and forms (Johnson, 1989; Ranade and Haywood, 1989; Saunders and Harris, 1990; Mohan, 1991).

New Right ideology, promulgating minimal state intervention and concepts of individualism, choice, competition, freedom and efficiency (Gamble, 1987; George and Wilding, 1994) must also be considered as a prominent influence on much of the Conservative governments' approach to domestic policy in this new 'enterprise culture'. This can be contrasted with the characteristics of collectivism, social rights, dependence, unresponsive services and lack of choice of the Keynesian welfare state (Farnham and Horton, 1993). Alternatively, this political transformation can be seen in the context of the wider move away from 'Fordist' production which was characterised by inflexible, remote and unresponsive service provision (Barnes and Wistow, 1992a; Jessop, 1994; Clarke and Newman, 1997). It is important to note however that the advantages to be gained from applying private sector style organisation and management to the NHS and Social Services were advocated from the 1970s (Allsop, 1995; Adams, 1996). That is, these initiatives are not solely a result of New Right Conservative ideology.

McCarthy (1989) believes 1979 marked a watershed in the development of the welfare state whilst Farnham and Horton (1993) saw it as 'a new stage in the development of the state' (p.4) due to subsequent changes in the size, composition and management of the public sector. Other authors however have commented on the relative lack of change, representing the period as one of policy continuity (Ranade and Haywood, 1989; Clarke and Langan, 1993). Wilding (1992) on the other hand believed the challenge to collectivism, the promotion of private provision and the mixed economy of welfare with a decreasing state role to be some of Mrs. Thatcher's most enduring legacies.

The Context of the Welfare State

The broad ideological standpoint and beliefs held by the Conservative government on ascension to power outlined provide a context for the subsequent policy initiatives implemented, detailed in this chapter. Whilst this chapter seeks to demonstrate how the change of government in 1979 marked the beginning of a distinct phase in the development of state welfare, wider economic, social and demographic influences are also relevant.

The 1970s witnessed debate about the ability to sustain the welfare state in its original form as resources fell short of anticipated expenditure (Ranade and Haywood, 1989; Clarke and Langan, 1993; George and Wilding, 1994). This was coupled with low economic growth, rising prices and high unemployment which had caused policy makers across the political spectrum to reconsider the costs of welfare provision.

More specifically, the welfare services were subjected to a level of debate rarely encountered in the previous twenty years and the needs, wishes and expectations of those using the services differed from those using the services during the period of comparative consensus which existed up to the 1980s (Ham, 1992). Changing patterns of ill health, technological advance, demographic change and economic demands have all created unprecedented pressure on the care services and were some of the reasons necessitating reform (Allsop, 1989; Robinson, 1991; Wells, 1992; Healthcare 2000, 1995).

As addressed in chapter 2, patterns of morbidity show how the incidence of chronic disease and disability for example, heart diseases, strokes and cancers, have replaced infectious diseases as major health problems. As a result, mortality rates have fallen, leading to an overall increase in life expectancy, whilst selected morbidity rates have risen, suggesting a decline in health for certain sectors of the population (Office for National Statistics, 1997a). Advances in medical knowledge and technology continue to be made and a greater variety of treatments have become available leading to more complex service development aims (Robinson, 1991). It must be noted however that these latter factors all initially stem from Department of Health decisions about resource allocation. The interaction of these factors has had implications both for the demand for, and the delivery of, health and social care services. They exert an upward pressure on the total demand for services but also have implications for how care is delivered, for example, community practitioners can readily manage chronic disease and disability. This, along with other factors, has meant that an increasing amount of care is now delivered outside the hospital setting (Boufford, 1994).

Demographic trends illustrate that elderly people are forming an increasing percentage of the total population. This is shown in Table 1 below.

Table 1:   Actual and Projected Percentages of the UK Population aged 65 years and over and 80 years and over

	1971	1993	2021
% of UK population aged 65yrs and over	13.2	15.8	19.4
% of UK population aged 80yrs and over	2.3	3.7	5.1

Source: Office for National Statistics, 1997a

The document 'Growing Older' (DHSS, 1981) acknowledged this trend and its implications mainly in terms of increased expenditure on services and increased demand for care, associations which have become increasingly important (see for example, Department of Health, 1996b; Office for National Statistics, 1997a). Characteristics of the older population of the UK and reasons for the choice of age group for this study are explored in Chapter 4 along with critical viewpoints regarding the economic and social position of elderly people in society.

These trends can all be argued to contribute to the increasingly costly, inefficient, bureaucratic, unresponsive and unaccountable nature of welfare delivery, often referred to as the 'crisis' in the welfare state (Loader and Burrows, 1994; O'Donovan and Casey, 1995; Clarke and Newman, 1997). It can be postulated that the 'marketization' of welfare has been encouraged to address the challenge posed by such a changing context.

This chapter now turns to address the framework of policy development between 1979 and 1997 and explores in particular those changes relating to an active role for service users.

1979-1986: Management Reform and Contracting Out

The early years of this period were mainly concerned with reforming the machinery of government whilst the whole period was dominated by questions of finance and calls for efficiency throughout the whole public sector. The overriding concern in 1979 was with controlling the growth of public expenditure (Clarke and Langan, 1993; Ham, 1994). Other important objectives were the desire to reduce bureaucracy, increase the role and influence of the private sector, create stronger management and increase local accountability and responsiveness (Jobling, 1989).

The consultative paper 'Patients First' (DHSS Welsh Office, 1979) (itself a landmark in that it was the first time policy makers had 'consulted' users of health services and health professionals) and the 'NHS Management Inquiry' (Griffiths, 1983) both suggested changes to strengthen the management of the NHS. 'Patients First' aimed to make the service more responsive to users' needs whilst Griffiths aimed to promote efficiency and effective management of manpower and resources.

'Patients First' advocated the benefits of decision-making '*by those who are close to and responsive to the needs of patients*' (p.5) in order to take their views and those of their carers into account. To this end, maximum delegation of responsibility and decision-making to local level was proposed. One tier of administration was removed and District Health Authorities (DHAs) were established (in 1982) whose management would enjoy a minimum of interference from any central authority as a move to strengthen local decision-making. Responsibility was also to be delegated to those in the hospital and community services within policies determined by the DHA altogether creating a less bureaucratic structure. The restructuring was presented as a means of moving decision making closer to where policy is implemented in order to more accurately reflect and respond to the local situation (Clarke *et al.*, 1994; Paton, 1996).

The outcome of the NHS Management Inquiry (Griffiths, 1983), appointed to advise on the effective use of manpower and related resources in order to enhance efficiency and accountability, was the organisation of the service along business lines and the introduction of *general* management to replace consensus management.

Griffiths reiterated the belief expressed in 'Patients First' that decision making power and responsibility should be delegated to the lowest possible level to ensure orientation and responsiveness to users and the community. This was coupled with accountability upwards with the appointment of one accountable general manager at regional, district and unit level. Accountability was also to be enhanced through for example the development of performance indicators, individual performance review, performance-related pay and short-term contracts. Of central importance to management in the planning and delivery of services was believed to be the acquisition of the experiences and perceptions of service users and the community (Griffiths, 1983: para. 13). These could be ascertained via Community Health Councils, surveys of public opinion and so on. Management could then '*respond directly to this information; act on it in formulating policy*' and '*monitor performance against it*' (Griffiths, 1983: para. 13). This is in line with the 'public service orientation' discussed by Stewart and Clarke (1987, in relation to local authorities) who believe that managers must know what services are wanted by the public, be close to their customers and seek out customer views, complaints and suggestions. Ranade and Haywood (1989) believe that while Griffiths emphasised control, consumer sensitivity, quality and efficiency, the reality was a major concern with the latter.

The introduction of general managers has been interpreted as presenting a challenge to medical dominance and autonomy (Hunter, 1994; Harrison, 1995) as it 'broke' established lines of professional responsibility and clinical freedom (Elston, 1991) and questioned traditional responsibilities of health authority members and staff (Levitt *et al.*, 1995). This is given as the reason for the opposition to it from health service workers, mainly the medical and nursing professions (Walby and Greenwell, 1994). Griffiths also introduced performance indicators, some of which were clinical which could further be construed as a 'challenge'. Ultimately however it was not believed to amount to the deprofessionalisation of medicine (Elston, 1991) or to the loss of autonomy of clinicians as general managers were not in a hierarchical relationship with medical professionals (Harrison, 1995) but dependent upon them for knowledge and to carry out their decisions. General management was not believed to provide the answer to the lack of managerial force and drive in the NHS whilst consensus management has been defended as representative of the multi-professional input necessary for effective patient care (Parston, 1988).

Further relevant viewpoints are that general management created a climate of opinion and practice that enabled the government to introduce plans for the 'internal market' (Butler, 1992), that it provided the roots for consumer ideology (Pfeffer and Coote, 1991; Rogers, 1993) and that it constituted a crucial element of the marketisation of the welfare state (O'Donovan and Casey, 1995).

The changes to management in the NHS can be paralleled with the New Public Management pervading the wider public sector during this period. Some of the main features of this public management were the disaggregation of units, clear goals and objectives, clear measures of performance, accountability and 'proven' private sector management styles (Hood, 1991; Ranade, 1994). Hood also provides a critique of public management believing it to weaken competencies at the front line, pursue efficiency at the expense of equity and to be a self-serving movement to promote the career interests of an elite few rather than public service customers and low-level staff.

A further initiative that provides an apposite example of an attempt to enhance efficiency, this time through introducing competition and reducing the role of the state, was the introduction of compulsory competitive tendering (CCT). This was introduced fairly extensively throughout the early 1980s for domestic services, such as laundry, portering and catering in the NHS and for catering and cleaning in education. It was also introduced widely in local government for cleaning, catering, repair work, refuse collection and so on and for 'meals on wheels' by Local Authority Social Services departments. The public, private and voluntary sectors were invited to tender for these functions, cost and quality presumably being the criteria on which contracts were awarded (Butcher, 1995). Marsh and Rhodes (1992) however question the ultimate success of this initiative as only a small percentage of contracts were awarded to private contractors (Key, 1988; Milne, 1992).

In relation to the NHS, competitive tendering was opposed on the grounds that the wages of already low paid staff would be further driven down, that an especially dedicated workforce was required, that domestic staff were viewed by patients as part of the health care team and more practically that there was unlikely to be sufficient alternative providers to offer ' real' competition (Allsop, 1995). Any savings that were achieved therefore may be at the cost of already low paid employees, by the substitution of full-time with part-time workers with fewer rights and benefits (Ranade and Haywood, 1989).

Whilst cost savings were made, the significance of contracting out has been presented as the principle established. In relation to health, Butler (1992) defines the important principles as firstly a demonstration that health authorities can fulfil obligations to the public just as well by *commissioning* as opposed to directly providing services and secondly the introduction of the cultures and mechanisms of the market place. In a later overview of the 'reforms' he sums up this significance as: '*The separation of purchasing from providing had begun*' (Butler, 1994: 15).

A further initiative to encourage private sector provision during this period was the state subsidization of private residential and nursing care for elderly people which considerably increased such provision (Lupton *et al.*, 1998).

It has been argued that the 'excellence' literature relating to lessons to be learnt from the management of responsive, successful organisations in the private sector (for example, Peters and Waterman, 1982; Goldsmith and Clutterbuck, 1984) was influential on the early changes initiated by Thatcher in the public sector (Hambleton and Hoggett, 1987; Young, 1991; Clarke and Newman, 1997). This stressed a commitment to quality and service and keeping in touch with customers in order to promote a 'user-oriented' approach to service delivery.

1987-1991: Market Mechanisms

There was a shift in emphasis in welfare policy as the Thatcher government moved into their third term of office. Market principles began to be implemented on a wider basis in order to achieve greater efficiency (McCarthy, 1989), increase choice and improve the quality of care (Ham, 1994). Changes now began to be made to the basic structures of welfare provision and the relationship between the State and the recipient of welfare (Deakin, 1994). In the provision of health and social care, the main piece of legislation was the NHS and Community Care Act 1990.

The NHS and Community Care Act, 1990

The two complementary White Papers 'Working for Patients' (Department of Health, 1989a) and 'Caring for People' (Department of Health, 1989b) contained the government's proposals for radical changes in the delivery of health and social care respectively. They were later consolidated as law in the NHS and Community Care Act 1990 (Department of Health, 1990). Market mechanisms were introduced into the delivery of health and social care through the separation of the purchasing role from that of the providing role and the introduction of contracts. According to New Right ideology markets would bring competition, increased choice, efficiency and responsiveness to service users.

Working for Patients

'Working for Patients' (Department of Health, 1989a) included a clear commitment to put service users first. *'Wherever they live in the UK'* people could expect *'better health care and greater choice of the services available'* (para. 1.8). The paper proposed the introduction of an 'internal market' into the delivery of health care with distinct and separate roles for those purchasing services from those providing services. It also introduced the opportunity for GP practices of a certain size to apply to manage their own budgets thereby becoming 'fundholders' and for hospitals to apply for self-governing status as NHS hospital 'Trusts'; these are further examples of devolved management. Initially only open to practices with list sizes of 11,000 or more, GP fundholding was subsequently extended greatly (see NHS Executive, 1994). Since election however the new Labour government have deferred further applications to join the GP fundholding scheme whilst health care commissioning is debated (Department of Health, 1997b).

GP fundholding proved to be one of the most debated aspects of the 'reforms'. Positive aspects included the potential to introduce innovation and flexibility and to enhance the efficiency and responsiveness of services (Glennerster, 1992). Concerns however included a 'two tier' system emerging in favour of patients of fundholders for example in relation to receiving preferential access to hospital services (Glennerster *et al.*, 1994; Whitehead, 1994), 'cream skimming' of the least costly users, cost shifting and underprovision (Mullen, 1993; Ham, 1994; Smee, 1995).

The last three must all be seen as ways in which fundholders may reduce their expenditure. Fundholding was also acknowledged as representing a substantial shift of power towards the primary care sector (Smee, 1995).

Fundamental features of the 'purchaser-provider split' were the existence of competition and the introduction of contracts. Contracts would be made between 'purchasers' (GP fundholders and health authorities) and 'providers' (self-governing Trusts and health authorities) for the supply of services. Competition for these contracts (to earn revenue) would encourage the supply of *efficient* services which were *responsive* to service users. For example, hospital Trusts were created in order to '*encourage local initiative and greater competition*' (Department of Health, 1989a: para. 3.3) with the aim of providing a better service to the public. The need to secure contracts would act as an incentive to provide the services that people want which would '*in turn ... stimulate other NHS hospitals to respond to what people want locally*' (para 1.9). Trusts were opposed by certain sectors however as examples of 'privatisation' (Levitt *et al.*, 1995: 81). In fact, 'privatisation' has been suggested as the ultimate aim of Working for Patients (Butler, 1992) a claim perhaps not unfounded give the flotation of a number of the public utilities throughout the 1980s.

A provision in 'Working for Patients' allowing money to cross administrative boundaries, in order for contracts to be secured between purchasers and providers in different health authorities (para. 6.2), further had the potential to increase competition, choice and efficiency by effectively increasing the amount of providers. The proposed income tax relief on private medical insurance premiums for retired people was also to encourage '*diversity of provision and choice*' (Department of Health, 1989a: para. 1.18) in health care.

It was proposed that it should be easier for people to choose and change their GP as they wish (para. 7.6). They would no longer have to go through the process of contacting their health authority; providing they are able to find a practice willing to register them, they can act independently. Further, capitation fees were to be increased from 46% of a GPs income to at least 60% in order to act as an incentive to satisfy users and accordingly, basic practice allowance would form a reduced proportion of remuneration (para. 7.3). In order for service users to utilise the provision to choose and change their GP, practices were to be encouraged to make information available including details of the services provided, doctors' qualifications and opening hours. These initiatives were all proposed earlier in the 1987

White Paper 'Promoting Better Health' which stressed the importance of the primary sector in the delivery of care and included the major objectives *'to make services more responsive to the needs of the consumer; ... to promote health and prevent illness; to give patients the widest range of choice and to improve value for money'* (Department of Health, 1987: para. 1.6).

The official view was that the user's position would be strengthened in two important ways by the heightened choice of family doctor. Firstly, they would be better informed and so able to exercise choice in a way related to his/her needs and secondly the financial incentives for doctors would encourage them to provide a better service creating a more competitive environment which would raise standards (Department of Health, 1987: para. 1.17).

Users of health services were to be provided with information about other aspects of services also to enable them to become more involved in their care and to assist them in any choices they may be given (Department of Health, 1989a: para. 1.13). Information leaflets about specific illnesses and treatments are examples, theoretically enabling service users to play a more active role in any encounters with the medical profession.

The 1987 White Paper had also proposed that complaints procedures were to be simplified. There would be a provision for verbal as well as written complaints to be accepted and an extension of informal conciliation procedures in an attempt to process grievances with greater speed.

Elderly people (defined as 65 years and over) had also been recognised as forming a distinct sector of the population with respect to primary care services both through being high users of such services and through forming a considerable and increasing percentage of the population (Department of Health, 1987: para. 3.17). They were seen as requiring assistance in maintaining a healthy lifestyle (para. 3.18) and it was proposed that some elderly people, along with other distinct sectors of the population, would be offered regular and frequent health checks (para. 1.15). In recognition of the time that this would demand, further changes were proposed in the remuneration of doctors.

Caring for People

'Caring for People' aimed to enable people to live as normal lives as possible in the community, to provide necessary care and support and to *'give people a greater individual say in how they live their lives and the services they need to help them to do so'* (Department of Health, 1989b: para. 1.8). It also stated how *'promoting choice and independence'* (para. 1.8) underlay all the proposals. The White Paper related to all people in need of care provided by Social Services departments; for the purposes of this study, the proposals relating to the delivery of care to elderly people with continuing care needs in the community, but not in residential or nursing homes, will be examined.

The changes proposed were similar to those in Working for Patients (above), that is, the separation of the purchasing and providing roles and the introduction of market principles to gain the benefits of competition. Social Services departments were to become *'enabling authorities'* (para. 3.1.3) by developing their purchasing and contracting role rather than, as was previously the case, being the sole, direct providers of services. Provision was to be encouraged by private, voluntary and 'not for profit' agencies where they represented cost-effective alternatives. Hence the use of the term *'mixed economy'* (Levitt *et al.*, 1995; Adams, 1996) or *'welfare pluralism'* (Pinker, 1992; Johnson, 1993). Many of these changes had been proposed earlier by Griffiths on the grounds that they would *'widen consumer choice, stimulate innovation and encourage efficiency'* (Griffiths, 1988a: para. 1.3.4).

The responsibilities of Social Services departments therefore would include assessing an individual's needs for social care in collaboration with other relevant professionals, designing 'packages of care' to meet the defined needs, securing the delivery of services in an efficient manner and regulating subsequent provision. In some cases, for example, where multiple needs were apparent, a 'case manager' may be appointed to ensure that needs were reviewed regularly and resources employed efficiently (para. 3.3). In all cases, whenever an individual's needs were assessed, *'the wishes of the individual and his or her carer'* should be taken into consideration and assessments *'should include their active participation'* (Department of Health, 1989b: para. 3.2.6). Social Services departments were also to have responsibility for establishing procedures for receiving comments and complaints (para. 3.1.3).

The changes outlined had the potential to bestow numerous benefits upon Social Services users similar to those resulting from the reform of health care delivery. These included *'a wider range of choice of services; services which meet individual needs in a more flexible and innovative way and competition between providers, resulting in better value for money and a more cost-effective service'* (Department of Health, 1989b: para. 3.4.3). As with the changes to the delivery of health care, these themes of choice, competition, efficiency and responsiveness reflect ways in which the position of the service user may be enhanced.

These White Papers (Department of Health, 1989a; Department of Health, 1989b) relate to the delivery of health and social care across the whole population in any encounters they may have with the services. Ways in which the role of (elderly) service users on discharge from hospital may be enhanced included increased levels of information about services (Department of Health, 1989a) and the design of packages of care to include their participation (Department of Health, 1989b). Guidance specifically relating to the discharge process is analysed later in the chapter.

'Quasi' Markets, Competition and Choice

It was always acknowledged that, whilst sharing many characteristics, markets for the provision of welfare would never be identical to their private sector counterparts. Hence the use of the term 'quasi' markets to describe the application of market mechanisms to the provision of health and social care (Le Grand, 1990; Bartlett *et al.*, 1994; Hudson, 1994).

The correctness of the term 'internal market' in health care has been disputed (Butler, 1992; Levitt *et al.*, 1995) on the grounds that it would not just entail competition between NHS providers but also between the public and private health care sectors. It is suggested here however that health care markets are largely made up of existing statutory providers while the potential for social care markets appears more diverse (Wistow *et al.*, 1992). There appears little role for voluntary, independent or informal sectors in competing for contracts for the provision of medical care whereas such competition forms the basis of the 'mixed economy' of social care. Other terms suggested for health care markets include 'managed competition' (Levitt *et al.*, 1995), partial deregulation (Hunter,

1989), planned markets and public competition (Robinson and Le Grand, 1995).

Competition has been shown to be one of the major objectives of the welfare policies implemented post-1987. It was believed that this would bring choice, efficiency and responsiveness in the delivery of care. A possible disadvantage of encouraging competition from a range of sources however is the *fragmentation* of services (Johnson, 1993; Munro, 1996). In addition it cannot be assumed that different service providers form complete substitutes as, with the personal nature of care, where the service is delivered and by whom can be fundamental features rendering the existence of perfect substitutes improbable. Some of the ways in which competition can be stifled are now summarised.

The purchaser-provider split has not always meant that these roles are distinct and separate. Many GP fundholders and health authorities fulfil both purchasing and providing functions and care managers have the potential to fill both roles in the field of social care. Health authorities maintain a provider role through the administration of their directly managed units and fundholders continue to provide GP services in addition to a new role in purchasing the services not provided in-house. Care managers may carry out both purchaser and provider functions as their role is to assess what care is needed and then arrange, purchase and monitor its provision (Lewis *et al.*, 1996).

The ways in which contracts could be set also served to limit competition. The use of block contracts, by which purchasers commit a large percentage of their budgets at the start of the year with given providers (Green, 1992; Paton, 1997) is an example. These may ensure efficiency and stability but hardly infer responsiveness to service users and place obvious restrictions on the level of choice available to the final user at the point of delivery. Similarly, the possibility exists of Social Services departments purchasing from a limited number of suppliers (Flynn and Common, 1990) in order to take advantage of economies of scale. The *patient* can be argued to follow the *money* rather than vice versa (Munro, 1996). Other reports show how five years of an internal market failed to significantly alter the established spending patterns of purchasers (Kennedy, 1996; Paton, 1997). This was possibly intentional however as health authorities were initially discouraged from making major changes to their spending patterns as this would threaten the financial position of providers (Harrison, 1995). Similarly the setting of block contracts tended to reflect existing patterns of activity (Robinson and Le Grand, 1995).

The practice of hospitals specialising and creating self-proclaimed 'centres of excellence' (Hayes, 1991) can also serve to limit competition by effectively creating a local if not national monopoly for that specialty. In a similar vein, Social Services departments as the dominant purchasers mean that there is less competition than might otherwise exist (Wistow *et al.*, 1994; Forder *et al.*, 1996). This concern may be assuaged somewhat by defining care managers as individual purchasers. In the field of social care also it must be considered that some providers, particularly in the voluntary sector, may not wish or be able to expand their provision (Wistow *et al.*, 1996). Also of concern is the haphazard nature of voluntary provision and its uncertain relationship with the statutory sector in both philosophy and practice (Leat, 1990) as well as the quality of voluntary and private sector provision (Wistow *et al.*, 1996).

Walker (1993) describes the whole aim of promoting a mixed economy of social care as 'bland' and considers a main underlying objective of structural change to be the residualisation of Social Services. He concludes the main reasons preventing a 'cultural revolution' from occurring to be underfunding, concerns about the quality of non-statutory provision and a desire by Social Services departments to remain as providers rather than managers.

Hayes (1991) believes the potential of market mechanisms to be heavily dependent upon peoples' ability and willingness to exercise a choice of GP with whom to register and along with Butler (1992) and Shackley and Ryan (1994) argue that choice for users of health care is possibly limited to this. Leavey *et al.* (1989) however believe that when choosing a GP, a range of accessible alternatives does not always exist due to factors including the geographical distribution of practices, the drawing of practice boundaries and the availability of public transport. They also believe that people are not motivated to change GP due to the infrequent nature of the patient role and the circumstances necessitating treatment precluding the possibility of 'shopping around'. With regard to any choice of treatment offered to potential service users, it is conceivable that possible choices would be pre-selected by the purchaser. Hunt (1990), in his analysis of patient choice and the NHS, even suggests that choice is only really available for (health) care suppliers and not for the final user. For public sector analysts, such a lack of choice for users makes private market ideas irrelevant (Hayes, 1991). Scrivens (1992) on the other hand suggests that increasing choice weakens the position of the service user as they become less able to determine their own needs and wants.

Le Grand (1993) considers that 'quasi' markets, with particular relation to community care, should be evaluated on the basis of efficiency, responsiveness, choice and equity, criteria which have also been applied to the evaluation of Trusts' performance (Bartlett and Le Grand, 1993). These criteria appear wider ranging than those used to assess the functioning of conventional markets where efficiency and profit maximisation are usually the overriding concerns (Lunt *et al.*, 1996).

Equity, a founding principle of the NHS, is not a consideration in many private markets; indeed allocation of resources by free markets is characterised by *inequality* (Levenson, 1992; Pierre, 1995). It is believed that social inequality and injustice are perpetuated by the allocation of scarce resources via market forces (Johnson, 1993) in that those with the purchasing power, knowledge and information to assume an active role are further advantaged by mechanisms encouraging them to do so (Pierre, 1995). On the part of purchasers, in the light of contracts and efficiency, the potential for 'cream skimming' or 'adverse selection', provides an example of positive discrimination in favour of the most lucrative users: the relatively healthy, the less needy, the more self-sufficient (Le Grand, 1993; Matsaganis and Glennerster, 1994). Such concerns are of particular concern in the provision of welfare (Light, 1992).

1991: The Charter Initiative

Changes within the Conservative Party saw John Major assume leadership in November 1990 marking a further shift in emphasis in relation to the public services. The Citizen's Charter White Paper (HMSO, 1991), one of Major's first initiatives, was proclaimed by Major himself as the centrepiece of policies in the 1990s (Drewry, 1993; Connolly *et al.*, 1994), as the 'big idea' of the Conservative government (Plamping and Delamothe, 1991; Lewis, 1993) and as one of his key policies (Jones, 1994; Tritter, 1994).

The 'citizens' in question were not defined, but it was clear that the White Paper actually referred to members of the public in their capacity as users of public services (Drewry, 1993; Connolly *et al.*, 1994; Pollitt, 1994). As such, the Citizen's Charter focused the management and delivery of public services on the position and perspective of service users (Bynoe, 1996). Quality, choice, standards and value were given as the main themes of the Charter which also claimed that public services would be more accountable and responsive to the wishes of users. It also aimed to sustain a number of principles of public service including information, choice, consultation, accessibility and redress. These objectives were to be achieved through mechanisms such as contracting out, competition, publishing performance targets and comprehensive complaints procedures. Many of these were of course already in place. It has been suggested that an aim of the Charter initiative was to define a role for the service user amongst the purchaser-provider split and the contract culture then in place (Bynoe, 1996).

Due to many mechanisms already being in place, it has been suggested that rather than representing an innovation in service delivery and management, it simply made explicit many of the changes which had hitherto been intimated (Hambleton and Hoggett, 1993; Lewis, 1993). That is, the Citizen's Charter initiative can be seen as a logical continuation of the reforms of the Thatcher governments. For example, quality assurance had been a recurrent theme in the provision of public services since 1979 (Kirkpatrick and Lucio, 1995). Similarly, the emphasis was largely on individual rather than collective service use which was consistent with New Right ideology, a strong influence on the policies of the Thatcher governments. Importantly, however, the Charter has been presented as demonstrating Major's genuine belief in (Doern, 1993), and his personal commitment to, the quality of public services (Drewry, 1993). It has also, albeit much less convincingly, been suggested as having established a direct relationship between providers and users of public services (Falconer *et al.*, 1997).

The intention was that most public services would observe the Charter principles and even produce charters for their specific area within national guidelines to include statements of their service standards.

Tritter (1994) claimed that one of the most positive aspects of the Citizen's Charter was the emphasis on disseminating information and laying down some of the basic principles with which public service providers should be concerned. The latter aspect would help develop 'customer' awareness which has been given as one of the main ways in which the Charter has impacted more on providers than on users (Pollitt, 1994; Falconer *et al.*, 1997). Further positive features include the fact that this was the first time that indicators of standards of service provision had been made public (Lewis, 1993; Falconer *et al.*, 1997) and the promotion of complaints procedures. The Citizen's Charter was criticised, however, for being little more than a public relations exercise. Indeed a survey carried out three years later found that many of the public plainly regarded it as essentially 'public relations' (Bellamy and Greenaway, 1995). Other less positive features were the 'top-down' setting of standards, rarely based on consultation with service users (Bynoe, 1996; Falconer *et al.*, 1997) and the confinement of performance indicators to aspects which could be easily measured and met.

The Charter initiative can arguably be regarded as a culmination of the 'reforms' to the public sector which had taken place throughout the 1980s its importance lay in its role in promoting the user-oriented nature of public services. For example, the Patient's Charter (Department of Health, 1991) can be seen as a mechanism for informing the public of what they could expect when using the NHS, particularly as a result of the policies detailed in this chapter so far. For this reason it can also be seen as a way of informing service users of policy change in an accessible way. Importantly, Ham (1994) believes that the Patient's Charter served to highlight those aspects of the NHS reforms concerned to improve the quality of services from the patient's perspective.

'The Patient's Charter' publicly expressed the NHS' aim of putting the patient first and making services more responsive to users' views and needs. As such, it may be viewed as an assertion of a potentially more powerful position for the users of health care; they had rights, they knew what to expect and could make a complaint if they were dissatisfied. It detailed seven existing rights of users regarding health care, three additional rights which were to be introduced in 1992 and nine National Charter standards of service provision. It also expressed the intention that local Charters would be published by individual hospitals and health authorities to reflect local circumstances, for example, expected waiting times in 'accident and emergency' units (Department of Health, 1991: 16).

The rights of service users included the right to have proposed treatment explained to them and the right to detailed information on health services. One of the further rights introduced in April 1992 was the right to have any complaint about the NHS investigated and to receive a full and prompt written reply from the Chief Executive or general manager (p.11).

The standards that service users could expect were also set out; many of which are particularly relevant to this study. Relatives and friends would be kept informed of progress, subject to the person's wishes; services were to be accessible to all, including those with special needs; a named qualified nurse would be responsible for care received and, before discharge from hospital, decisions would be taken with regard to continuing care and the necessary services arranged.   In respect of decisions regarding discharge, service users and, with their consent, their carers would be consulted and informed at all stages (p.15).

This Charter was distributed widely amongst health professionals, relevant organisations and to all households. It actively called for people to offer their views and suggestions about its content and also expressed the intention to continue to search for users' views in order to improve services. For example, by encouraging health authorities to use surveys and questionnaires. This was in line with the broader policy permeating the NHS of consulting local communities about service provision (NHS Management Executive, 1992).

Similar to the Citizen's Charter, a positive feature of the Patient's Charter was the fact that standards were set and published. However, the standards were set by policy makers and enforced 'top-down' and the 'rights', many of which were already in existence, were not legally enforceable (Falconer *et al.*, 1997). It is also possible that the indicators, for example, waiting and appointment times (which are easily measurable) were not the priorities that service users would have identified. The priorities can even be argued to distract from more fundamental issues, for example, efficacy of treatment (Hogg, 1994). Almost dismissing the specific content of the Patient's Charter, Hogg (1994) argues that its true value lay in its representation of a means of negotiation between service providers and users and the implications for a more equal relationship.

Following on from the original Charter, a further edition 'The Patient's Charter and You' (Department of Health, 1995a) was published. This was noticeably more extensive than the first and claimed to have incorporated the comments and suggestions received in response to the original. Additional rights included the ability to choose and change GP easily and quickly if desired, the publication of information by GP practices to enable people to make such choices and the right to detailed information on local health services. Significantly, these had all been addressed in 'Working for Patients' (Department of Health, 1989a). The 1995 Charter claimed that '*The NHS now gives you more information than ever before*' (Department of Health, 1995a: 7). This included the right to information on local Charter standards and the performance of individual hospitals, access to annual reports and NHS Comparative Performance Tables (commonly known as 'League' tables).

Additional standards that NHS users could expect included a maximum wait of twenty six weeks for a first outpatient appointment, a choice of food whilst an inpatient and home visits by community health services to be at a convenient time for the recipient (about which they would be consulted) and to be seen within two hours of that time. Again, these are indicators which can be quantified and so represent limited aspects of receiving health care. The intention to produce local community care Charters, covering rights and standards with regard to home care services, aids and equipment for daily living, was also stated and guidance had been formerly published (Department of Health, 1994a).

The local Charter standards of individual service providers to supplement those to be achieved nationally should be seen within the broader context of devolved management and decisions being taken closer to where care is delivered. Although guidance was issued centrally, individual purchaser and provider units appeared to have much more freedom in how the guidance should be interpreted locally in response to the needs of the local population. The setting of national guidelines within which local provider units were to work has the potential to create pressure for individual units in meeting national targets and to distort their own priorities (Bynoe, 1996).

From the standpoint of public participation the Charter initiative can be cautiously applauded as a way of potentially increasing the involvement of service users, of increasing accountability to service users and thereby creating a new relationship between service providers and users (Lewis, 1993). In short, making the public sector more user friendly (Connolly *et al.*, 1994). The many limitations however demonstrate that whilst it represented a noble attempt at redefining the relationship between public services and their users, its significance in promoting substantial change in the relationship between providers and the public remained limited.

Specific Policy Guidance

The legislation outlined so far concentrated on policy change in a broad sense both to establish a context within which to locate more specific policy guidance and to illustrate prevailing attitudes and values regarding the delivery of care. It also analysed ways in which the criteria identified throughout this study as indicative of a stronger position for users of public services namely, *participation, representation, access, choice, information* and *redress* were promoted repeatedly. Whilst this provided a framework within which to conduct the empirical study, specific guidance regarding hospital discharge was also issued which addressed these criteria. This is now analysed with particular reference to the subjects of this study, elderly people with continuing care needs on discharge from hospital, but not into residential or nursing home care.

The demographic and economic trends outlined earlier in this chapter coupled with the changes introduced in the NHS and Community Care Act (Department of Health, 1990) made this a particularly pertinent area for study. The cumulative trend had been for people to stay as inpatients only for as long as was medically necessary and for much of their rehabilitation and continuing care needs to be met in the community (NAHAT, 1994, 1995b). The result has been a steady reduction in the average length of inpatient stay, the closure of many hospital beds and an increase in throughput (largely due to the expanding role of day surgery). These trends were particularly marked in the care of elderly people throughout the 1990s.

Reductions in the length of hospital stay have been apparent since 1979 when the average length of stay in a geriatric ward was 77.5 days compared to 1989 when it was approximately 37 days (Audit Commission, 1992). The 'average daily available beds' for geriatrics decreased by 28.6% between 1982 and 1992-3 whilst the throughput increased by 149% and the number of day cases increased by 700% (Department of Health, 1996b).

The Discharge Process

Discharge from hospital and the period shortly afterwards can be a very significant time for the service user and their family and can be resource intensive for care providers. As such the process needs to be managed effectively to ensure that users are satisfied, their needs are met appropriately and there is an efficient deployment of resources (Waters, 1987; Henwood and Wistow, 1993; Chapman and Jack, 1996; Armitage and Kavanagh, 1998). Later policy guidance acknowledged hospital discharge as an issue of 'central strategic concern' and a critical 'litmus test' against which service users and their carers judge the quality of services (Department of Health, 1994b).

The Government circular HC (89)5 'Discharge of Patients from Hospital' (Department of Health, 1989c) attempted to promote good practice. It emphasised the importance of ensuring that before people are discharged, arrangements should be made for their return home and any continuing care needs they might have. It stated that planning for discharge should begin at the earliest possible stage and that '*the patient, and if appropriate, the family or carer(s) must be at the centre of the planning process*' (para. 3). The roles of health and social care staff who may become involved as appropriate were also outlined including medical, nursing and social work staff; they may be involved either in discharge planning or in care delivery on, or after, discharge. Information, written if deemed necessary, to service users and their families was cited as an important aspect of discharge.

A booklet also entitled 'Discharge of Patients from Hospital' (Department of Health, 1989d) was designed to assist health authorities in drawing up guidelines for discharge to meet the requirements of HC (89) 5. The booklet acknowledged that special care was needed in the discharge arrangements for certain groups of people. Although not recognised as a group by virtue of their age, people of 70 years and over probably constitute a high proportion of a number of the groups specified, for example, people who are living alone, people with a continuing disability or people who have been in hospital for an extended stay.

The 'Hospital Discharge Workbook' (Department of Health, 1994b) was later compiled as a result of a project established by the Department of Health which consulted experienced individuals (health and social care professionals and academics) and considered examples of good practice. The workbook, which lacked the status of policy guidance, provided a framework for good practice but recognised that all people have different needs on discharge; some being relatively straightforward while others are more complex. It identified the responsibilities of the major 'stakeholders' involved in the discharge process namely senior managers, hospital and Social Services managers, community based practitioners and hospital based practitioners and established a checklist for each to ensure that all aspects were addressed. Although acknowledging that '*the most important stakeholders in hospital discharge are service users and their carers*' (p.3), it is significant that their role is not addressed due to having no explicit responsibilities to uphold.

The workbook claimed to have the needs of the service user and resource effectiveness at its core both of which are consistent with market principles and broader government philosophy shown throughout this chapter so far. The trend for an increasing level of care being provided outside the hospital sector was also reflected.   Firstly, the workbook advocated that admission to hospital should only take place when all other alternatives had been explored and it was found to be the most efficient and appropriate option.   Secondly, people should only stay in hospital for as long as they are in need of specialised medical care, a belief which is highlighted by the closure of many long stay, particularly geriatric, hospital wards and a reduction in the average length of stay, shown above. The need was also addressed for people to be provided with information before admission about their condition and the likely course of action to be taken and that preparation for discharge should begin on or before admission to hospital.   This was highlighted as particularly important in cases where people were likely to have continuing care needs or their care needs were likely to be complex, for example, in the case of some elderly people.

The workbook further addressed the need to inform and seek agreement from inpatients and their families about the day of discharge in advance.   It stated how service users with continuing care needs should have care plans devised (with their participation) before they are discharged from hospital.   They should agree to the plan and they and their carers should retain a copy of it.   In addition, individuals and their families should have a named contact and telephone number in case of any difficulties.   These are all factors which have since been identified by groups of elderly people as particularly important in relation to hospital discharge (Barnes and Cormie, 1995).

The explicit definition of roles which was introduced by the NHS and Community Care Act (Department of Health, 1990) through initiatives such as the purchaser-provider split and contract setting for the delivery of services has necessitated a corresponding need for explicitness in defining responsibilities.   Where the responsibility of the NHS ends and that of Social Services departments begins and vice versa was one area that needed clarification.   In some ways, this is a positive move by ensuring that responsibilities are honoured but also can be seen as threatening the concept of 'seamless' care and placing emphasis on budgets at the expense of care.   In addition, real and potential difficulties due to clashes of interests between the NHS and Social Services departments were apparent (Cervi, 1996).

Health Service Guidelines (95)8 'NHS Responsibilities for Meeting Continuing Health Care Needs' (Department of Health, 1995b) superseded the criteria in HC (89)5 and was more specific in its delegation.

The guidance referred most directly to older people (as a specific client group and those suffering from mental illness); people with dementia; younger adults requiring care due to illness or accidents and children (para. 7). As the title suggests, the guidelines attempted to clarify responsibilities for meeting continuing care needs. NHS purchasers were to retain full responsibility for arranging and funding care to meet physical and mental health care needs whether people were cared for as inpatients or in the community. Other important NHS responsibilities covered rehabilitation, palliative health care, respite health care and community health services support (para. 1). Social Services departments also had a role to play in continuing care; as such, collaborative working was considered essential between the NHS and Local Authorities, a development envisaged in the proposals in 'Caring for People' (Department of Health, 1989b). A crucial distinction between the different sectors is that care provided by the NHS continues to be free of at the point of delivery whilst care commissioned by Social Services departments may be means tested.

The document (HSG (95)8) also reiterated the need for decisions regarding continuing care on discharge from hospital to be taken following an appropriate multi-disciplinary assessment of the patient's needs (Department of Health, 1995b: para. 17) which should take into consideration *'the views and wishes of the patient, his or her family and any carer'* (para. 19). Hospitals were to provide written information about needs assessment and discharge procedures to 'patients' and should ensure that they, their families and carers were provided with the information required to participate in decisions. Before the discharge was implemented, the patient and his or her representative(s) would be given the right to seek a review of the decision and could expect a response in writing and an explanation of the decision within two weeks (para. 30). In many instances an independent panel would consider the case (Department of Health, 1995c).

As a result of the guidance in HSG (95)8, individual health authorities were required to produce by September 1995 draft local policies and eligibility criteria for continuing health care (para. 9a). Public consultation was then to take place in each health authority and local policy finalised by 1st April 1996. The rationale behind developing local criteria within national guidelines is to ensure flexibility in responding to local needs. The same reasoning was given for the devolution of power and responsibility advocated in earlier legislation and reports documented in this chapter and for the devising of Charter standards by individual provider units.

The consultation document produced by the local Health Authority within which this study takes place (Sefton Health, 1995) proposed that care would continue to be funded by the health authority and provided as an inpatient if an individual needed specialist care which could only be provided by a consultant or GP-led team or otherwise required health care equipment or treatment. Other specialist health services and home loans would be provided in the community. The document also stated the intention of the health authority to have in place by 1 April 1996 a process for reviewing decisions regarding eligibility for NHS continuing health care to comply with the national criteria (Department of Health, 1995c).

Further reform of the management and delivery of health and social care nationally was introduced on 1 April 1996. This included the abolition of the fourteen Regional Health Authorities to be replaced by eight NHS Executive regional offices and the merger of the District Health Authorities and the Family Health Services Authorities into a single Health Authority. The latter would have responsibility for commissioning all primary and secondary care services. The new health authorities assumed responsibilities previously held by each of the two separate bodies and worked within the guidelines outlined above. These changes appear to be a move towards centralisation in that policy implementers are further removed from service provision which suggests distance from and less responsiveness to local needs.

A further proposal of the last Conservative government relating to continuing care is the 'Community Care (Direct Payments) Bill' (Department of Health, 1995d). This bill proposed that in certain circumstances those in need of care provided by local authorities could be given cash payments in order to buy the services directly. Needs would continue to be assessed by the statutory authority and those in receipt of 'direct payments' must use them to purchase services to meet those needs. Individuals could supplement the payments received in order to obtain extra care or upgrade their care. If introduced, the scheme was to be piloted on adults aged under 65 years who were physically disabled and who were able and willing to manage direct payments with the intention to ultimately extend its scope to most other groups in receipt of local authority care. Whilst this proposal is not of direct relevance to this study because of the limited coverage suggested initially, the potential of such a scheme in enhancing the role of the service user in relation to health and social care is obviously huge. However, this may transfer both financial and quality risks to the service user (Saltman and von Otter, 1995).

The Labour Government (from May 1997)

The general policy guidance outlined so far in this chapter shows how market ideology was implemented widely in the distribution of scarce welfare resources between 1979 and 1997. The Labour government which assumed power in May 1997 pledged to end the 'internal market', claiming it to be expensive to administer and that it distorted clinical priorities and fragmented care (Department of Health, 1997a; The Labour Party, 1997). An accessible and responsive NHS with quality and efficiency at its core were adopted as the aims guiding. *New Labour's* proposals for the delivery of health care.

Commissioning, based on co-operation rather than competition between Health Authorities, Social Services, GPs and NHS Trusts to achieve truly 'seamless' care was to be introduced over a number of years, during which time public consultation would take place (NHS Executive, 1997). A further policy initiative was the setting up of Primary Care Groups comprising GPs and community nurses to commission services for local populations in order to heighten responsiveness. Proposals for a new NHS Charter developed in partnership with users and carers and a new annual National Survey of patient experience to provide a voice in shaping the NHS (Department of Health, 1997b) provide strong indications that the perspectives of service users are destined to be given even greater emphasis than ever before.

Summary

Both the broad ideological and philosophical shift which has been apparent in the delivery of health and social care over the last twenty years and the legislation during this time have shaped the changes have been explored in this chapter. The main policy changes of relevance to this study have been analysed, that is, those aspects which seek to enhance the position of the service user in their encounters with the NHS and Social Services departments, with particular reference to hospital discharge. These include an increase in the level of information and an accessible complaints procedure.   Emphasis has also been placed on those areas which have created a new or more influential role for the service user or their carer(s); for example, participation in decisions about care on discharge and a simplified procedure for choosing and changing general practitioner. Collectively, a more active role is envisaged for service users as a result of the policies outlined. In addition, many incentives have been introduced to encourage service providers and policy makers to heed the wishes and needs of the final user of the service. Examples of such initiatives are the introduction of contracts for service delivery and an increase in the proportion of a GP's funding derived from capitation fees. It was within this policy framework that the present study took place.

The subjects of the study are people of 70 years and over recently discharged from hospital, in 1996. Guidelines for good practice envisaged that they should be given information before admission to hospital; given a choice of hospital to enter (unless an emergency admission); should be consulted regarding the care they are to receive on discharge; given a copy of their care plan on discharge from hospital and have a named professional to contact if necessary on their return home. The empirical study investigated the way in which the recommended procedures were applied in practice along with the views of both service users and NHS and Social Services professionals about the introduction of user-oriented principles. The study also sought to explore the ways in which the defined group of service users were willing and able to assume an active role in the process of using health and social care.

Chapter 4 now provides an analysis of the position of elderly people in contemporary society, presenting them as a 'critical case', and arguing that they are the *least* likely age group to assume an active role in using health and social care.

4 The Position of Elderly People in UK Society

Introduction

The argument so far has examined the changing position of users in relation to the formulation and implementation of public sector policy. Chapter 2 explored the concept of user *participation*, mainly in relation to health and social care, along with the associated issues of *representation, access, choice, information* and *redress* as indicators of a strengthening position for service users. Chapter 3 then analysed policy initiatives (mainly between 1989 and 1997), which aimed to introduce user-oriented initiatives and to encourage an active role for users of health and social care services, highlighting references to the above concepts. Chapter 3 also served to focus the study on the process of hospital discharge and, where possible, on elderly people.

In order to further contextualise the defined area of study, an appraisal is now provided of the position in UK society of people of 70 years and over; the group which was sampled for this study. Chapter 2 intimated that not all sectors of society are equally able or willing to participate whilst Chapter 3 demonstrated briefly how elderly people are an increasingly prominent age group. They form a large and growing percentage of the population, they are the group who make the greatest use of NHS and Social Services provision and as such are the sector most likely to be affected by the policy changes outlined. It is posited that elderly people constitute an ideal, indeed *critical*, group for the purposes of this study (see also Chapter 1) in that they may be *less* able or willing to assume an active role in the use of welfare services than other age groups in society.

This chapter analyses relevant literature and statistics relating to elderly people (operationally defined as 70 years and over) in order to explore the theoretical feasibility of them assuming an active role on discharge from hospital and in the short period afterwards. It discusses differing perceptions of elderly people as a distinct sector of society, provides data on the social and economic circumstances of people in the older age groups, explores the concepts of 'ageism' and 'burden' in relation to elderly people and examines the notion that elderly people have a socially constructed dependent status. The implications of these factors for older age groups participating in the ways envisaged in the policy documents outlined in Chapter 3 are then discussed. A critical review of primary research which contributes to knowledge in this area, highlighting those aspects that this study aims to expand upon is also incorporated. These previous studies are drawn upon in Chapters 7 and 8 when discussing the findings.

Critical Case Rationale

In order to undertake a comprehensive and in-depth analysis of the utilisation of health and social care services, a specific user group was required to provide a sufficiently defined focus. This chapter demonstrates why the age group selected is the most appropriate for such a focus and also why it forms a *critical case* in this analysis. The focus taken of people of 70 years and over on discharge from inpatient care and in the short period afterwards was felt to contain a number of important features which may influence both their ability and willingness to assume an active role. These are shown throughout this chapter.

An adaptation of the *critical case* concept as defined in Chapter 1 is employed in this study as the rationale for the selection of the age group. The original idea of a critical case was to investigate a population amongst whom the phenomena being studied was felt to be most likely to be evidenced. This research uses a population group which can be assumed to be the *least* likely amongst whom to witness the phenomenon under study. This chapter provides comprehensive supporting evidence for this assumption, that is, that the elderly age groups contain some of the most vulnerable and dependent members of society. However it also demonstrates that there is such diversity in circumstances and experiences across the whole population that the assumption cannot blindly be applied. This diversity is incorporated into the research design and is analysed in Chapter 8 when discussing the findings of the study.

Classifying Older People

> A sociological view of age ... regards it as one of the key variables in the
> understanding of social structures and cultures ... as the proportion of old
> people has steadily risen over the course of the 20th century, so too has
> age become one of the critical social distinctions (Bury and Macnicol,
> 1990a: viii).

Defining a group on the basis of a single variable for example age, as this
study does, obviously assumes a degree of commonality within that group.
It must be stressed however that no assumptions are made here as to
elderly people (70 years and over) forming a homogeneous group. Indeed
the research approach and analysis comprehensively sought to consider
demographic and social differentials in order to ascertain any such
influences on experience and behaviour in the use of welfare services.
Victor (1994) identifies four approaches to the definition of old age, the
first two of which are important in the analysis in this chapter: chronology;
the political economy approach, biological age and as a lifecyle stage.
Chronological age was employed in this study as an arbitrary constant in
the absence of more meaningful or reliable variables on which to define
the sample. It represented the most straightforward way by which to group
a sample of elderly people for an in-depth exploration of service utilisation
and participation. (See Chapter 5 for full information regarding the
sampling procedures employed.) It also allowed an analysis of the
findings of the empirical study by a number of other variables rather than
narrowing the sample at too early a stage.

The age range of 70 years and over used in this study shows a
discrepancy with that most commonly used in government produced
statistics, official legislation and most authors which adopt 65 years and
over, the state retirement age for males, as demarcating 'elderly people'.
Such publications are referred to throughout this chapter for information
on the circumstances of elderly people. The use of age 70 years and above
is an attempt to focus the study as specifically as possible yet retain the
potential for splitting the group into two age groups for the purposes of
analysis.

The increase in life expectancy outlined in Chapter 3 has resulted
in retirement periods spanning up to thirty years or more, effectively two
generations. This provides a further reason for selecting an age range of
70 years and above and is the reason for the increasingly common

distinction between 'elderly' or 'young elderly' people at 65 years and above and 'very elderly' or 'old elderly' people at age 80 years and above (Tinker *et al.*, 1994). Other authors have used the terms 'third age' to cover the period after retirement but before dependency and 'fourth age' as that of dependency leading to death (Laslett, 1987; Carnegie UK Trust, 1993). This study uses the two age groups, 70-77 years and 78 years and above, for the purposes of analysis; the latter age, used as a cut-off point, is derived from the mean age of questionnaire respondents and so was retrospectively applied. Coincidentally, the defining age of 'geriatric' in the acute hospital Trust under study is also 78 years.

Related to chronological age is the state's formalised response to older people, for example, exclusion from the labour force, exemption from prescription charges and eligibility for benefits including the state retirement pension. Such factors can also be used to categorise groups of people, for example, according to whether they participate in the labour force or not and if so by socio-economic grouping. In terms of this study, the age group selected, the general trend towards early retirement and the prerequisite for inclusion in the study as the possibility of having continuing care needs make it likely that the majority, if not all, of the sample will no longer participate in paid employment. Official retirement ages in the UK at present are 65 years for men and 60 years for women, although this will be equalised at 65 by 2020 (Whitting *et al.*, 1995). On reaching these ages people become eligible for social security benefits including the state retirement pension and occupational or private pension if applicable.

As stated at the beginning of this chapter, older people do not constitute a homogeneous group. As such, the classification of 'elderly people' here on the basis of age alone (or by any other single factor) can fail to take account of the huge diversity of attributes and experiences present within the group defined as such. There is scope for variations in such factors as access to resources, health experience and social support within all age groups. Three attributes often cited as major determinants of life experience are class, race and gender (Giddens, 1989; Williams, 1989). Socio-economic group or social 'class' and gender are two aspects which this study explores as potential influences on user experience and behaviour. Ethnicity or race, although acknowledged as an important potential influence on experience and behaviour, is not a factor which this study explored due to necessary constraints on the breadth of the investigation in addition to the relative lack of cultural diversity in the geographical area studied. The fact that these variables can be major determinants of life experience at all ages suggests the logical corollary that experience in old age may simply be a continuation of that throughout life.

The social dimensions of ageing are therefore important considerations and are central to 'social gerontology' on which there is an increasing volume of literature (Bond and Coleman, 1990). Two dominant themes of this relatively new academic discipline are the increasing numbers of elderly people and the generally negative public attitude towards old age in Western societies. That is, the classification of elderly people as a distinct sector of society and as 'different' is one of the baselines of social gerontology (Higgs, 1995); the belief that they should not be forms one of the central tenets.

Approaches which view elderly people as a distinct sector of the population can be argued to marginalise them relative to other age groups (Victor, 1994). They imply that the needs of people who have reached a certain age are uniform and are different from the needs of younger people. Such approaches tend to focus on the needs of elderly people, representing this age group as a 'problem' and viewing their increasing needs in a negative way (Arber and Evandrou, 1993). Discussion of elderly people in terms of their problems and needs holds the risk of 'welfarising' the group (Fennell *et al.*, 1988), a patronising approach, inevitably resulting in a diminution of the group under study. In addition, by focusing on needs and problems, such approaches can divert attention away from the wider social context or causes of such need or even obscure more positive attributes of the elderly population. Such approaches also grossly overgeneralise about a huge percentage of the population and facilitate the application of stereotypes relating to the behaviour, attitudes and expectations of elderly people. Wells and Freer (1988) firmly argue that increasing numbers of elderly people need not be viewed negatively and indeed the 'problem' that they represent is exaggerated.

More positive approaches suggest that classifying elderly people as a group with similar needs and experiences enables the provision of specialised services to be more accurately tailored to their specific needs, for example, 'geriatric' care. Similarly, Bytheway (1995) argues that approaches which seek to *integrate* elderly people into the wider society along with all other age groups risk negating the particular needs and desires of older people. In addition, grouping elderly people together can be seen positively in a political sense; raising the profile of the particular needs of older people may prevent relevant issues becoming subsumed under wider welfare issues and may ultimately help to further their cause. This has particular potential in the light of demographic change and elderly people as a growing proportion of the population and therefore the electorate. Examples from the United States show the success of organised movements of older people such as the Gray Panthers.

In this research a firm rationale has been provided for defining the population to be studied on the basis of chronological age whilst recognising that for an analysis of experience and behaviour in relation to service utilisation and participation few generalisations can be made about whole groups of people (Horton, 1984). Service users are a heterogeneous group even for very narrowly defined services due to differences in resources, experiences, needs and so on. It is argued here that focusing on a specified user group undergoing a narrowly defined phase in their care allows an in-depth exploration to take place. In this case the specified user group is people of 70 years and over and the defined phase in their care is discharge from inpatient care and the short period afterwards.

The user group or the service being obtained could obviously be defined more specifically, for example, by considering sufferers of a certain illness or users of a specified service. However this was felt to be too specific and therefore too limited for the purposes of the study. In addition, limitations were in place over initial sample selection (see Chapter 5). An in-depth view is sought instead of a stage in the lives of people who are, or have recently been, receiving care and who are experiencing a change in that care in which policy directives indicate that they should play an active role (see Chapter 3). Analysis of the findings takes place using various social, demographic and health-related variables and links between these variables to demonstrate the heterogeneity of the sample (see Chapters 6 and 8).

Profiling Older People

In order to provide a general impression of the circumstances of elderly people and to contextualise the study, relevant data from routinely compiled information is now summarised. Data for the country as a whole is combined with more specific data relating to the area where the study took place (Southport and Formby). Certain trends relating to increasing years, income, ill health and indeed the links between these variables are noteworthy.

As already outlined briefly in Chapter 3, decreasing mortality at all ages since the turn of the century has had major implications for the composition of the population of the United Kingdom. Coupled with a downward trend in the birth rate, a general ageing of the population has resulted. Life expectancy, an indicator of the overall health of the nation, has been increasing and is expected to continue to do so. This is shown in Table 2.

Table 2: **Actual and Projected Life Expectancy at Birth of the UK Population by Gender (Years)**

	1961	1991	2021
MALES	67.8	73.2	77.6
FEMALES	73.6	78.7	82.6

Source: Office for National Statistics, 1997a

Older people today form a larger group both in absolute terms and as a percentage of the total population than ever before (Laing and Hall, 1991); this trend is increasing and is projected to continue to do so. In 1971 approximately 13.2% of the population of the UK were aged 65 years and over; by 1991 this had increased to almost 16% and is projected to increase to 19.4% by 2021 (ONS, 1997a, see Table 1). The peak of this trend is estimated for 2036 when the 65 and over age group is projected to reach 21.6% of the total population (Laing and Hall, 1991). The 1991 Census reported that 21.4% of the population of Southport and Formby were aged 65 and over. Perhaps of greater significance to policy makers and service providers, due to correspondingly higher demand for care, is the percentage of the population aged 80 years and over. In 1971, this age group made up 2.3% of the population of the UK, by 1991 this figure had risen to 3.7% and by 2021 it is projected to have reached 5.1% (ONS, 1997a, see Table 1). In Southport and Formby in 1991, 5.9% of the total population were aged 80 years or above.

The differences in life expectancy by gender are reflected in the gender composition of the older age groups. In 1995, 48% of the UK population aged 65-69 years were male and 52% female; of people aged 70-74 years, 45% were male and 55% female whilst of people aged 75 years and over the difference was more dramatic with only 37% of the population male and 63% female (ONS, 1997b). In Southport and Formby in 1991 these figures were 43% of the population aged 65-74 years were male and 57% female and for the population aged 75 years and over, 30% were male and 70% female. As a result, there are more older women than older men living alone. In 1995, 36% of women aged 65-74 years lived alone compared to 17% of men; 62% of women aged 75 years and over lived alone compared to only 33% of men of the same age (ONS, 1997b).

Whilst morbidity rates are high amongst older people, it is difficult to determine whether the health status of the elderly population has improved, deteriorated or remained constant during the decades of declining mortality due to the lack of data over the period (MRC, 1994). As would be expected, morbidity rates are highest amongst people in the older age groups with self-reported long-standing illness and health status serving as useful indicators. In 1995, 55% of people aged 65-74 years in the UK reported a long-standing illness compared to 63% of those aged 75 years and over. These figures showed little change over recent years and little change by gender. Thirty seven percent of people aged 65-74 years reported a *limiting* long-standing illness compared to 48% of people aged over 75 years (ONS, 1997b). Martin *et al.* (1988) in the Disability Surveys report an exponential increase in disability with advancing years and very elderly people were found to predominate amongst the most severely disabled. Thirty two percent of people aged 65-74 in Southport and Formby reported a *limiting* long-standing illness in 1991 compared to 54.8% of people aged 75 years or above. In addition to greater experience of illness with increasing age, the number of conditions experienced at any one time also increases with age that is, the needs of elderly people tend to be multiply pathological (Young and Olson, 1991; Victor, 1994).

Self-reported health status over the previous year tended to worsen with age although such reports are generally fairly positive. Of people aged 65-69 years, 46% reported their health as 'good', 35% as 'fairly good' and 19% as 'not good'. Of people aged 85 years and over, 29% reported their health as 'good', 45% as 'fairly good' and 26% as 'not good' (OPCS, 1996). In addition, women tended to report their health less positively than men, particularly in the older age groups. Of people aged 85 years and over, 37% of men rated their health as 'good' compared to 26% of women and 17% of men rated their health as 'not good' compared to 30% of women (OPCS, 1996). Cox *et al.* found similar trends in the comprehensive Health and Lifestyle Survey (1987).

The high use of services by older people was recognised in much of the policy documentation analysed in Chapter 3. The General Household Survey reported that in 1994, 47% of people aged 65 years and over had consulted a GP at the surgery and 11% had received a visit at home in the previous three months whilst of people aged 85 years and over, 37% had consulted a doctor at the surgery and 31% had received a home visit in the three month period (OPCS, 1996). Similarly, the proportion of people who attended an outpatients department during the three months prior to the interview was highest among the 65 years and over age group at 21% (ONS, 1997b). Moreover, inpatient stays show how people of 65 years and over were most likely to be admitted as inpatients, again a trend which increased with age. They were also the age group who spent the longest period in hospital, a factor which differs by gender; elderly men spent an average of 11 nights in hospital and women an average of 14 nights (ONS, 1997b). This difference in length of hospital stay could possibly be accounted for by the fact that older women are more likely to live alone than older men and the implications this has for the availability of informal care.

The statistics for hospital bed availability and throughput however show how both the number of available beds and average lengths of inpatient stay are decreasing whilst day case rates are increasing resulting in a huge expansion in throughput (Department of Health, 1996b; see Chapter 3). Apparent for all age groups, these trends are particularly marked in geriatric medicine and have been described by Jennings (1993) as examples of 'rationing' services away from elderly users.

The General Household Survey also shows how contact with community health practitioners increases with age; 19% of people aged 85 years and over had used the services of a district nurse or health visitor in the previous month compared to only 2% of people aged 65-69 years. Local Authority home help services had been provided to 27% of people aged 85 years or over compared to 2% of people aged 65-69 years whilst no-one aged 65-69 years received 'meals-on-wheels' compared to 12% of people aged 85 years and over (OPCS, 1996). These differences in service usage by age suggest increasing levels of dependency with advancing years and are a factor supporting the choice of age group (70 years and over) slightly above that used conventionally (65 years and over).

These trends are obviously too broad to provide confident predictions of the health of older people in the UK. In addition, other analyses of age and ill health suggest that for many elderly people, morbidity is experienced for a very short period during the terminal phase of life (Fennell *et al.*, 1988). Debate exists about the validity of competing models of health and age employing expressions such as a 'compression of morbidity' (Fries, 1980; Bury, 1988) or the 'terminal drop' model of ageing (Wilson, 1991). Fries rests his argument regarding the 'compression of morbidity' on the assumption of a fixed human lifespan and morbidity from chronic diseases, the onset of which may be delayed. In addition, Freer (1988) argues that the proportion of elderly people rating their health positively is high despite the presence of ill health and that incidence of ill health does not necessarily equate with dependency or vulnerability.

General economic trends relating to elderly people as individuals also merit consideration. Although official retirement ages exist, it is becoming increasingly common for people to leave the labour force before having reached these ages (Taylor and Walker, 1995) making the use of state retirement age problematic in defining 'old age'. In 1994, only 51% of men aged 60-64 years were economically active compared with 83% in 1971 and among men aged 65 years and over, participation rates had declined from 19% in 1971 to 7% in 1994 (Tillsley, 1995). Corresponding figures for women show trends in the same direction but not of the same magnitude. Such trends can be interpreted in various ways for example, a desire for leisure or forced unemployment due to illness or to meet the needs of the economy; the latter of these is central to the 'political economy' approach to ageing (Walker, 1981) explored later in this chapter.

Former occupation can be used to determine the socio-economic grouping of elderly people although it is not always a reliable measure due to changes in employment in later years, for example, between industries or from full to part-time employment. An indication of the level of resources available to households containing elderly people can instead be gained from proxies such as housing tenure, ownership of consumer durables and receipt of a pension other than the state retirement pension. In 1994, little difference was observed in tenure between households containing a member of 65 years or over (64% lived in owner-occupied accommodation) and households with no elderly people in them (68% were owner occupied) (OPCS, 1996). It must be remembered that the General Household Survey only includes private households and so no indication is obtained of the percentage of elderly people living in institutions.

Possession of consumer durables, the ownership of which strongly reflects levels of income and standards of living (Askham *et al.*, 1992), tends to be lower by households containing an elderly person compared to other households although the gap is lessening. Car ownership also decreased with age with only 35% of people aged 75 years and over living in a household with a car, compared to 51% of people aged 65-74 years (OPCS, 1996). Availability of public transport and restrictions placed on the driving certification of elderly people will also be important factors in determining older peoples' car ownership and mobility, factors which are beyond the scope of this study.

The Family Expenditure Survey (ONS, 1996) reports actual income distribution and shows how in both one and two person households, income distribution is concentrated at the lower end of the income range in retired households compared to non-retired households. This is particularly marked in one adult households and amongst elderly disabled people (Victor and Vetter, 1986). One adult retired households mainly dependent upon state pensions had the lowest average gross income (ONS, 1996) and the proportion of income from wages and salaries decreased as the age of the head of household increased. Research also shows how most elderly people are dependent upon the state retirement pension and on other state benefits (Walker, 1982; Victor and Vetter, 1986). Males are slightly more likely to be members of a pension scheme than females (ONS, 1997a, 1997b) whilst those in non-manual occupations are more likely to be members than those in manual occupations.

Access to a low level of resources by older people is not a recent finding. Old age has long been recognised as a lifecycle stage during which poverty may be experienced (Booth, 1889; Rowntree, 1901; Royal Commission on the Distribution of Income and Wealth, 1978; Townsend, 1979).

These figures provide evidence for the assertion that people of 65 years and above constitute an increasingly prominent sector of the population. The statistics outlined also show many differences within the group, for example, life expectancy by gender and the resulting effect on the gender composition of the population at the older ages. There are more older women than there are older men; they tend to live alone more than older men; have access to a lower level of resources; report their health less positively and tend to stay as inpatients longer than elderly men.

These differences are particularly apparent at the higher end of the age scale. The possible ways in which these factors affect users' ability or willingness to assume an active role may therefore be exacerbated for older females as opposed to older males. This is explored in the empirical phase of this study along with possible differences by socio-economic status, differences between the behaviour of 'young elderly' people and 'old elderly' people and differences by household composition. This section has shown how all these variables are inter-related.

The Dependent Status of Older People

The statistics explored above examining the circumstances of people aged 65 years and over in the UK present a fairly pessimistic view of their economic, social and health status although this is not universal across the population of elderly people. From the broad profile given, dependency may be perceived in a number of forms in a culture where independence is valued. 'Dependency' has been defined in various ways, all of which imply a depressed status for the recipient: a power relationship (Walker, 1982), an asymmetrical relationship (Lloyd, 1991) or a subordinate relationship (Tinker, 1997).

Consideration of the degree of dependency in the UK often uses the 'dependency ratio', which relates dependents, or the economically inactive, to the economically active, that is, those in paid employment and is usually calculated on the basis of age (Johnson and Falkingham, 1992). This may be particularly relevant in the light of an increase in life expectancy (Fletcher, 1996), yet a degree of this may be offset by a falling birth rate. It must also be acknowledged that demographic factors alone are increasingly inappropriate in calculating the ratio of workers to non-workers due to such factors as early retirement, unemployment and the complex employment patterns of women. Whilst the dependency ratio predominantly relates to financial dependence, physical dependence can also be assumed in many instances, particularly in the case of elderly people.

Johnson (1990) believes that a dependent status has parallels with that of a 'deviant' status, that is, someone who no longer enjoys a place in the mainstream of society and whose behaviour is 'abnormal'. The sociological literature on such a phenomenon covers anyone who is dependent on others on a daily basis. Johnson concludes however that the application of such a theory to elderly people is inappropriate. Interestingly, given these definitions, although 'dependent' and 'deviant' statuses also have application to children, younger age groups tend not to be viewed in a negative way. Indeed, Walker (1982) perceives that *'the 'problem' of dependency has been treated exclusively as a problem of old age'* (p.131). This can be argued to be related to a representation of elderly people as a 'burden'.

The notion of 'burden' has been applied in terms of either the fiscal load (Gough, 1990; Jefferys and Thane, 1991; Evans, 1996), particularly in terms of pensions, or in terms of care-giving efforts and stress or indeed both (Warnes, 1993) although some authors believe it to be exaggerated (Freer, 1988; Laing and Hall, 1991; Victor, 1994).

Views of elderly people as a 'burden' have been influential in creating the discriminatory concept of *'ageism'*. Ageism is a term used by many commentators to describe the discrimination suffered by older people or the potential for such discrimination (Butler, 1969; Bytheway and Johnson, 1990; Bytheway, 1995). Butler, a psychiatrist, who was the first to use the term (in 1969), defined ageism as *'a process of systematic stereotyping and discrimination against people because they are old'* (Butler, 1987: 22).

Parallels have been drawn between 'ageism' and the concepts of racism and sexism in that a group is discriminated against by virtue of a common characteristic: age, ethnicity or gender. However, there are also many differences between the groups suffering discrimination such that the concept is not identical. Obviously, no one is born into the age group and the majority of life is spent as 'not old' particularly if the qualifying age is taken as 65 or 70 years. In addition, 'elderly people' are a group to which the majority of the population will eventually belong if they survive, unlike females or ethnic groups. This suggests that females and those from ethnic groups may experience double discrimination on reaching a certain age.

Perceptions of individuals or groups as 'dependent' do not fit easily with the promotion of an active role in the use of (public) services. However it has been argued that dependency is not an inevitable aspect of old age and that it is social and economic processes which serve to heighten dependency.

The Construction of Dependency

There are persuasive viewpoints claiming that dependency and negative perceptions of old age, potentially giving rise to ageism, are socially rather than biologically constructed and, as such, can be redefined through social and economic policies (Walker, 1980; Townsend, 1981). Developments in social welfare and employment policies, are argued to determine the distribution of power in society and assign dependent status. As such, they reinforce the stereotypes of elderly people as a distinct group having special needs and problems. This has been termed *institutional* ageism, relating elderly people to the means of production, or the demand for labour, and is central to the *political economy* approach to old age (Walker, 1981; Estes *et al.*, 1982; Phillipson, 1982). Moving away from viewing elderly people as a homogeneous group, such an approach considers older people as an integral part of society.

The status of a person defines their position within society along with certain expected rights and obligations (Harris, 1990). Employment is the main source from which people derive their economic status (Townsend, 1981; Macnicol, 1990) in addition to psychological qualities such as social status, self esteem, social interaction and so on (Pratt and Norris, 1994). It is also the main basis on which people are assigned to a socio-economic group or social 'class' (Reid, 1977). Retirement from the labour force can therefore be argued to be a major life transition affecting social, psychological and financial circumstances. Declining financial status may be the most readily apparent change given the low incomes of many elderly people illustrated earlier. An important feature of financial status is that the state retirement pension constitutes the largest percentage of the average income of those over retirement age.

These two major determinants of economic status, that is, employment status and state retirement pension (Walker, 1990) are both defined by state policy. Imposition of an arbitrary age at which participation in paid employment should cease shows how central government can determine the participation of older people in the labour market. It deprives them of the vital opportunity to sell their labour and suggests that age rather than ability should be the basis on which people are retained in employment (Laczko and Phillipson, 1990). The level of the state retirement pension and other social security benefits that elderly people may be entitled to and which constitute such a high proportion of their income are also state determined as are the criteria for eligibility.

In terms of the level of social security benefits that elderly people may claim, including the state retirement pension, the intention has always been for the state to provide a minimum level which could be supplemented by private means (see Beveridge, 1942). This however seems illogical and unfair given that the concept of a 'pension' is to provide post-employment income in recognition of years of service and suggests that pension policies are concerned with regulating the economy and labour force rather than meeting need.

Phillipson (1982) expands the relationship between older people and the economy by considering that the nature of capitalist society is such that people are only valued for the contribution they can make in the labour force. Exclusion from paid employment therefore imposes an inferior social status. A further aspect of Phillipson's argument showed how elderly people could be manipulated as a reserve 'army' of labour for managing the labour supply in response to cyclical movements in the economy. That is, they could be encouraged to continue working when there was little unemployment and high demand for labour yet encouraged to leave when unemployment was high in order to provide vacancies for younger workers. This represents older workers as passive rather than active in their labour market activity.

An early analysis of the relationship between elderly people and the means of production was given by Cowgill and Holmes in 1972 who devised the 'modernisation theory' arguing that as the degree of modernisation increases in a society the status of elderly people declines. More recently, Bond and Coleman (1990) have argued that industrialisation has resulted in a loss of respect for elderly people, with 'old' having acquired negative connotations. Modern technology has reduced the demand for workers and seen the evolution of new occupations. This can further be interpreted as a manipulation of the demand for labour with preference given to younger workers and classed as an example of society devaluing its older members.

A prominent sociological view of ageing, or indeed of older people's place in society, applies the theory of *disengagement* (Cumming and Henry, 1961) defined broadly as '*decreasing participation in the larger society by older persons*' (Sherman and Wood, 1979: 193). It is seen as a gradual but inevitable process resulting in decreased interaction between the ageing person and others in the social systems to which they belong (Cumming and Henry, 1961). Importantly, it is a process to be viewed positively by both individuals and society, as ensuring the smooth functioning of society.

From a functionalist perspective, loss of roles and therefore identity must be considered as central to disengaging from former aspects of life (Fennell *et al.*, 1988); roles being defined as expected behaviour derived from status (Harris, 1990). For males, the major life role was traditionally taken as employment whilst for females the major role was that within the family (Victor, 1994) or indeed marriage. In contemporary society it may be realistic to define employment as a person's main status, the male experience of which continues to be more comprehensively documented than that of females. The disengagement theory may appear credible given trends showing a fall in labour market participation with age but also trends showing how participation in leisure pursuits declines markedly with age (Askham *et al.*, 1992).

A further feature of *disengagement* is that it may be initiated by the individual or by others in the situation. This relates to the political economy analysis of old age in that withdrawal from employment may be enforced rather than the result of individual choice. Similar to the modernisation theory, in terms of labour market interaction, disengagement suggests that society ceases to depend on older people in fulfilling various roles. In terms of employment, younger people are preferred largely for the skills they are believed to possess (Sherman and Wood, 1979). This blatantly devalues the wisdom, skills and experience of older people and can even be argued as justification for their exclusion from the workforce in capitalist society.

Disengagement is generally viewed as a positive move for older people, yet retirement is viewed ambiguously. A trend towards early retirement may be interpreted as evidence of it as a desired status yet at least some of this may be accounted for by ill health or redundancy. Although retirement has been classed as a *'universal social institution'* (Townsend, 1986: 22), there is now a growing volume of literature relating retirement experience to former employment experience which has in turn been shown as related to pension rights. Pension entitlement and subsequent access to resources is documented by many authors as a major factor determining quality of life in retirement (Victor and Vetter, 1986; Walker, 1990; Wilson, 1993). Retirement has been interpreted as:

> ... the final confirmation of the advantages and disadvantages attached to given social and class positions: once the advantages accruing to a

particular position are consolidated they are likely to be sustained even into very old age (Fennell *et al.*, 1988: 93).

The theories and viewpoints analysed so far present a negative portrayal of old age along with an attempt to illustrate that it is not a uniform experience. Yet positive interpretations of the ageing experience and the social and economic circumstances of elderly people do exist. Although it would perhaps be reasonable to solely assume role *loss* on reaching old age, particularly in relation to paid employment, widowhood or physical activities, new roles may also be acquired. These include the important roles elderly people play within their families in addition to volunteering, charity work (Arber, 1996; Tinker, 1997), part-time paid work and perhaps pursuing less strenuous activities. Tinker (1997) considers that these new roles could give the feelings of self-esteem and status usually derived from employment and are important in elderly people being contributors as well as recipients, a central determinant of their status in society. In terms of contributing financially, this can be presumed throughout their working lives in National Insurance payments and through general taxation. Hence the process is one of role *orientation* rather than simply *loss*. This view can be related to classifying older people by virtue of the stage reached in the lifecycle and the associated cultural norms of behaviour and attitude to be witnessed (Victor, 1994).

The portrayal of elderly people as having a socially constructed dependent status, a perspective which appears to equate work with independence and retirement with dependence, has attracted a degree of criticism. The most notable critic is Johnson (1987) who uses as a central theme the argument that all throughout life people are dependent and only on retirement do they move from being dependent upon finding and retaining employment to being dependent upon social security benefits. He even suggests that retirement lessens an individual's dependency as the independent income they receive on retirement is guaranteed by the taxable capacity of the state rather than the uncertainties of the labour market. As such, receipt of state benefits allows them to retain independence as far as possible rather than fostering dependence (Johnson, 1991). Equally, arguments relating to financial dependence are not solely applicable to elderly people. There are numerous groups within society who are financially dependent upon state benefits, for example, unemployed people, some groups of informal carers and some groups of disabled people.

The structured dependency arguments assume financial dependence on state benefits and although income from the state retirement pension constitutes a high proportion of the income of elderly people, other sources are available. The viewpoint takes no account of peoples ability to save or otherwise prepare for their future, which most people try to do. The growth of occupational and private pension coverage and the increases in owner occupation are evidence of this, again factors determined by former occupation (Johnson, 1991). Interestingly, the proportion of post-retirement income made up from sources other than the state retirement pension is increasing.

The earlier arguments examining the relationship between elderly people and the means of production focused on the idea of social control, the state and on employers who were perceived to control the situation. No account appeared to be taken of the strength of influence of individuals' choice as to whether to make themselves available to employers. Although not always possible in times of high unemployment and uncertainty in the labour market, the trends towards 'early' retirement demonstrate that this is an option open to and taken by many.

Dependency is not just definable in financial terms although this has arguably attracted the most attention. Physical and mental dependency, as related to advancing years, may also be apparent. Also, it is not just on entering old age that people are dependent upon the state for the provision of welfare services. The nature of statutory provision in the UK is such that everyone is entitled to care from the NHS and Social Services in proportion to need and regardless of the ability to pay. Obviously those suffering from most ill health are most dependent at any one time but, at the point of delivery, service users are equi-dependent, that is, elderly people no more so than any other sector of the population (Jeffreys, 1991).

Whilst dependency as a concept does not appear compatible with that of playing an active role in relation to using welfare services, ways in which elderly people may be defined as independent have been shown.

Possibilities for Elderly People Assuming an Active Role

The exploration of the health, economic and social circumstances of the elderly population of the UK in the chapter so far is now analysed to briefly consider possible ways in which the defined age group may assume an active role in the use of health and social care. This also demonstrates possible differences within the sample classed as a 'critical case', reinforcing the need to consider social, economic and health-related differentials as associated with user experience and behaviour.

The policy initiatives outlined in Chapter 3, aiming to enhance the position of service users in relation to the provision of care, may be considered as more advantageous to elderly people than other age groups due to them being the highest users of many welfare services. It could be postulated that elderly people have the greatest opportunities to engage in all the aspects of service use explored by this study by virtue of having the most regular contact with service providers. It follows that they may for example have the most opportunities to *participate* or be *represented* in any decisions about their care, to have *access* to services, to gather *information* and to *choose* what services they wish to receive and how they will be provided. In terms of *redress*, recent guidelines advocate immediate informal conciliation by staff when patients make dissatisfaction known. Although elderly people may have the highest probability of experiencing dissatisfaction, due to being the highest users of services, this also gives them the greatest opportunity to have grievances dealt with promptly.

Extending the association between the experience of ill health or the use of services and opportunities for assuming an active role, a number of differences may be expected by various demographic characteristics. It is likely that elderly women will have both different experiences and behave differently compared to elderly men in terms of service use as will 'old' elderly people compared to 'young' elderly people and people living alone compared to people living with others due to their higher and more regular contact with welfare services.

High levels of contact with health and social care professionals and with the process of receiving care could conceivably place elderly people in a favourable position for assuming an active role. They are likely to gain familiarity with the system and its procedures in addition to familiarity with and knowledge about their condition and treatment. In addition, any knowledge or information that is acquired may be used in future encounters as many conditions are likely to be long-term. Statistics also show how elderly people are the group who spend the longest period in hospital. Therefore, in addition to having the most regular contact with health and social care professionals they also appear likely to have the most sustained contact, which may serve to further enhance the above advantages.

A high prevalence of ill health or disability and the possible resulting physical dependency can alternatively be hypothesised to reduce the potential for an active role. A less than optimum health state may make service users unable or unwilling to assume an active role, a factor likely to be compounded in the case of elderly people. This may further be exacerbated by the possible presence of mutliple pathology.

The care needs of elderly people may require multi-disciplinary input increasing the likelihood of a case conference, at which the service user may be present (Hughes, 1995). This can be viewed positively in that it provides a defined forum for the expression of views, or participation in decision making, by the service user. Such a situation may not be available to, or required by, many other sectors of the population. Alternatively it could be that the greater the number of professionals involved, the less influence the service user may have. The number of providers of services is also likely to be increased for elderly people due to the complexity of needs. This may simply increase the amount of negotiation for the elderly person to be involved in, further complicating the process for those wishing to play a role. The increasingly indistinct health-social care boundary, having the potential to complicate the process of using services, is also of particular relevance to elderly people who, as has been shown, are likely to use care provided by both the NHS and Social Services.

Access to welfare services, one of the fundamental principles of both the NHS and of this study, is on the basis of professionally assessed need. With finite means and increasing demand however priorities are being widely established and employed for the distribution of resources and prioritising or 'rationing' is taking place (NAHAT, 1995a). Such rationing tends to focus on the outcomes of interventions and will automatically discriminate against populations who are unlikely to enjoy a full recovery, for example, elderly people, around which debate exists (Evans, 1997; Williams, 1997). This may serve to restrict opportunities for an active role amongst such populations.

One of the main developments contributing to the existence of 'markets' in the provision of welfare is an increase in the number of suppliers. It was suggested in Chapter 3 that the 'mixed economy' of social care had greater potential than the 'internal market' of the NHS. The mechanisms of the 'mixed economy of care' appear to provide numerous opportunities for people willing and able to purchase required services independently due to the possible availability of providers other than those in the statutory sector. Even if this were to prove the case, the traditional concentration of elderly people at the lower end of the income distribution suggests that elderly people may be unlikely to assume such a role. The analysis of the incomes of elderly people given above however presents an increasingly optimistic picture. A large proportion of the income of older people is guaranteed, namely state benefits, which can be argued to provide greater security in addition to facilitating long-term planning of welfare. Interestingly also, an increasing proportion of the income of older people is made up from private sources. Access to resources in later life including entitlement to a pension other than the state retirement pension has also been shown to differ by gender and by occupational group. As such, the ability and willingness to pay for services may differ accordingly.

Choice, an important principle of service use explored by this study, may be stifled in additional ways for elderly users to those already outlined in Chapter 3. The chapter considered one of the major choices that people may have in relation to welfare is choice of a GP with whom to register. It was further argued that this choice could be reduced by 'cream skimming' by practitioners who may favour 'inexpensive' patients. If this is apparent, elderly people again may find themselves discriminated against due to their high use of services. A further way in which choice has ostensibly been increased is by money to pay for treatment being able to cross administrative boundaries, thereby effectively increasing the range of providers. Availability of transport however will be a major determinant of whether people can take advantage of these opportunities. Due to illness, frailty or disability and state restrictions on driving certification for older people, again elderly people may find their choices restricted to a greater degree than those of younger people.

'Dependency', analysed earlier along with its many facets including financial, physical and structural, is difficult to interpret in a positive light; it was defined as being in a subordinate power relationship. Wiles (1993) cites four factors creating an imbalance of power between service users and providers of health and social care, one of which was the dependence of the recipient at the point of service. Whilst it is debatable whether elderly people are more dependent than other age groups at the point of service delivery, possible ways in which this may be the case are the increased number of services used at any one time, the frequency of service use and the length of time over which services are used. The possible resulting imbalance of power between elderly service users and providers does little to suggest an active role in the use of welfare.

The experience of this age group prior to the creation of the welfare state and the resulting expectations must also be a consideration in influencing the behaviour of the sample in this study. That is, they will have experience of individual responsibility for welfare via private, informal or charitable provision. This may mean that they are more able to play an active role in assuming responsibility for securing care through prior experience of having done so. Alternatively however it may mean that they are less willing to do so, seeing it as a return to the pre-welfare state situation. It is suggested here that older people have lower expectations of the state provision of welfare which may stem from having experience of welfare provision prior to 1948. As such, they may be less assertive and assume a more passive role than younger people with no such experience.

Previous studies that have considered the role of elderly people in the process of using health services mainly conclude that older people appear less likely than younger people to assume an active role. This gives further support to the application of the 'critical case' rationale in this study.

Previous Research

A general survey carried out in Australia used questionnaires to explore the level of 'consumerism' amongst a cross-section of attendees at general practices by focusing on respondents' choice and continuing use of a GP (Lloyd, Lupton and Donaldson, 1991 also reported in Lupton, Donaldson and Lloyd, 1991). A further report of the same study (Donaldson, Lloyd and Lupton, 1991) emphasised the behaviour of elderly people (65 years and over) compared to other age groups.

The overall findings from the study revealed that most of the respondents displayed characteristics pertaining to the 'traditional' model of medicine based on trust of the practitioner and dependence of the patient. By age group, these characteristics were most pronounced amongst older people (65 years and over) who tended to always use the same practitioner and had not changed practitioner in the previous 12 months. The authors acknowledged that older people were more vulnerable and physically dependent and so may be more trusting of their doctor than other groups. They believed that as such older people may not be as willing to undertake an assessment of their GP.

An American study (Beisecker, 1988) focused on the relationship between older patients and a desire for medical information and input into medical decisions at an outpatients clinic. The methodology was extensive including questionnaires and tape recordings. The questionnaires covered thirteen areas where decisions are made and asked who they thought should make the decisions: doctor, patient or jointly, in addition to ranking the importance of obtaining information on each of the thirteen areas on a five-point scale. The recording of the medical encounter was analysed by classifying patients' comments which were 'information seeking', 'assertive' or 'suggestions', categories derived from Haug and Lavin's study (1983). The latter of these was used as evidence of a desire for input into the decision-making process.

Age was found to be significantly related to many of the attitude measures. Those of 60 years and over (n=21) were less likely to suggest alternative treatments and so more inclined to wish the medical professional to assume the dominant role. Older patients in particular wanted health professionals to make decisions on their behalf; indeed only 52.4% of those aged 60 years and over wanted any input in medical decisions compared to 81.2% of younger patients. Beisecker concluded that elderly patients did not want responsibility for medical decision making and did not believe that patients should challenge the medical practitioner. She provides two possible explanations for this. Firstly, their experience of the traditional 'doctor' and 'patient' roles precluding any questioning by the patient and secondly that with increasing age, people wish to have lower levels of responsibility and to rely more on the expertise of others. Haug and Lavin (1983) also concluded that older people were less likely than younger people to express attitudes questioning the doctor's authority.

These studies focus on the way that elderly people themselves act in the medical encounter. The way in which professionals behave towards patients is a further aspect of service utilisation. 'Ageism' was explored by Greene *et al.* (1986) by analysing audio taped encounters between primary health care practitioners and patients at a teaching hospital in New York. Twenty elderly patients (65 years and over) were matched with twenty younger patients (45 years or younger) for sex and race and an additional forty interviews between physicians and elderly patients supplemented this data. The Geriatric Interaction Analysis instrument was used to analyse the interactions.

Greene *et al.* (1986) found that more medical and fewer psychosocial issues were discussed with elderly patients than with younger patients and the differences were largely attributable to issues raised by the physician. Topics discussed and physician response revealed significant differences between elderly and younger patients with physicians being more responsive in terms of information giving, questioning and support to young patients. This was most marked when patient-raised topics were examined suggesting that elderly people find it more difficult to get the physician to address and discuss their concerns. The researchers classed this as subtle 'ageism'. Overall ratings of the encounter showed how physicians were less respectful, less patient, less engaged and less egalitarian with their old than with their young patients.

An American study of elderly patients (65 years and over) on discharge from hospital examined their participation and influence and that of their family and of health professionals in the discharge process (Abramson, 1988). Information on the participation and influence of service users (n=148) in the planning of discharge was provided by social workers through the use of questionnaires. The social worker also estimated a percentage figure for the level of patient participation on a scale and provided information on the number of discharge planning options they had discussed with patients and families and the amount of time they spent with patients and families. Finally an evaluation was carried out of the level of influence over decision making, particularly the final decision, held by the patient, the family and the professionals respectively.

The study found a general high degree of participation in decision making by patients and that the patient or their family controlled discharge decisions in most cases. Differences were apparent however by medical condition with those in the poorest mental and physical condition having the lowest participation rates. Social workers were found to spend substantially more time with family members than with patients in large part due to the patient's physical and mental condition precluding their participation. The main limitation of this study of course, which is acknowledged, is that service users and their families were not involved in providing data; the perceptions of participation and influence were those of social workers.

A further American study (Hibbard and Weeks, 1987) investigated the extent to which insured people behave as 'consumers' of health care and attempted to identify factors associated with this behaviour. All data was collected by face to face interviews. The study examined four measures of behaviour: information seeking, exercising independent judgement in accepting physician advice, knowledge about health care and cost sensitivity and four groups of explanatory variables in relation to these measures: socio-demographic, attitudes toward medical care and physicians, health status and experience of health care. Elderly people were found to be substantially less likely to undertake any of these behaviours. The authors suggest that *'older cohorts may have a substantially different perception that younger cohorts of the proper 'patient' role in health care'* (p.1030). They also suggest that a significant barrier to adopting an active role is a high degree of faith in, and dependency on, physicians. Elderly people were identified as the group with greatest experience of health care and as such the most likely to have developed attributes considered 'consumer-oriented' yet concluded that few elderly people had these attributes.

The studies reviewed above all contribute to the present state of knowledge in this area. They also give credence to the assertion upon which this study is based that elderly people may be the least willing or able to assume an active role in their use of welfare services. Participation, information and choice have been common themes throughout however none have surveyed the perceptions of elderly users themselves. The present study explores six criteria in relation to service use: *participation, representation, access, choice, information* and *redress* and as such goes beyond the scope of these previous studies.

In addition, whilst the most pertinent research that has been carried out in other countries needs to be acknowledged, it is of limited application due to widely differing systems of health service provision. Further the emphasis has consistently been on 'health' provision and largely in the primary care sector with no attention paid to Social Services provision. It is vital to combine study of both particularly since the divide between health and social care is becoming less clear and with decisions about continuing care made by a multi-disciplinary team as an integral part of the discharge planning process. This study considers 'discharge' as part of a continuing process and the receipt of continuing care as a continuation of that process for those elderly people requiring further care.

This study incorporates the views of service users themselves, those acting in a corporate capacity as local managers and implementers of policy, as well as health and social care professionals having daily contact with elderly users of care.   In this way it is much broader and more comprehensive than previous studies and attempts to reconcile the experience and behaviour of services users with that of service providers. Both qualitative and quantitative methods are utilised in order to gain first hand in-depth insights in addition to descriptive and quantifiable data.   The design of the research and rationale are explored in the following chapter to demonstrate how the research questions were comprehensively addressed.

Summary

This chapter has provided a broad, general view of the position of elderly people in contemporary UK society, critically analysing their position from social, economic and structural perspectives.   The viewpoints relating to the general ageing of the population which tend to portray elderly people in a negative light include their relationship to the labour market, levels of dependency and notions of social and economic 'burden'.   Such theories, however, tend to encapsulate elderly people as a homogeneous group suggesting that they share uniform characteristics, have access to the same level of resources and so on.   It would follow therefore that they would all assume the user role in a standard way.   Recognition of the diversity of the elderly population however has been attempted throughout the chapter.

Classifying a group on the basis of a single characteristic, such as the 'critical case' approach adopted here, can quite readily be classed as 'ageist'.   This heightens the importance of undertaking a comprehensive analysis of user experience and behaviour based on a variety of other social, economic and demographic variables including gender, age, socio-economic grouping, household composition and self-reported health status *within* the defined group.   The associations of these variables with user experience and behaviour found by this study are reported in Chapters 6 to 8.

5 Research Design and Methodology

Introduction

Chapters 2 to 4 have collectively created the analytical framework within which this study took place. Ways have been explored in which users of public services, specifically health and social care, have played an increasingly active role and in which recent policies have ostensibly encouraged and provided opportunities for them to do so. Chapter 4 then narrowed the focus to users of 70 years and over and examined various viewpoints which may impact upon the ability and willingness of this age group to play an active role. It is within this framework that the empirical study was designed and executed.

This chapter describes how the present study was carried out in order to address the specific aims of the research. It explores the methodologies selected, designed and utilised, the sampling procedures undertaken, the logistics of administering the research tools and the analysis performed. The importance of this stage of the process is succinctly stated by Yin (1984) who claims that: '... *the* [research] *design is the logical sequence that connects the empirical data to a study's initial research questions and, ultimately, to its conclusion*' (p.28). That is, the research design phase is central to the successful progression from existing knowledge and theory to making a contribution to advancing the overall state of knowledge. In addition, the research findings may ultimately '*suggest new problems for theory, invite new theoretical formulations, and lead to the refinement of theories themselves*' (Denzin, 1989: 67).

This very close link between concept formation and research requires that appropriate and well-designed empirical work takes place within a well-defined analytical framework upon which the research will ultimately build (Fawcett and Downs, 1986).

Defining the Focus

The conceptual phase of this study included forming broad research questions, developing an analytical framework and subsequently narrowing the focus of the investigation. Many factors helped determine the focus of the study within the broad area of service utilisation and participation. These included personal interest in the user-oriented nature of welfare reform and literature searching which helped in identifying gaps in previous research, determining the existing state of knowledge and in refining the analytical framework within which to conduct the study. Policy initiatives, detailed in Chapter 3, plus demographic trends and trends in the use of health and social care services, detailed in Chapter 4, led to defining the most appropriate population for this study as people of 70 years and over discharged from hospital to their own home.

Hospital discharge was shown in Chapter 3 to be an increasingly crucial point in the use of care due to the interaction of trends such as shorter hospital stays and an increasing level of care provided in the home environment. It is also a defined point at which decisions are taken which can straddle both NHS and Social Services care. People of 70 years and over were defined as a 'critical case' and assumed the least likely age groups to assume an active role in the use of welfare services (see Chapters 1 and 4). Only people discharged to their own home were considered in this study in order to define the sample as narrowly as possible but also in the knowledge that certain services may not be available to those in residential or nursing homes. As such, opportunities for an active role in the use of care may not be a possibility. These services include meals on wheels and home helps, both services that would be provided 'in house', whilst other opportunities such as contacting care providers or searching for information may also be assumed by employees of the establishment.

The broad aim of this research was to explore service utilisation and participation during and in the short period after hospital discharge among a sample of people aged 70 years and above. The specific aims, as stated in Chapter 1 were finalised as:

1.   to explore the experience and behaviour of elderly users of health and social care services with regard to criteria indicating user influence or control (namely *participation, representation, access, choice, information* and *redress*);

1.1   to compare the experience of elderly service users with regard to stipulated policies for service delivery;

1.2   to explore the ability and willingness of elderly service users to assume an active role in the use of health and social care;

2.   to determine the experience of health and social care professionals (managers and front line workers) regarding the introduction of user-oriented services including the ability and willingness of elderly service users to assume an active role;

3.   to explore perceived barriers to the introduction of user-oriented health and social care services from the experience of elderly service users and health and social care professionals.

The design phase of this study involved choosing, developing and finalising the research tools, determining the sampling plan and carrying out the pilot study along with many administrative details. The completion of both the conceptual and design phases was fundamental to the form of the empirical study, and the ensuing phases of data analysis and interpretation to meet the aims of the study. The research area and questions determine to a great extent the subsequent design of the empirical study. Specifically, the aims of the research determine the type of study or research methodology employed (Hakim, 1987). The selection of an appropriate methodology also helps to enhance the validity of the results and overall credibility of the research.

Research Methodology: Service Users

Portrayed in most of the research literature as opposite approaches to the collection of data and indeed being useful for different types of study (Fielding and Fielding, 1986; Bryman, 1988), this study utilised both *qualitative* and *quantitative* methodologies. These distinct approaches to social research have been referred to as subjective – objective, interpretive – positivist and inductive – deductive demonstrating major differences in both approach and outcome. Where literature advocates that both approaches are employed, one is often presented as forming the preparatory stage for the other, or one as the dominant or more credible approach. In this study the phases of data collection by questionnaire and interviews took place almost simultaneously and the data generated were deemed to be of equal weight when reporting the findings.   This complementary approach is explicitly addressed in a growing body of literature (Brannen, 1992a; Weinholtz *et al.*, 1995; Pearson, 1997). Discussion surrounding the use of such a multi-method approach is given later in this chapter.

The different approaches to data collection were used to address the same as well as different aspects of the overall aims outlined above. That is, questionnaires were used to gain a general understanding of the experience of hospital discharge whilst a qualitative approach was used to gain a deeper understanding of the complexity of the issues surrounding hospital discharge (aim 1.1).   As such, a degree of corroboration was sought to increase the validity of the findings.   However, an interview setting was felt to be more suitable to studying the ability and willingness of respondents towards assuming an active role hence contributing to the roundedness of the overall findings (aim 1.2).   An interview setting was also felt to be appropriate for exploration of perceived barriers to the introduction of user-oriented health and social care from the experience of service users (aim 3).

Despite acknowledging limitations in their use, a postal questionnaire was selected as the most efficient method of collecting quantifiable data from a relatively large number of respondents.   The advantages to be gained in this instance were that it was relatively cheap and easy to administer and would allow comparisons to be made between different groups of respondents (Oppenheim, 1992; Polit and Hungler, 1993).   Possible disadvantages, however, included the potentially low response rate, dependency upon accurate recall and that they are not always effective for dealing with sensitive or personal issues.   It was recognised that these limitations can be exacerbated when used with elderly people who may additionally be suffering from ill health or have sensory impairments or loss of memory function (Rodgers and Herzog, 1987; Bowsher *et al.*, 1993).

For these reasons the questionnaire was short and deliberately straightforward consisting largely of closed response questions although attempts were made to also collect qualitative data by its use.   A comprehensive covering letter was enclosed explaining the purpose of the research, how names had been selected, exactly what was required from the respondent, assurances regarding confidentiality and a pre-paid envelope for reply.   Details of how to contact the researcher were included on all correspondence.

The questionnaire began, after a short introduction, with two straightforward tick-box questions about the services the respondent had been in contact with since leaving hospital. The main purpose of these was to provide a gentle lead into the questionnaire. Other functions that these questions may have served include focusing the individual on the receipt of welfare services or possibly thinking back to their hospital stay and discharge when the use of services may have been discussed.

The questionnaire next turned to explicitly considering the discharge process and the subsequent use of welfare. Seventeen statements were listed to be answered on a 'yes/unsure/no' scale. These statements were devised on the basis of the policy documentation relating to hospital discharge and subsequent care analysed in Chapter 3 and addressed the criteria for assessing user influence or control in the use of welfare services (aim 1). For example, involvement in needs assessment (3.3) (*participation*), involvement of carers in decision making (3.6) (*representation*), the provision of *information* (3.5) and the provision of *choice* regarding care delivery (3.10 and 3.15). Perceptions of *participation* and *information* respectively were also surveyed (3.7 and 3.17). Whilst answering in the affirmative to these statements (particularly 3.3, 3.10 and 3.15) *may* signify users being willing and able to play an active role such activity is likely to result from opportunities provided by those in positions of authority. Also important for this study were ways in which users may take the initiative in assuming an active role suggested by for example, knowledge of where to obtain information about available care (3.11) and who to contact with any questions (3.16), both of which relate to both *access* and *information*. Aspects of wider service use which it was felt may impact upon overall ability to assume an active role in the use of health and social care were also addressed. These included ability to express wishes when in hospital (3.4) and to social workers (3.13) and knowledge of service entitlement (3.8 and 3.12). The issue of *redress* was surveyed by asking respondents if they would make a complaint in the event of dissatisfaction with care received (3.9) and whether they would know how to do so (3.14).

Care was taken over the ordering of the statements, starting and ending with questions that would not cause offence or be threatening; indeed those regarding 'complaints' were the only ones which could be deemed 'sensitive'. Items relating to the same principle, for example, 'information', were separated in order to encourage respondents to consider each statement carefully. The item asking whether needs assessment had taken place (3.2) was included in order to lead onto further questioning about the assessment process. These statements were all one directional, therefore no check was made for consistency; that is, whether people would answer with the same meaning when the question was asked from the opposite direction. However, there are advantages of such an approach to be realised during analysis.

The possibility remains that people may answer in the affirmative if they feel that the opposite may display ignorance or a passivity which may be deemed undesirable. Indeed, elderly people have been shown to be more inclined to overreport desirable information (Rodgers and Herzog, 1987). With health services research inherent difficulties are noted in asking 'patients' to evaluate services (Williams, 1994), particularly when asked for their 'satisfaction'. The neutral category of 'unsure' was included so that respondents would not be forced into definite response categories although in many instances 'unsure' was actually meaningful. However, the possibility must be anticipated that respondents may use such a category in order to avoid committing themselves or giving items full consideration (Oppenheim, 1992).

Three open-ended questions were next included on the questionnaire relating to respondents' involvement in decision making (*participation*), information received (*information*) and perceptions about the level of care received (*access*) allowing respondents to answer in their own words. This was to supplement the quantitative data. These areas again related to the policy guidance analysed in Chapter 3 and the criteria for user influence or control.

The last page of the questionnaire asked for a number of demographic details which were to be used in the analysis as potential associations with user experience and behaviour. At the end of the questionnaire was an invitation to the respondent to take part in a semi-structured interview for the purposes of the research although making it clear that they were under no obligation to do so.

Reminder letters were sent, along with a second copy of the questionnaire and further pre-paid envelope, after a period of approximately three weeks to people who had not replied to initial correspondence. Questionnaires had been coded numerically in order to identify non-respondents. As expected reminders increased the response rate quite markedly. A second reminder was felt to be both costly and risk becoming an imposition upon people and so was not issued. Again, this was a particular concern with elderly people as vulnerable subjects of research.

The font size used and the spacing on the letter and questionnaire were given specific consideration given the age of the recipients, who could be visually impaired. The four-page questionnaire was administered as double-sided in an A3 sized (folded) booklet to appear both less complex and less lengthy.

The semi-structured interview schedule addressed the same criteria of user influence or control and aimed to expand on the responses gained to the postal survey. The broad outline of the interview schedule again led in fairly gently with two general questions, this time relating to respondents' perceptions of adequate service delivery. These were explored in detail with respondents as the responses were felt to underlie the process of service utilisation, that is, whether respondents had access to the services they felt they required or would like. Whilst these are slightly more sensitive than the first questions on the questionnaire, which called for objective responses, they were felt appropriate in a face-to-face encounter. The interview schedule was then structured according to the six criteria indicating user influence or control addressing the ways in which the policy documentation advocated an active role for users of health and social care. These questions largely related to specific aspects of hospital discharge but also extended to the subsequent use of welfare.

In addition to gaining service users' detailed experiences of service utilisation (aim 1.1), interviews also attempted to ascertain respondents' ability and willingness to assume an active role in the use of health and social care (aim 1.2). Such views were not addressed on the postal survey as it was felt that statements regarding being involved in decisions, being provided with choice or information, having greater access to services and so on would meet with overwhelming support and yield low discrimination. An interview setting was felt to be more appropriate to questioning about attitude, providing the opportunity to explore issues in greater depth rather than reducing them to single statements. Similarly with perceived barriers to the introduction of user-oriented health and social care (aim 3) which were implicitly rather than explicitly addressed with service users. This further demonstrates how the research strategy employed was chosen as appropriate to the questions to be answered. Hakim (1987) reports how qualitative research is of use in gaining '*reports of individuals' perceptions, attitudes, beliefs, views and feelings ... as well as their behaviour*' (p.26).

The semi-structured interview schedule used was, by definition, not rigid and so was flexible in adapting to the individual circumstances of each respondent. This was fundamental given that nothing was known about the personal circumstances, health state or likely hospital experience of the interviewee before the encounter.

Some of the numerous advantages of collecting data face-to-face were realised through carrying out semi-structured interviews, particularly pertinent with the age group under study. These included the chance for the interviewer to also assume the role of observer, the opportunity to clarify areas of uncertainty or ambiguity thus avoiding potential misinterpretation, allowing the interviewer to probe the respondent to expand on relevant issues and the likelihood of respondents providing longer, more in-depth responses than they would have written on a postal questionnaire (Burgess, 1984; Barker, 1991; Marshall and Rossman, 1995; Mason, 1996). These can be deemed to far outweigh the disadvantages of interviewing, two of which are that they are costly and the data obtained is both difficult and time-consuming to interpret (Seaman, 1987; Patton, 1990). Both of these factors have an obvious influence on the sample size which can be taken.

All interviews took place in the home of the respondent. Logistically, this was felt to be the most convenient for interviewees but an informal setting was also thought to be important in placing the respondent at their ease and making them more willing to converse than a clinical or unfamiliar environment. All meetings were tape recorded, with the respondent's consent, then transcribed *verbatim* by the researcher. Brief field notes were also taken as a reminder of the context of the interview, to supplement the 'observer' role and as a precautionary measure in instances when a respondent was softly spoken or there was intrusive background noise.

Important considerations were necessary at interview due to the age group under study. These included allowing the respondent sufficient time to answer, making encouraging remarks and taking time to listen to what the respondent wished to talk about rather than sticking determinedly to the areas on the interview schedule (Domarad and Buschmann, 1995). These are all features of good research interviewing but arguably need reinforcing with older adults. Emphasis was therefore given to these communication aspects at the same time as taking care not to enter the situation with expectations as to how this age group would assume the user role and risk influencing the overall findings.

The phase of quantitative data collection began before the qualitative for a number of reasons, most fundamentally that the questionnaire phase acted as a 'screening' mechanism in identifying those who wished to take part in the interview stage of the research. Also, it seems logical that an 'in-depth', exploratory phase should follow rather than precede the more general phase.

Interviews were staggered throughout the quantitative phase of data collection. This was to prevent a time delay being experienced by those respondents to the first batch of questionnaires who were selected for interview but also in the knowledge that recall of hospital discharge would fade with time.

The strengths and weaknesses of the different research approaches utilised have relevance to the validity of the findings. No regulation can be exercised over the responses to postal questionnaires, including whether they are completed by the intended recipient, or any check made as to the consistency or honesty of findings. Certainty as to the identity of the respondent is guaranteed by face to face interviews whilst careful questioning and probing can ensure a greater degree of accuracy and consistency of responses.

Research Methodology: Professionals

A quantitative approach was not deemed appropriate when seeking the views of professionals. A postal questionnaire would probably have found its way into the waste paper bin along with the ever-growing amount of paperwork in circulation and given that the sample size was modest, face to face interviews were sought. The professionals were contacted by letter to explain the purposes of the research and exactly what would be required of them. This was followed by a telephone call approximately ten days later to arrange a meeting.

Interviews with professionals were completed before those with service users in order to ensure a thorough understanding of contemporary issues surrounding the discharge process and continuing care. They also provided, in many cases, further areas to explore with service users. Interviews with professionals addressed their experience regarding the introduction of user-oriented services, including the ability and willingness of service users to assume an active role (aim 2) as well as perceived barriers to the introduction of user-oriented health and social care services from their experience (aim 3).

The interviews were slightly more structured with health and social care professionals than with service users. This was because the researcher could be better prepared for the situation when meeting professionals in terms of what to expect due to general knowledge of what lay within their professional remit. However, this did not mean that the research tool was inflexible.

The preamble aimed to focus the interviewee on the post-1989 reforms to welfare and on the user group under investigation. As professionals were relating their experience to general rather than specific incidents, discharge was explored as a *process* which encompassed the six criteria under investigation rather than addressing each in turn. Firstly, experience of the discharge process and associated decision making was discussed as an event, with aspects of 'good practice' from the policy guidance specifically addressed. Then the use of care following discharge was addressed along with more general questioning for example about contact points available to users and complaints procedures. This was so that hospital discharge was not treated as an end in itself in addition to exploring other ways in which service users may be able to assume an active role. It also encouraged both health and social care professionals to consider the delivery and use of care across the health-social care divide. Barriers to the implementation of user-oriented services from both within the organisation or service and stemming from service users themselves were also discussed.

Further questioning addressed the views of professionals regarding how far the criteria of *participation, representation, access, choice, information* and *redress* should realistically be applied to the delivery and use of care services. The main changes to working practices and the receipt of care were also addressed to consider the wider context of greater user-orientation.

Many of the professional interviewees, particularly the managers, were asked at the end of the interview for a further contact for the researcher to approach (see 'Sample Selection: Professionals' below).

Interviews with health and social care professionals took place in the work place of the interviewee. Convenience for the interviewee was again a consideration. All encounters were tape recorded, with the respondent's consent, then transcribed *verbatim* by the researcher.

Methodological Pluralism

These three sources of information, incorporating both qualitative and quantitative enquiry, could be broadly classed as 'methodological triangulation' (Denzin, 1989) or 'multiple sources of evidence' (Yin, 1984, in discussing case study research). These are processes which use different methods and perspectives in order to ascertain as accurate a picture as possible of the situation studied, limit errors and improve the credibility of the information obtained (Corner, 1991; Robson, 1993). Brewer and Hunter (1989) believe that: '*The multi-method approach is a strategy for overcoming each method's weaknesses and limitations by deliberately combining different types of methods within the same investigations*' (p.11).

This study had no prior expectations of producing data from different sources which tallied which appears a common assumption when using a multi-method approach (Fielding and Fielding, 1986; Mason, 1994). Indeed such is the basis of using the method to enhance validity. However, it can be argued as '*relevant to, rather than constitutive of*' validation (Bloor, 1997: 38) as the differences between the various sources of data must be as important as areas of agreement (Kellaher *et al.*, 1990). In this aspect, a benefit of using different methods to study the same phenomenon is that it may allow the researcher to regard the data more critically and to identify weaknesses.

In this study, the use of both questionnaires and interviews to overcome the weaknesses peculiar to each single method highlighted was only possible in those areas where the topics covered overlapped, that is, *experience* of hospital discharge. This is consonant with the belief that no single research approach is sensitive or flexible enough to ascertain all the required data. Corner (1991) believes that few studies are so 'purist' as to employ only one method totally.

The use of different sources of data and methods can also be seen as a way of exploring data with greater depth and breadth in order to produce a deeper analysis (Fielding and Fielding, 1986; Pope and Mays, 1995). In this instance, quantitative data provided the structure of the findings whilst qualitative data provided the meaning. Similarly, a combination of methods can be used to study different levels of enquiry in order to expose different aspects of the same problem (Brannen, 1992a). This *complementary* approach is based on the belief that data are constituted by the method used and that different data sets do not therefore add up to some rounded unity. Rather, a multi-method approach should permit a sharper focusing upon the reference points around which the research is constructed (Kellaher *et al.*, 1990). In this study of service utilisation a qualitative inquiry was used to explore in greater depth the processes surrounding hospital discharge which had been addressed on a more superficial level via questionnaires. Exploration of *behaviour*, including the ability and willingness to assume an active role, and barriers to doing so was possible via qualitative research to supplement data about *experience* of playing an active role during the discharge process collected by questionnaire and at interview.

Different approaches therefore can be used to investigate the same phenomenon to increase validity or to explore a different aspect of the same phenomenon to create greater understanding. This study uses multi-methods in both of these ways.

The data collected from professionals was also used to supplement the data regarding experience of the discharge process in addition to providing a different perspective on the introduction of and perceived barriers to user-oriented services.

Sample Selection: Service Users

Elderly people (of 70 years and over) on discharge from hospital to their own homes were the subjects of this research. The sampling method employed aimed to provide a single stage analysis of this specific age group, using them as a 'critical case' in the analysis of service utilisation (see Chapters 1 and 4). The geographical area under study is particularly pertinent due to its skewed age profile also shown in Chapter 4. The diversity of the elderly population, illustrated in Chapter 4, has been claimed as a factor making sampling procedures difficult (Bowsher *et al.*, 1993).

Little control could be exercised over the selection of potential respondents to whom to administer the postal questionnaire. Compilation of lists of recently discharged people to contact for inclusion in the sample was reliant upon the co-operation of managers and staff at the District General Hospital. This co-operation was very kindly and willingly given. The two main concerns of the researcher however were with making a minimum demand on the time of hospital staff and, of course, with confidentiality. The acute hospital Trust supplied the name, address and date of birth of all people of 70 years and over who had recently been discharged from hospital to their 'usual place of residence' from routinely compiled databases. No information was therefore obtained regarding the reason for hospitalisation of potential respondents, their likely state of health or whether they were in receipt of continuing care. Some of the names had to be excluded due to their 'usual place of residence' being a residential or nursing home. (A list of all private and Local Authority residential and nursing homes had been secured from the local Social Services department for this purpose.)

A convenience sample was used for distribution of the postal questionnaire in that all people who met the criteria, that is, in the defined age group being discharged from inpatient care to a private address within a specified time period, were included irrespective of their care needs. It had originally been envisaged that all respondents would have continuing care needs but this information had not been available. Retrospectively however inclusion of those with different levels of need proved useful as a wider range of health states were included which were then considered for potential associations with user experience and behaviour. (This information was only available for interviewees.)

The time of year during which the questionnaire was distributed could potentially have an effect on the sample. Hospital activity is cyclical in that there tend to be more admissions over the winter months, particularly of elderly people. This sample was made up of those discharged from hospital over the spring and summer months, thereby avoiding the busiest period. As such it must be borne in mind if making any claims of the representativeness of the findings, that they cannot be deemed applicable to all those discharged from hospital in any typical month.

For the purposes of interview, service users were purposively sampled (Patton, 1990; Mason, 1996) on the basis of age, gender and household composition; this information was obtained from the questionnaire responses. Random sampling may not have yielded a sufficiently broad range of these characteristics. Every attempt was made to match the respondents selected for interview with the characteristics of the potential respondents to whom the questionnaire was initially sent. In terms of socio-demographic characteristics, the three groups of people (that is, the total sample to whom questionnaires were sent, the questionnaire respondents and the interview sample) were fairly well matched (see Table 3). However, no claim is made about the ability to extrapolate the data to the wider population. By the very nature of the criteria for inclusion, that is, people of 70 years and over on discharge from hospital, there will be over representation of those who are ill than would reasonably be expected in this age group.

The process of sampling for interview purposes was interactive in that the size of the interview sample was finalised during the qualitative phase of the study. Once interviews had been started, judgements were made as to the sample size required to sufficiently explore the processes under study and enable comparisons to be made. Mason (1996) explores how purposive sampling enables meaningful comparisons to be made in relation to the research questions, the theory and the type of explanation sought. Data can be generated to explore processes, similarities and differences in order to test and develop theory and explanation to account for these similarities and differences. Yet no claims to representativeness can be made.

Lack of control over the selection of the sample to whom to administer the postal questionnaire resulted in a very diverse sample. Purposively sampling interviewees on the basis of demographic characteristics of questionnaire respondents therefore also resulted in a degree of heterogeneity. This was utilised effectively during the analysis phase however in that demographic and social characteristics were explored as possible associations with user experience and behaviour.

Response Rates

The questionnaire was distributed initially to a total of 518 people of 70 years and over on discharge from a large District General Hospital over a 5-month period in 1996. A response rate of 55% was achieved. Of these, 260 were valid and sufficiently complete, giving a final response rate of just over 50%. One hundred and thirty four (51.5%) respondents agreed to be contacted further for the research.   Thirty respondents were then interviewed; demographic and social characteristics (gender, age and household composition) being the basis on which they were selected. Interviews lasted between 40 minutes and 2 hours; the time-consuming nature of such a method of data collection necessarily imposed limitations on the sample size. As such, emphasis is given to validity of interview data at the cost of representativeness, a common feature of a qualitative approach. The characteristics of the various samples are shown in Table 3 below.

Table 3:   Characteristics of Samples

	TOTAL SAMPLE (N=518)	QUESTIONNAIRE RESPONDENTS (N=260)	INTERVIEW SAMPLE (N=30)
MALE	231 (45%)	125 (48%)	14 (47%)
FEMALE	287 (55%)	135 (52%)	16 (53%)
AGED 70-77 YRS	299 (58%)	131 (50%)	17 (57%)
AGED 78 YRS AND ABOVE	219 (42%)	129 (50%)	13 (43%)
LIVES ALONE	NOT AVAILABLE	103 (40%)	15 (50%)
LIVES WITH OTHERS	NOT AVAILABLE	152 (60%)	15 (50%)

(Totals Vary Due To Missing Data)

Although this table demonstrates similarities between the samples, as there are many other variables on which the groups could differ caution dictates that it would be unwise to suggest that the respondents were representative of the wider population. In addition, a response rate of 50% can be classed as relatively low and means that the views of half of the total sample were not represented. It may be possible that this non-response was due to ill health but nothing definite is known about the non-responders other than that which can be derived from Table 3. The study was also limited to one locality. These factors limit the potential for extrapolation of the findings to the wider population. Accordingly this study makes no definitive claims to be representative of the total population of people aged 70 years and above discharged from hospital. Emphasis is given instead to the composition of the samples in order that comparisons can be made between sub groups and similarities and differences exposed in order to provide explanations of the processes under study.

Sample Selection: Professionals

Knowledge gained from working within the NHS and consultation with colleagues provided an initial list of senior job titles, whose post holders within the local area would be essential to speak to for the purposes of the study. Perusal of the Health and Social Services Yearbook (IHSM, 1996; Mould *et al.*, 1996) followed by consultation with relevant personnel at the local hospital and the local Community Health Council provided contact names for these posts.

It was also considered essential to gain the views of front line workers who are in daily contact with elderly people and have some bearing on the discharge process. It was assumed that they may have a different perspective of hospital discharge from that of policy makers and implementers. Again, a list was compiled of professions, representatives of which needed to be surveyed for their views to be included in the research. Access was gained via the relevant managers (as interviewees or otherwise) who identified a named member of their staff to approach. Approaching front line workers on the recommendation of line managers or equivalent was an important way of enhancing the credibility of the project and helped secure the co-operation of these workers. In addition to providing contact names for job titles identified by the researcher, there were instances when professionals, as interviewees, suggested a further contact name or profession not originally conceived of. In all cases these were pursued and an interview secured.

It was at the point that no new names or job titles were emerging from interviews that the sample was considered exhaustive. A total sample of 21 professionals were identified and interviewed representing a 100% response rate.

Such a method of gaining further contacts to research is often referred to as 'snowball' sampling, that is, early members of the sample population are asked to identify others who meet the eligibility criteria for the study (Polit and Hungler, 1993). Often used for populations whose traits may be difficult to identify or with 'closed' populations, this method proved very effective in this instance. The way in which the 'snowball' was used in this study was quite strict in that a representative from a specific occupation was sought.

Potential bias is introduced by this sampling method in that most front line workers were selected specifically by those in more senior positions, the researcher having no control over the criteria used in that selection. However, it constituted a quick and effective method of securing the co-operation of relevant respondents and given that it was not a very contentious area of practice, no real difficulty was posed by such a method of selection. Although it was felt that all the managers wished to help the progress of the research as much as possible, as indeed all respondents did, the possibility remains that they may have provided names of front line workers sharing similar views to their own.

Pilot Study

Colleagues within the academic institution and contacts within the health service and voluntary organisations were consulted at various stages of designing the research tools and invited to critically review both the proposed method of data collection and the specific tools. Pilot studies were then carried out in order to assess the extent to which the required data would be collected.

The questionnaire was piloted at two local day centres where the organisers kindly identified appropriate attendees, that is, of 70 years and over and recently discharged from hospital to their own homes. The covering letter and questionnaire to be issued to ex-patients were shown to the person after a brief introduction. There was then minimum intervention other than when questions were asked or clarification was needed regarding specific questions. Comments gained and clarifications needed were incorporated into subsequent versions of the questionnaire which were then also piloted. Three pilot phases in all were carried out, with each of the three versions of the questionnaire being piloted on three or four individuals.

Although not identical to the way in which respondents would actually receive the questionnaire, this method was thought to be as effective, if not more so, as carrying out a postal pilot questionnaire. Immediate feedback was gained, which proved to be mainly on the phrasing used. Verbal comments were also sought on the aesthetics, the areas researched and general views on receiving questionnaires.

Piloting of the interview schedule for use with service users was also carried out but on a more modest scale. It was deemed less important to stringently pilot a deliberately flexible research tool and informal meetings with three of the first questionnaire respondents proved to be sufficient. Again terminology and phrasing were issues that proved to need attention. The main reasons for 'piloting' the interview schedule were to sample the logistics of carrying out tape recorded interviews and to ensure the sensitivity of the recording equipment with potentially frail, hard of hearing or softly spoken respondents.

In a quantitative context, validity refers to the ability of the research tool to measure what it aims and professes to measure whilst in qualitative terms, it refers to the ability to represent an accurate picture of reality (Dempsey and Dempsey, 1992). The comprehensive pilot study carried out for this research can be seen as instrumental in ensuring the subsequent success of the study; enhancing the validity of the main study is a fundamental objective of any pilot study (Yin, 1984).

Piloting of the semi-structured interview schedule for use with professionals was considered neither feasible, in that all named respondents needed to be included in the final study, or necessary, in that there were unlikely to be problems of sensory impairment or vulnerable respondents.

Ethical Considerations

Ethical dilemmas will arise in any research involving human subjects. This is particularly the case when research involves medical interventions or treatment other than would normally be received. Neither of these was the case in this study which solely involved asking about care already received. The main concerns in this case were with questioning about a personal subject, that is, health and social care, inconveniencing the respondent and with raising expectations about services. Ethical approval was sought, and obtained, from the relevant local Research Ethics Committee as soon as was practicable.

By definition, those recently discharged from hospital have experienced, or are experiencing, health problems and so could possibly be vulnerable. Elderly people are also more likely to be confused or otherwise have problems with recalling events. This heightens the potential for an 'exploitative' relationship to develop, a possibility with any research involving those receiving a service. Therefore, particular consideration needs to be given to ethical issues when including elderly people as the subjects of research. However, this assertion is disputed by Butler (1990) who classes such 'special' consideration as a form of 'ageism' claiming instead that all social research should be conducted in the light of a strict ethical code.

Respondents who omitted to complete their name and address on the questionnaire indicating that they did not wish to be contacted further received no more correspondence; identification on their completed questionnaires was solely by means of a number. For those respondents completing their name and address, assurances were given that their names would not be recorded and would at all times be kept separate from the information supplied. A telephone call was made to arrange appointments for interviews, yielding a further opportunity for questionnaire respondents to decline to be further involved. People with no telephone or who had included an incorrect contact number were contacted by letter suggesting a time for the interview to take place. The contact number of the researcher was included on all correspondence should further information be required.

Robson (1993) believes a major ethical consideration to be whether respondents can rationally, knowingly and freely give informed consent. Informed, voluntary written consent was obtained from service users before an interview commenced following a detailed verbal explanation. Respondents were assured regarding confidentiality. It was also made clear that any questions they had would be answered and that they were free to withdraw at any stage without providing a reason and with no detrimental effect on their care. Interviews were tape recorded, with the respondent's consent, transcribed and the recording destroyed within six weeks of the date of interview. Information collected was used for research purposes only.

Bowsher *et al.* (1993) believe that elderly people are particularly likely to feel that they have been 'researched' and then left, once the interview is over. This heightens the importance of 'debriefing' or other method of terminating the interview encounter. In this study, at the end of an interview, the use to which the information would be put was reiterated along with further opportunities to ask questions or raise issues with the researcher.

Ethical concerns were not of such urgency with health and social care professionals as no danger could be seen of an exploitative relationship developing. A copy of the research protocol was provided to all professionals and assurances were given regarding confidentiality and anonymity. Again, encounters were tape recorded, with the respondent's consent, transcribed for analysis and the recording destroyed within six weeks of the date of the interview. Information collected was used for research purposes only.

Analysis of the Data

Consideration was given to the analysis of the findings from the beginning of the project particularly in relation to how the findings were to be presented in response to the specific aims of the study.

A data file was created using SPSS 6.1 for Windows, into which questionnaire data could be entered as it was returned. Variables were created and defined on the basis of the individual questions on the postal survey. In the case of qualitative comments, only an indication could be entered into the programme as to whether a response had been completed or not. Two such responses were following filter questions, being 'not applicable' in some instances, they were coded as such. Individual questionnaires were consulted when seeking to analyse *verbatim* comments.

The respondents were dichotomised on the basis of the mean age of the questionnaire respondents; the two age groups were 70-77 years and 78 years and over. This was devised from the mean age of questionnaire respondents and the defining age of 'geriatric' in the geographical area under study. 'Pension', the dichotomous variable indicating whether respondents were in receipt of a pension other than the state retirement pension, was used as a rough proxy of socio-economic status. The questionnaire findings showed how pension entitlement was significantly associated with former occupation ($p < 0.05$) and housing tenure ($p < 0.05$), further potential indicators of socio-economic status. An abbreviated version of the Registrar General's classifications was used to group respondents on the basis of former occupation. These associations are shown in Tables 4 and 5 below.

The dichotomous variables of gender, household composition (whether the person lived alone or not), pension and age group were then considered in all instances to assess whether they were associated with user experience and behaviour. All of these form categorical or nominal data and as such could only be subjected to non-parametric testing (Bryman and Cramer, 1997).

Table 4:   **Occupational Group and Pension Entitlement**

	NO OCCUPATIONAL OR PRIVATE PENSION	OCCUPATIONAL OR PRIVATE PENSION	TOTAL
PROFESSIONAL	6	30	36
SKILLED NON-MANUAL	7	24	31
SKILLED MANUAL	38	28	66
UNSKILLED	19	8	27
NO FORMER OCCUPATION GIVEN/ HAD NOT WORKED	52	12	64
TOTAL	122	102	224

(Pearson chi-square value = 54.972; degrees) of freedom = 4; p< 0.05
(36 missing cases)

Table 5:   Housing Tenure and Pension Entitlement

	No OCCUPATIONAL OR PRIVATE PENSION	OCCUPATIONAL OR PRIVATE PENSION	**TOTAL**
OWNER-OCCUPIED	76	96	**172**
NOT OWNER-OCCUPIED	52	25	**77**
TOTAL	**128**	**121**	**249**

(Pearson chi-square value = 11.605; degrees of freedom = 1; $p < 0.05$)
(11 missing cases)

Simple frequency distributions of the questionnaire responses were obtained. These were explored for any notable patterns. The data was also cross-tabulated to ascertain any relationships between the variables and any relationships with the demographic and personal characteristics listed above. The Chi-Square test with an alpha value of 5% was used to demonstrate the presence or absence of a relationship between variables. This test compares the observed frequency against the expected frequency of two or more unrelated samples on a variable which may have two or more categories (Cramer, 1994). It aims to assess the extent to which any differences are 'real' rather than occurring by chance, that is, as a result of 'sampling variability' (SPSS, 1994). Tables and charts are used as appropriate in the presentation of quantitative findings.

Adjusted standardised residuals were also calculated for all cells in contingency tables. These measure the level of deviation of the findings from the mean, again testing the difference between the observed and expected frequencies, and give the clearest picture of the relative contributions of each cell to the overall result. Any observed value of two standard deviations or more (+/- 1.9) from the mean can be concluded to be contributing to the overall effect. The magnitude of the score indicates the degree of the discrepancy and the sign indicates the direction, that is, whether the observed score was less than or greater than expected (SPSS, 1994). A positive residual indicates that there are more observed cases in a cell than would be expected if there were no association between the variables whilst a negative residual indicates that there are fewer observed cases than would be expected.

Content analysis was employed to analyse the findings from the qualitative phase of this research. Q S R Nud Ist (version 3) was employed in the analysis of the in-depth interview data largely to organise the dataset and make it amenable to analysis. The data from interviews with service users and that from interviews with professionals were treated as separate datasets. As such, two 'projects' were created in Nud Ist.

All transcripts were read through thoroughly and an initial list of themes or 'analytical categories' (Strauss, 1987; Miles and Huberman, 1994) were developed. The research questions from the interview schedules provided a structure for guiding this categorisation and all subsequent analysis and interpretation. Further exploration of the written transcripts produced an annotated list of categories and sub-categories to index the data in addition to revealing relationships between them.

A list of 67 categories was devised from the interviews with service users. This included both descriptive and conceptual categories (Mason, 1994), the latter of which are grounded in the analytical background of the study. All transcripts were then coded manually on this basis and entered into the computer package. Relationships were explored between the categories and with social and personal characteristics of respondents, those above plus self-reported health state (either positive or negative), in order to gain a more complete understanding of the data and thereby the experience and behaviour of service users.

A list of 64 categories was devised from the interviews with professionals. Again, both descriptive and conceptual categories were devised and the data was coded manually accordingly and entered into Nud Ist.

Nud Ist was used to list appropriate sections of text as appropriate for the subsequent selection of pertinent quotes. This provided a comprehensive means of accessing information and also provided the possibility of quantifying comments, methods which are addressed by Silverman (1993). This study focuses on the richness of the data provided by the qualitative approach yet also presents the strength of evidence by simple counting procedures.

Summary

This chapter has given consideration to all aspects of the research process and the rationale for the selection of the various approaches. It has shown how the implementation of different types of research methodology and the collection of data from different sources serve both to contribute to the validity of the findings and also provide a greater depth and breadth of understanding of the phenomena under investigation. The importance of ethical considerations and of carrying out a comprehensive pilot study are also highlighted. The procedures undertaken during analysis are also detailed.

The data accruing from these processes are presented in the following chapter. This is followed in Chapters 7 and 8 by a discussion and interpretation of these findings, particularly in relation to the original aims of the study and analytical framework. The data collected by questionnaires and gained through in-depth interviews with service users is incorporated in reporting the overall findings insofar as they researched the same issues. In most instances, there is an attempt to reinforce the findings from one source with those from the other, reinforcing the utility of combining quantitative and qualitative methodology. With regard to findings revealing the behaviour of service users, only qualitative data was available. Data collected from health and social care professionals is presented separately from that from service users in Chapter 6 yet interpreted alongside that from service users in Chapters 7 and 8.

6 Findings

Introduction

Selected observations are now reported from carrying out the empirical study detailed in the previous chapter, in order to address the specific aims of the project (see Chapter 1). The findings are presented using the criteria indicating user influence or control, addressed by the study, of *participation, representation, access, choice, information* and *redress*. These were all promoted by the policy initiatives and guidance analysed in Chapter 3.

The findings relate to the three sources of data detailed in Chapter 5, namely a) postal questionnaire data completed by users of health and social care (n=260) b) semi-structured interviews with service users (n=30) and c) semi-structured interviews with health and social care professionals (n=21). This chapter attempts to reconcile these data sources, in addition to drawing links between the six criteria outlined above. The findings presented consider the variables of age group, self-reported health status, gender, household composition and pension entitlement (as a rough proxy of socio-economic status) as possible associations with user experience and behaviour. Chapters 7 and 8 provide discussions of the position of the service user in relation to the main issues of service use revealed by the present chapter and by these variables of social differentiation respectively.

Participation and Representation

'Participation' was used in this study as the central concept in investigating the experience and behaviour of users of health and social care. The empirical study explored participation by the respondent and by their family and friends (as representation) in assessment and decision making regarding continuing care on discharge from hospital and in the period shortly afterwards.

Service User Responses

Sixty three percent of questionnaire respondents stated that they had been involved in decisions about the care they would receive when they returned home (question 4) but feelings about how much their views had been taken into consideration (question 4a) varied. Of those who felt that they had been involved, few thought that their views had not been considered. Comments included *'not much'* (8 respondents, 3%); *'satisfactorily'* or *'adequately'* (16 respondents, 6%); *'quite good'* or *'fairly well'* (15 respondents, 6%); *'considerably'* or *'very much'* (26 respondents, 10%) and *'completely'* (11 respondents, 4%). A selection of other pertinent comments is given below.

> Not sure, social worker liaised with [friend] on my behalf (female, 82 years, lives alone).

> Very much, my wife and I were told exactly what was happening and what after care treatment was available (male, 72 years, lives with wife).

> Everyone listened to what I wanted and discussed it with my family (female, 81 years, lives with husband).

> Even though I was so ill my views were openly discussed when my wife was present (male, 72 years, lives with wife).

An important observation to note here is the seemingly advantageous position of respondents who have family or friends (as *representatives*) to articulate on their behalf or otherwise help or provide support in their contacts with care professionals. This is reinforced by examining the association between respondents' living arrangements and involvement in needs assessment (question 3.3), shown below in Table 6. Using adjusted standardised residuals, a significant association was found between respondents living alone and feeling that they were *not* involved when their needs were assessed.

Table 6: **Household Composition and Involvement in Needs Assessment, Questionnaire Respondents (n=260)**

INVOLVED IN NEEDS ASSESSMENT	LIVES ALONE	LIVES WITH OTHERS	*TOTAL*
NO	**31 (30%)**	29 (19%)	**60 (24%)**
YES	63 (61%)	98 (65%)	**161 (63%)**
UNSURE/NOT APPLICABLE	9 (9%)	25 (16%)	**34 (13%)**
TOTAL	**103 (40%)**	**152 (60%)**	**255 (100%)**

(Pearson Chi-Square value = 6.01; degrees of freedom = 2; $p<0.05$)
(5 missing cases)

Splitting the data by selected variables provides more of an insight and permits further identification of user groups and their likely experience and behaviour. For respondents aged 78 years and above, a significant association was found between the gender of the respondent and whether they felt that they had been involved in the process of needs assessment. Males in this age group were much more likely to feel that they had been involved in the process of needs assessment than females. This is shown in Table 7 below.

Table 7:   **Involvement in Needs Assessment by Gender,**
Questionnaire Respondents aged 78 years and over
(n = 105)

INVOLVED IN NEEDS ASSESSMENT	MALE	FEMALE	TOTAL
NO	8 (19%)	18 (29%)	**26 (25%)**
YES	**32 (74%)**	30 (48%)	**62 (59%)**
UNSURE/NOTAPPLICABLE	3 (7%)	14 (23%)	**17 (16%)**
TOTAL	**43 (41%)**	**62 (59%)**	**105 (100%)**

(Pearson Chi-Square value = 7.85; degrees of freedom = 2; $p<0.05$)

Also of relevance here is the significant association ($p<0.05$) between gender and household composition with males much more likely to live with others than females. Only 23% of males lived alone compared to 56% of females. Of respondents aged 78 years and above, 42% of males lived alone compared to 64% of females.

Reinforcing the questionnaire findings, most interviewees reported having been consulted, or at least spoken with, about their discharge from hospital. Most (73%) had spoken with a social worker or other front line worker before or very shortly after discharge about their perceived needs and service requirements. The only dissatisfaction emerging amongst a small minority of interviewees (17%) regarding the discharge process was with shortfalls in subsequent care provision which most recognised as due to lack of resources, for example:

> [social worker] said 'there's no money'. She as good as said she was asking us but there wasn't any money for anything (male, 84 years, lives with wife and son).

One gentleman succinctly gave what appeared a widespread perception of what 'involvement' could entail.

Up to now I think I have been pretty well involved. They've told me what they were going to do and they've done it (male, 74 years, lives alone).

All interviewees (100%) had been keen to return home, stating as much to the professionals when their discharge was discussed. A few interviewees (7: 23%) even felt that they had initiated the discharge process or at least asked when they could expect to return home and expressed an unprompted desire to do so. All were aged 70-77 years and all rated their health positively. Perhaps unsurprisingly, all waited for 'permission' from the doctor or consultant before leaving inpatient care. Those living with others again faced a different situation to those living alone as shown by the following comments.

When they said to me 'you're fairly stable, is there somebody to look after you?' and my wife was, so they said 'you can go if you wish to' and I went (male, 72 years, lives with wife).

... they said I was going to be discharged and was there somebody to look after me. I said 'yes', so they said I could go home (male, 76 years, lives with wife).

Attitudes towards participating were also explored at interview. Understandably service users felt that advice from professionals was valuable and many were content for them to take decisions on their behalf often not feeling competent to have an active role. The following comments illustrate this:

I left it entirely to them. They ask you what you want ... and I said 'well you know more about it than I do'. They're the experts so I left it to them and I'm quite happy ... (female, 72 years, lives alone).

[district nurses] ... it was just decided that they would come and see me, I wasn't consulted, but I didn't want to be. I was quite happy with what they were doing, more than happy (male, 70 years, lives with wife).

Other comments such as *'they're the experts', 'they know best', 'it's naturally better to take their advice'* and *'I haven't sufficient knowledge'* were typical. Health status was found to affect willingness to play an active role, with interviewees suffering from poor health being less inclined to participate than those in better health. Eighteen interviewees (60%) made specific comments, when questioned, regarding wishing to be involved in decisions about their care, whilst 23% definitely did not wish to be, largely on the grounds of poor health.

With regard to expressing an opinion to care professionals, over half of interviewees (53%) felt that if asked they would do so, the majority of whom rated their health positively. Ill health was specifically cited by three interviewees (10%) as a reason for not expressing an opinion.

Broad issues which were felt to underlie respondents' whole attitude towards assuming an active role and their ability to do so were also explored. These included reported knowledge of entitlement to care and the ability to express wishes to care professionals. Whilst they have implications for service users participating, these factors also impact upon users *accessing* services.

With specific regard to entitlement to statutory care, 50% of questionnaire respondents expressed confidence in their knowledge of service entitlement (questions 3.8 and 3.12). This is shown in Table 8.

Table 8: **Knowledge of Entitlement to Care, Questionnaire Respondents (n=260)**

	I KNOW WHAT HEALTH CARE I AM ENTITLED TO	I KNOW WHAT CARE I AM ENTITLED TO FROM THE SOCIAL SERVICES
No	42 (16%)	53 (20%)
YES	130 (50%)	129 (50%)
UNSURE/ NOT APPLICABLE	88 (34%)	78 (30%)
TOTAL	**260 (100%)**	**260 (100%)**

Pearson Chi-Square value = 107.55; degrees of freedom = 4; $p < 0.05$)

A significant association was found between these two statements with those knowledgeable of one sector also being knowledgeable of the other and vice versa. In these areas it can reasonably be assumed that 'Unsure' was meaningful, that is, people were not totally sure of what care they were entitled to. Interview data mirrored these responses. Half of interviewees (50%) felt that they knew what care they were entitled to whilst half did not and a close relationship was revealed between knowledge of entitlement to care from Social Services and from the NHS.

Working on the basis of adjusted standardised residuals (see Chapter 5), questionnaire respondents living alone were significantly more likely to claim that they did not know what care they were entitled to than those living with others (+/- 2.2). By gender, males were significantly more likely to claim to know what care they were entitled to than females (+/- 1.9) and by age group, 'young elderly' people (70-77 years) were significantly more likely to claim to know what care they were entitled to than 'old elderly' people (78 years and above) (+/- 2.0). These results were again strengthened by interview findings as shown in Table 9.

Table 9: **Knowledge of Care Entitlement by Gender, Household Composition and Age Group, Interviewees (n=30)**

	KNEW WHAT CARE ENTITLED TO (N=15)	DID NOT KNOW WHAT CARE ENTITLED TO (N=15)
MALE	9 (60%)	5 (33%)
FEMALE	6 (40%)	10 (67%)
LIVES ALONE	6 (40%)	9 (60%)
LIVES WITH OTHERS	9 (60%)	6 (40%)
70-77 YEARS	10 (67%)	7 (47%)
78 YEARS AND ABOVE	5 (33%)	8 (53%)

A number of interviewees' views regarding entitlement to care demonstrated how many had not considered attempting to obtain further care although in many instances this was obviously related to perceived need. Some examples are given below.

> Well I'm not entirely sure of all the services, I've never gone into it, if you know what I mean. I haven't looked at it as yet (female, 72 years, lives alone).

> I've got to be content with what I get haven't I? There's no other help I'm entitled to, I'm not entitled to anything else (female, 76 years, lives alone).

> I'm not terribly interested, if I was interested I'd soon be aware [of available services] but no, I'm not. If I was on the bread line I suppose I'd have to be, but I'm not (male, 70 years, lives with wife).

For some interviewees (3: 10%), attitude towards obtaining further care was related to the importance of retaining independence, as illustrated below.

> As long as I don't need them, I don't want to know (male, 86 years, lives alone).

> ... being the independent type people used to say to me 'you're entitled to this, that and the other' and 'you'll get help if you only ask for it' but I didn't need any help. I can manage to clean the house and I can cook and feed myself (female, 87 years, lives alone).

> I can't think of anything else that I need, I don't want anything else (female, 81 years, lives with husband).

Communication with care professionals was explored as a fundamental aspect of *participation* but must also be considered as having implications for *access*. The questionnaire item. *'I felt able to express my wishes when I was in hospital'* (question 3.4) produced the results in Figure 1.

This was deliberately a very general and broad statement which could encompass both medical and non-medical issues with a variety of medical and non-medical personnel. It was solely intended to give a general idea of respondents' comfort in communicating with 'professionals' when in a less than optimum health state and in unfamiliar surroundings.

Figure 1: **Respondents Able to Express their Wishes in Hospital (n=260)**

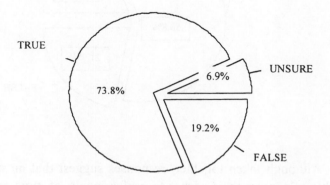

Responses to the more specific questionnaire item, 'I am able to express my wishes to social workers' (question 3.13) produced the results shown in Figure 2.

Figure 2:   **Respondents Able to Express their Wishes to Social Workers (n= 260)**

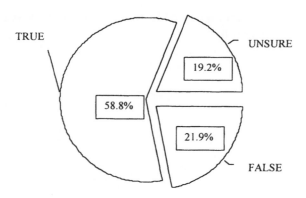

Although taken together, responses suggest that most people feel quite able to express their wishes to professionals, of more concern is the sizeable minority who were unsure of this ability.   The statistically significant association between Figures 1 and 2   (p<0.05) reveals how almost 20% of questionnaire respondents felt unable to express their wishes to hospital or social work personnel.

At interview, a distinction was made between doctors or consultants and other front-line workers in terms of communication. Only 33% (10) of interviewees felt able to communicate with doctors or consultants, compared to 63% feeling able to communicate with other front-line workers.   The characteristics of those feeling able to communicate with doctors or consultants are quite different from those of interviewees feeling not able to communicate with these professionals, as shown in Table10.

Table 10: **Characteristics of Interviewees able/not able to Communicate with Doctors or Consultants**

	INTERVIEWEES ABLE TO COMMUNICATE WITH DOCTORS/ CONSULTANTS (N=10)	INTERVIEWEES NOT ABLE TO COMMUNICATE WITH DOCTORS/ CONSULTANTS (N=20)
HEALTH RATING: POSITIVE	10 (100%)	12 (60%)
HEALTH RATING: NEGATIVE	0 (0%)	8 (40%)
OCC / PRIVATE PENSION	10 (100%)	9 (45%)
NO OCC/PRIVATE PENSION	0 (0%)	11 (55%)
LIVES ALONE	3 (30%)	12 (60%)
LIVES WITH OTHERS	7 (70%)	8 (40%)
MALE	7 (70%)	7 (35%)
FEMALE	3 (30%)	13 (65%)

This table shows how it was interviewees rating their health positively, interviewees in receipt of a private or occupational pension, interviewees living with others, and males who were most likely to feel able to communicate with doctors or consultants.

Interviews with Professionals

Overall, the majority of health and social care professionals surveyed (81%) stated quite clearly that service users and their carers (as representation) were consulted regarding their care. Although participation was perceived as desirable, many professionals acknowledged that the ultimate *influence* that users may have over decisions may be limited by resource constraints.

With regard to the discharge process and opportunities for participation, managers and professionals not having daily direct contact with elderly people were only able to relate second-hand experience. Reassuringly, nobody simply reiterated the policy documentation regarding what *should* happen.

> They are involved in the assessment stage and I'm persuaded by talking to our team leaders that it happens (Acting Assistant Director, Older People and Hospitals, Social Services).

> The nursing plan that we sign up then there is always carer and patient involvement ... what the level of care is going to be, how long the involvement is for and what the review process is. The evidence I have seen ... demonstrates that that's happening (Director of Community Services, Community Trust).

Front line workers, having daily direct contact with older people, were able to be more specific as illustrated by the following comments.

> We do spend a lot of time with patients, with carers ... it's a fact gathering exercise and perhaps tentative plans are talked about ... but there is high consultation with the patients and their carers (Senior Practitioner, Social Work Department, NHS Trust).

> ... we look at the situation, see how she or he is, we wait for them to tell us how they're managing, what they can do, what they can't do (Senior Home Care Assistant).

> ... whether the patients themselves have a say I'm afraid, because if it is a frail condition or they do not know whether they can cope or not, they would be consulted by their family or the doctor but it's difficult to say (Ward Manager, NHS Trust).

An awareness that consultation may raise expectations which can then not be met due to limited resources was also apparent.

... we have to balance what the patient really wants and what we can afford... Expectations are rising all the time and can we meet them within a very tight budget? (Business Development Manager, Medicine, NHS Trust).

... by the fact that I consulted them and asked for their views I have further raised their expectations that by expressing their expectations we are going to do something about it (Executive Director, NHS Trust).

All professionals perceived resource limitations as an underlying factor in decision making and a number (20%) even believed that decisions about discharge started by looking at resource availability, that is, were supply-led as shown by these comments.

... it goes off to the panel and we lose it at that point really because then it's down to what's available, financially. We're moving away from needs-led to service-led really (Senior Practitioner, Social Work Department, NHS Trust).

... we're always thinking 'well have we got enough money in the budget?' (Senior Home Care Assistant).

Within this however there appeared a genuine desire to recognise the wishes of the service user.

... as far as we can, we at least try and keep them up to date with what's happening and involve them ... even though their wishes can't always be followed (Named nurse, NHS Trust).

... [we're] obviously not always able to give them what they wish but we try to do as near as possible to their wishes and if they do want to go home then we go out of our way to make sure they can (Team Manager, Health Visiting).

The majority of professionals (57%) stated that they were keen for service users to have a degree of influence over continuing care. They felt that once it was established that care was required, the wishes of users with respect to 'what' and 'when' should be honoured, particularly given the fact that the services would be delivered to the home of the user. These are issues of both *participation* and *choice* and as such are explored in greater depth later in the chapter.

Regarding the possible involvement of third parties, 33% of professionals mentioned potential conflict between the service user and their family regarding care requirements. A cause of conflict identified was family members having vested interests, that is, being the ones on whom caring responsibilities would fall in the event of a shortfall in services. All professionals stressed the service user's needs taking priority over those of their representatives in such instances. The availability of informal care was also shown to impact upon the level of *choice* provided to service users and is explored later in this chapter.

Significantly, many professionals felt that users were beginning to realise that they could assume an active role. That is, the culture within which care is delivered is beginning to change. A need to further change the prevailing culture however was also highlighted, although it was acknowledged that this would only happen over time.

Access

Access in the field of health and social care can be defined in many ways and is closely related to peoples' right to receive care. As such, many of the above factors are relevant to ways in which access may be secured, including whether people are knowledgeable of the services that they are entitled to, in addition to ease of communication with professionals. Further issues of access which are now explored include knowledge of how to obtain services and whether respondents felt they were in receipt of all the services they needed. That is, whether they were able to *access* them. Although recognised as indicators of responsiveness to users, physical issues of access, issues relating to convenient opening hours, transport considerations or obtaining appointments and so on were not addressed, nor did they emerge from any of the interviews.

User Responses

Twenty five percent of questionnaire respondents felt that they were *not* receiving all the health and social care services that they needed (question 6). Eighty five percent of these respondents (56) were able to provide an explanation for this shortfall (question 6a). Table 11 indicates that males and those living with others were more likely to feel that they were in receipt of sufficient services than females and those who lived alone. The differences were statistically significant. No differences were revealed by age or pension entitlement. Again, the association between gender and whether respondents lived alone or not is relevant.

Table 11:   Receipt of Adequate Care by Household Composition and Gender, Questionnaire Respondents (n=260)

'DO YOU RECEIVE ALL THE HEALTH AND SOCIAL SERVICES THAT YOU FEEL YOU NEED?'

	No	Yes	Total
LIVES ALONE	31 (52%)	69 (37%)	100 (40.5%)
LIVES WITH OTHERS	29 (48%)	118 (63%)	147 (59.5%)

(Pearson Chi-Square value = 4.11; degrees of freedom = 1; $p < 0.05$)

	No	Yes	Total
MALE	22 (34%)	101 (53%)	123 (49%)
FEMALE	41 (65%)	88 (47%)	129 (51%)

(Pearson Chi-Square value = 6.49; degrees of freedom = 1; $p < 0.05$)
(totals vary slightly due to missing data)

The qualitative comments obtained explaining why respondents were not receiving sufficient care (question 6a) provided useful insights into the relationship users *expect* to have with health and social care providers and where they feel responsibility lies in accessing services. Some people felt that it was their role to initiate gaining access to services, and had indeed tried, whilst others felt that this lay within the remit of professionals. For this analysis of user behaviour and attitude, feelings regarding activity or passivity were fundamental. Problems with access appeared to stem from lack of knowledge about availability and about how to access services (see comments below). As such, it may be related to the provision of *information*, which is explored later.

> I don't know what's on offer (male, 72 years, lives with wife).

> I don't expect any (female, 87 years, lives with daughter).

> None has been offered (female, 74 years, lives alone).

> Nobody has discussed the possibilities of what is or may be available to me (female, 77 years, lives with husband).

> I am still waiting for an assessment (female, 87 years, lives alone).

There were a number of interviewees (57%) who were making use of private resources to access care or who had bought aids or adapted their homes in some way in response to perceived need. Eighteen percent of these respondents received Attendance Allowance, 65% were in receipt of a private or occupational pension, and some received both. Importantly, many interviewees (37%) were aware that statutory 'home helps' were only available for those needing personal care and no longer carried out domestic duties. Some of these interviewees had been refused the service, or indeed had refused the service, on these grounds.

Whilst respondents able and willing to pay privately were found to have heightened *access* to domestic care, the levels of *choice* available regarding delivery of such care were also increased, a factor explored later in this chapter. Although this can be equated with private sector markets, where access to services is dependent upon ability and willingness to pay, there are still limits to the extent to which private resources can secure access to statutory care.

Sixty three percent of questionnaire respondents felt that they would know who to contact if they had any questions about their care. This was explored further at interview. With regard to accessing health care, interviewees inevitably identified their GP, or professionals based at the GP's practice, as contact points, most being confident that they would receive a home visit. Regular attendees at outpatient clinics mentioned hospital contacts whom they could approach with health care needs.

In the case of social care, however, points of contact were less well defined. When asked where they would seek care other than to meet health needs, most interviewees (63%) identified 'Social Services', although a minority were unsure about how to go about this or what services were available. Twenty three per cent identified their GP after initially stating that they 'did not know' whom they would contact. Seven per cent of interviewees stated that they had information which they would consult in order to access further care and 7% identified Age Concern. (Information provision about service availability is discussed later in this chapter.) Comments relating to seeking help from different sources are given below.

> I don't know, I think I should have to go to the health centre, they deal with all that kind of thing, well they would (male, 86 years, lives alone).

> I don't know really I would probably go to this place down there, Age Concern, it's only up the road (female, 87 years, lives alone).

> Yes I've got a list of places that I can ring up, they're agencies evidently, I haven't enquired about that yet (female, 70 years, lives alone).

> I would just ring [Social Services] and contact someone if I needed something (female, 80 years, lives with sister).

It seems that whilst none would be at a loss as to who to approach, a general lack of precision was evident. Reassuringly, a number of comments were made suggesting peoples' willingness to assume an active role: *'I'd soon find out'; 'We could soon find out'* or *'I could look up the 'phone number'*. A few interviewees (10%) mentioned that their sons or daughters would assist in defining or contacting care professionals.

Whether respondents would contact service providers is an indicator of their attitude towards assuming an active user role. The provision of names and contact numbers is user orientation but whether service users utilise the opportunity is a separate issue. Many interviewees stated that having a contact name provided a degree of security should the need for additional care arise.

Interviews with Professionals

The issues that arose with professionals regarding access to care centred around the ease with which services could be secured by users and the ease with which professionals could be contacted. As found with service users, a distinction was apparent between care provided by the NHS and that provided by Social Services on these issues. This 'divide' and resource limitations were overwhelmingly cited as barriers to access. The earlier findings around *participation* demonstrated how resource limitations could limit the influence of service users in decision making around their care which may impact upon their *access* to services.

Access to continuing care is based on an assessment of need. Such an assessment however does not necessarily mean that access to services will ensue nor at the level required. Overall, there seemed to be no dispute regarding individuals' need for care, only difficulties in securing it. Ninety five percent of professionals interviewed mentioned the desperate financial situation facing Social Services departments in providing continuing care. An insight into this is gained by the following comments.

> Ideally people who meet the eligibility criteria should have immediate access to services but we're in a desperate imbalance between supply and demand. They haven't got access ... (Acting Assistant Director, Older People and Hospitals, Social Services).

> Obviously at times a patient going home may be assessed as needing more care than we can provide, because we do have limits on our care packages to the amount we can go up to. So you will get a patient who needs a lot more care, or even a little bit more, than we can provide ... (Team Leader, Social Work Department, NHS Trust).

> ... we haven't delayed anybody at all, maybe a few days. The delay now is Social Services support for the elderly being discharged back home, It's getting almost to crisis point now (Discharge Planning Co-ordinator, NHS Trust).

> ... there's an awful lot of patients blocking beds in the hospital ... they just have to sit there if they are expecting funding, everything is prioritised, they can sit there for up to 7 weeks (District nurse).

Professionals who had been in post during the implementation of the NHS and Community Care Act, 1990, were able to effect historical comparisons. The broad consensus seemed to be that eligibility criteria for services had been tightening with people prioritised immediately on being referred to Social Services and only those classed as top priority securing services. Front line workers in particular reported a huge difference in levels of access. Some examples are given below.

... it used to be just a matter of going out, visiting people, you could come back and really they could have everything, but now the restraints are there (Senior Home Care Assistant).

... when Community Care first came in there were no restrictions. So if that had continued it would have been great, but it was never going to continue, we never thought it would ... (Senior Practitioner, Social Work Department, NHS Trust).

As revealed from service users, the services that people want are no longer available, the one most commonly cited (by 29% of professionals) being domestic cleaning.

... they say they need things like they want someone to clean their house because that's important to them, but people don't do that any more ... We perhaps feel it's their need as well but because it isn't there they can't have it (Manager, night services and specialist services, Community Trust).

... what they want is help with hoovering, cleaning and that is exactly the services that have been stopped (Director of Community Care, Health Authority).

... they're not getting the service they want ... the home help service will not clean and it just seems ludicrous to me that they're not being provided with the service they need ... The clients generally are not getting the service that they want, they are getting the service that's given to them (Community Staff nurse).

Such help was reported as available privately for those able and willing to pay. Yet, payment for some statutory services was recognised as a feature of welfare largely due to means testing and pressure on statutory funding. The majority of professionals, most of who were front line workers, made comments stating as much (below). This has obvious implications for *accessing* care.

The resources are being tightened and tightened ... I have very serious concerns about it ... people are having to try and use their own money to look after themselves, to care for themselves (Occupational Therapist, NHS Trust).

... if they are self-funding which would mean they would pay full cost for our service ... they're independent purchasers I suppose so they can go to the agencies and they can get what they want but if they're on Income Support it's slightly different (Senior Home Care Assistant).

When they've been discharged and it's been deemed a nursing problem and we've looked after them, then it becomes a social problem ... suddenly they have to pay for it so suddenly they don't want it or we get the abuse at times ... (Manager, night services and specialist services, Community Trust).

Twenty four per cent of professionals mentioned Attendance Allowance as a potential source of income in order to access necessary care, most of whom provided examples of themselves or colleagues encouraging service users to apply for the benefit.

With regard to service users contacting providers should the need arise, no professionals foresaw any problem. All felt that their particular service was accessible and that their contact details were known by users. Front line workers in particular specifically provided names and contact details to users, 86% of whom were able to report instances of users contacting them which is encouraging even though some were felt to be inappropriate, for example:

We get people ringing up saying the home help hasn't arrived ... (Senior Practitioner, Social Work Department, NHS Trust).

... they're sticklers for time, so it's usually '[home help] is usually here at 25 past 8, it's 28 minutes past, nobody's turned up' (Senior Home Care Assistant).

Due to staff shortages, answering machines had been introduced for many services namely the community liaison department, social workers, health visiting and district nursing to cover out-of-hours and peak times. Although acknowledging the reluctance of some elderly people in using the service, most professionals felt that it was an efficient system with all messages promptly acted upon.

The issue of seamless care again arises in that as long as there is one point of access, this should theoretically lead to provision of all necessary care. This was raised with one professional in particular although others spoke of how they often direct service users to appropriate contacts.

> I think it would be nice to have people treated more holistically ... I don't think people really want to know about the different places you need to go depending on what's wrong with you, whether it's health or social services or the benefit office. I think there should be a common point of access for people requiring health and social support (Director of Community Care, Health Authority).

The distinctions in terms of responsibility, accountability and finance between the NHS and Social Services department could prevent such a policy being implemented. Given the difficulties outlined, 'professional boundaries' could be deemed an inhibiting factor in many areas of access.

Choice

The concept of *choice* is very closely related to *participation* (and *representation*); it is now shown that the two principles are part of the same process. Opportunities for exercising choice can only arise when there is participation (or representation) and likewise, the very act of choice means that there has been a degree of participation (or representation). In turn, both are related to the other principles of *access, information* and *redress*.

User Responses

Quite evidently, most respondents felt that they had been involved in the discharge process, however the issue of *choice* was soon revealed not to be the fundamental issue that had at first been anticipated. Questionnaire responses and interview piloting confirmed this at an early stage.

It is presumed that those who were engaged in discussions around continuing care were provided with a degree of choice regarding the care to be provided, including whether to receive any care. With regard to decisions about continuing care, 35% of questionnaire respondents felt that they had been given choices about what services they wished to receive (question 3.15), whilst 40% felt that this had not been the case. This refers to any services that people may receive to enable them to stay at home, the services that perhaps would have been suggested in discussions with social workers or other professionals before their discharge. For those with no assessed continuing care needs, this would be 'not applicable'.

Choices could also feasibly be given regarding more specific details of care delivery. Whether respondents had been given choices about who would deliver the care they needed (question 3.10) refers to how users wish their care needs to be met and incorporates informal care. The findings showed a highly significant association between being given choices about the services to receive and being given choices about who would deliver them (p<0.01). This is shown below in Table 12.

The questionnaire data was split by the variables gender, household composition, age group and pension entitlement and notable differences were revealed in all cases. Males, respondents living with others, respondents aged 78 years and above and respondents in receipt of an occupational or private pension reported experiencing the greatest opportunities for exercising both aspects of choice. The latter two of these were statistically significant.

Table 12: **Questionnaire Respondents Given Choices Regarding their Care (n=260)**

CHOICE OF WHAT SERVICES

		No	Yes	Unsure/ NA	Total
Choice of	No	76	23	18	117 (45%)
who will	Yes	7	43	8	58 (22%)
deliver	Unsure/NA	21	25	39	85 (33%)
	Total	104 (40%)	91 (35%)	65 (25%)	260 (100%)

(Pearson Chi-Square value = 90.58; degrees of freedom = 4; p<0.01)

Interviews revealed the existence of three broad types of people: those not wishing to receive any care; those who accepted what was offered and those who felt that they needed additional help but were unable to obtain it. Those in the latter category obviously had the least opportunities for *choice*. These distinctions are also important in terms of *access* to care.

Ten interviewees (33%) had accepted the help that was offered to them, that is, they chose to receive it, all expressing high levels of satisfaction with the subsequent care provided. Accepting what was offered can be viewed in the light of lay people leaving decisions regarding their care in the domain of the professional, explored earlier as an issue of *participation*. That is, they may have been either unable or unwilling to become involved in decision making, preferring to leave final decisions in the hands of the 'expert'.

One gentleman (74 years, living alone) who stated '*I didn't wait for them to ask me! I stated categorically that I wanted to go into permanent residence*' had visited several care homes in order to select the most suitable. His choice was unable to be honoured however, due to restrictions on statutory funding.

Thirty percent of interviewees (n = 30) had exercised their right to choose by declining to receive the care offered. Reasons for declining services included the availability of other sources of help (either informal or private), wishing to retain independence and feeling the services were unnecessary. For example:

> No I can clean myself, I'd rather keep going. If they came they wouldn't satisfy me ... they wouldn't do it right for me so I'd rather do a little bit on my own (male, 86 years, lives alone).

> [home help] would have been available, but I'd have had to pay for it just the same so I might as well carry on with [private cleaner] (female, 81 years, lives with husband).

Almost half of the interviewees (47%) had private help around the home, whilst others (20%) were dependent upon means-tested Social Services 'home helps'. Those paying for private help were in an advantageous position in terms of determining both the timing of service provision and the duties that would be performed by service providers. As explored earlier, there are obvious issues of *access* surrounding the distinction between those paying for private care and those receiving statutory care.

Timing of care was not found to be an issue with the respondents to this study who often had very few other demands on their time although courtesy should demand that they are given an approximation. All interviewees seemed flexible and willing to accommodate the service provider. One gentleman had arranged for agency help for assistance with getting up and dressed in the morning following the end of the four week post-hospital statutory provision. Immediately after discharge he had also received help with getting into bed at night, the timing of which had been fortuitous:

> ... luckily they didn't come too early, about 9pm. A few years ago I had help like this and the girls were coming at 6pm ... so I used to put my dressing gown on and stagger out again (male, 75 years, lives with friend).

When subsequently arranging agency help for mornings he stated:

> I may have mentioned it in talking to the head of [agency] that 9 to 9.30am would be a suitable time but I don't remember making a specific point of it but I probably did.

One off visits such as district nurses or chiropodists tended to be by specific appointments whilst more long term care such as daily nursing or home help services were more flexible in the timing of their visits. Respondents knew generally what time to expect them, understanding that the service was in demand.

> She comes at about 9am to do breakfast ... I think she comes back about 11am to give me my lunch ... Now this week she's coming later, she's got an extra case on, an old man that's poorly ... (female, 75 years, lives alone)

In terms of the role of domestic help, again those with private arrangements inevitably had greater control over what was included. However, once people received (statutory) home care there seemed to be flexibility over the duties performed. Some respondents remained unsure about what fell within the remit of the workers.

Within reason they'd do anything, you know, a bit of washing, ironing, dusting (female, 82 years, lives alone).

... she just came and asked me what I wanted doing (male, 74 years, lives alone).

Well she knows now what to do ... She knows that anything she sees needs doing, needs doing (female, 75 years, lives alone).

The overall feeling was that people valued being provided with choices although there were few areas in which this was available. In some cases it appeared that service users did not see the concept of choice as a valid one, feeling that the professionals 'know best', not feeling sufficiently competent to partake or that their choices may not be honoured.

Interviews with Professionals

Professionals viewed the concept of *choice* in the use of care in a different way to service users. They felt that it was more apparent, that is, greater opportunities existed for exercising choice than were perceived by the actual users and also more valid, that is, choices made would be honoured. Resource limitations, identified by professionals as constraining user *participation* in decisions regarding care and in accessing care were similarly given as restricting opportunities for choice for service users. Recognised by service providers and users alike, opportunities for participation and choice in clinical areas are obviously limited.

With reference to continuing care, most professionals believed that a degree of choice was available regarding the services to be provided. However many stressed that choices could only be given from what is available and, more importantly, within the resources. '*Options*' within '*given parameters*' was identified as a more achievable aim than 'choice' *per se*.

... we can't give them as broad a choice, it's a narrow choice, it's perhaps still a choice but it's narrowed down considerably (Senior Practitioner, Social Work Department, NHS Trust).

> ... we tell them what is available and they can choose from what is available but they can't actually choose what they want (General Manager, Medicine, NHS Trust).

The choice of service provider was also expressed as being limited. One Social Services manager mentioned 'block contracts' limiting choice for managers and ultimately for those using the service but went on to say:

> ... I have to then balance restricting choice and giving more services to more people. In which case maybe I do have to restrict choices a bit. Then it's choice within narrower parameters (Acting Assistant Director, Older People and Hospitals, Social Services).

Even given the 'mixed economy of care', choices are restricted.

> Normally there would be very little choice ... if our own services are available then it would be our own services that would be provided. We would not give them a choice of private agency, resources do not allow that (Team Leader, Social Work Department, NHS Trust).

As deduced from service users, professionals reported how users with other sources of care available or able and willing to pay for private care have a higher degree of choice than those reliant upon statutory provision. This was found to be in terms of both choice of services to use and choice of service provider. Self-funding service users would be provided with the necessary information and advice and would be free to act independently, choosing which services to use and from where to purchase them. Similar to findings already presented, more opportunities for such choices were perceived when seeking social care as opposed to clinical care.

Service users' desire to maintain independence, or at least return home, was acknowledged by a number of professionals.

> ... there are a lot of older people who don't want anything that makes them look disabled and they'll manage ... Some people really need help and equipment but they won't have it, it's their pride you know (Occupational Therapist, NHS Trust).

> A lot of patients are realistic ... There are other patients ... that are unrealistic about their abilities ... so you're working with them, counselling them to let them make the decision ... and if it is still something, well people have to accept what they're doing (Senior Practitioner, Social Work Department, NHS Trust).

> I feel a lot of elderly people want to get home and they'll do anything. They'll say 'yes, we've got all this help, all this support' ... and they'll have said anything just to get home (Health Visitor).

These comments demonstrate possible ways in which users may exercise choice in decision making regarding the services they wish to receive. The comments however also demonstrate a perceived need amongst professionals for 'expert' input in determining both need and appropriate service delivery.

Choice with regard to residential care was mentioned by a number of professionals (57%). Although technically outside the scope of this study, the findings are relevant insofar as residential care presents an alternative to continuing care provided to people in their own homes. Yet this study revealed no real consensus about whether choice was available or not between these alternatives, seen as dependent on funding. Thirty eight percent of professionals believed that there was scope for choosing a residential home, over half of whom were front line workers. Some examples are given below.

> ... they are always given [choice] ... he or she is given the leaflet by the social worker about all the details and names of the rest homes. He or she is at liberty to go and visit the place ... and make up his or her mind, they are given the choice (Consultant Physician in Elderly Medicine, NHS Trust).

> ... they will be given the choice if they are going into a nursing or a residential home, they are given the choice of those homes as a rule ... They are given that sort of choice, once the funding is in place (District nurse).

The last phrase of this of course shows where the limitations may lie. Further financial factors were also identified, this time by those in managerial roles.

> ... Social Services determine what homes they go to ...   Finances will dictate the type of nursing home and the 'deals' they've got with nursing homes. So that again I believe limits choices (Executive Director, NHS Trust).

Even though stating:

> The biggest choice happens when there is a distinction between a patient going home or going into a nursing home.

Again, however this choice would often be determined by cost. Some professionals expressed this is terms of a similar level of continuing care being provided in their own homes as in a residential setting.

> ... it all hinges on money. They can have a care package at home up to a certain level but after that it's nursing home care because it's cheaper (General Manager, Medicine, NHS Trust).

> To be offered the choice of a residential care home where you'd be looked after when you know you need support without being offered the choice of that support in your own home is not a choice (Director of Community Care, Health Authority).

Information

User Responses

Forty percent of questionnaire respondents stated that they were given written information to take home from hospital whilst 55% stated that this had not been the case. Questionnaire data also determined whether respondents felt that they had received sufficient information about the care that they received and whether they would know where to get information about the care services that are available to help them in their daily life. The results shown in Table 13 were obtained.

Table 13:   Questionnaire Respondents Receiving Sufficient Information and Knowledge of Where to Obtain Information (n=260)

	HAVE RECEIVED SUFFICIENT INFORMATION ABOUT CARE	KNOW WHERE TO GET INFORMATION ABOUT CARE
No	57 (22%)	52 (20%)
Yes	153 (59%)	156 (60%)
Unsure/NA	50 (19%)	52 (20%)
Total	**260 (100%)**	**260 (100%)**

Although not quite reaching statistical significance, questionnaire respondents aged 70-77 years felt less knowledgeable of where to obtain information about care than respondents aged 78 years and above. In addition, those in receipt of an occupational or private pension felt more knowledgeable of where to obtain information than those with no such pension.

Open-ended questions regarding information asked respondents what information (verbal or written) they had received about their care (question 5) and how useful they found it (question 5a). Seventy eight percent (203) of respondents made a comment regarding receipt of information, 63% of whom (127) went on to state its perceived usefulness. Very few respondents who made comments (8%) were negative about the usefulness of the information supplied. Equal numbers of respondents (46%) rated the information as '*good*', '*adequate*' or '*satisfactory*' as rated it '*very good*', '*very informative*' or '*very helpful*'.

Most information received was regarding specific health conditions including medication and dietary advice although in many cases details were also given of care services. For a small number of respondents, approximately 5%, information provided on discharge amounted to a follow-up appointment with outpatients or another service. Examples of some of the information provided are given below.

Information and guidelines for people with diabetes (male, 80 years, lives with wife).

Usual advice before leaving hospital (female, 94 years, lives alone).

Diet advice (male, 86 years, lives alone).

I was given a book about heart treatment (male, 71 years, lives with wife).

Social Services leaflets (female, 74 years, lives alone).

Seventy seven percent of interviewees gave instances of being provided with information. Consolidating the questionnaire data, interviews revealed that the majority of information provided was concerning medical condition. Although a similar number of respondents had received information about services as received information about medical condition, that provided about the latter, both written and verbal, appeared the most substantial. Consulting information about available services was mentioned earlier as a way in which users may attempt to *access* (social) care.

Of those interviewees who mentioned information about their condition, 21% did so regarding its paucity; a further 21% rated the provision very highly whilst 58% felt overall 'satisfied' with the provision. Those who rated this provision very highly, all (100%) rated their health positively compared to 71% of those who were 'satisfied' and only 60% of those who felt information was lacking. A selection of responses demonstrating dissatisfaction with levels of information about medical condition are given below.

It's lack of attention isn't it? That's all I could say and lack of divulging to you your condition. In other words not saying what's wrong with you (female, 75 years, lives alone).

It would have been nice to have been told a little more about what they were doing you know and what all these tests were for and when they did get the results what was it (female, 77 years, lives with husband).

... they weren't forthcoming with the information, we had to go and ask. We had to ask 'what is it?' 'what are you doing?' 'what are your recommendations?' Then they were fine, yes, they told us ... but we had to ask (female, 89 years, lives alone; 'we' refers to son and herself).

With respect to information provided about welfare services available, of those interviewees who commented, 18% rated the provision very highly whilst an equal number (41%) stated overall satisfaction with the information as were dissatisfied or were negative in their judgement. Again, those rating the provision very highly, all (100%) rated their health positively as did 89% of those who were 'satisfied' compared to only 33% of those who were dissatisfied. The following comments were made by two of those who felt that the information supplied was 'adequate'.

> Meals on wheels were suggested. [Health visitor] sent me a list of places that you can go to, where you can go for the day and it's to get you out instead of being on your own and to mix (female, 70 years, lives alone).

> The surgeon told me about the rehab. [sic.] course at the hospital ... the lady who runs it came to introduce herself to me at Christmas, she came to each one who'd had heart trouble (male, 70 years, lives with wife).

In addition to the *provision* of information, whether people actively seek out information which they feel to be lacking or feel that they would benefit from, provides a useful indicator of user behaviour. Just over half of the interviewees (53%, 16) reported seeking out information about an aspect of health and social care.

The sub-group reporting information seeking behaviour (n=16) proved fairly similar to the sub-group who did not seek out information (n=14) on a number of demographic characteristics. Breakdowns of respondents by age group and pension arrangements were similar across the two groups. However, by gender, there was a disproportionately high number of males reporting information-seeking behaviour and by household composition, a disproportionately high number of people living with others positively reporting such behaviour. This is shown in Table 14.

Closely linked to *access*, knowledge of where to obtain information must be fundamental in seeking it out. Indeed, quite logically, many of the individuals or services mentioned as access points to receive care from the NHS or Social Services department were also identified by interviewees as potential sources of information.

All interviewees identified their GP, professionals based at the GP's practice or possible hospital contacts as sources of health information whilst for Social Services, as with the identification of contact points, where to obtain information was less straightforward.   Seventy nine percent of interviewees named a specific service provider from whom they would seek information about social care, mainly *'the health centre'*, *'social services'*, *'home help department'*, *'the clinic'* or *'the social people'*, whilst 21% 'did not know'.

Table 14:   **Demographic Characteristics of Information Seeking and Non-Information Seeking Interviewees**

	INTERVIEWEES WHO SOUGHT OUT INFORMATION (N=16)	INTERVIEWEES WHO DID NOT SEEK OUT INFORMATION (N=14)
MALE	**11 (69%)**	**3 (21%)**
FEMALE	**5 (31%)**	**11 (79%)**
70-77 YEARS	10 (63%)	8 (57%)
78 YEARS AND ABOVE	6 (37%)	6 (43%)
OCC./PRIVATE PENSION	11 (69%)	8 (57%)
NO OCC./PRIVATE PENSION	5 (31%)	6 (43%)
LIVES ALONE	**6 (38%)**	**9 (64%)**
LIVES WITH OTHERS	**10 (62%)**	**5 (36%)**

From the trends given so far, it appears that users appreciate being provided with information about aspects of their care.   When specifically asked for their attitude towards the provision of information, interviewees overwhelmingly reported that they valued it, or would value it, if it were provided.   Understandably people were interested in their condition, their treatment, what services were available and what benefits they were entitled to.   Some examples of pertinent comments are given below.

I would sooner, even if I had cancer and heaven forbid that I don't have it, I would much prefer to be told quite frankly what the situation is so that I can adjust my life accordingly (male, 72 years, lives with wife).

You see I've asked the doctor today what's wrong ... and she's explained the condition of my heart so that we know my limitations ... Now I've been told not to do these things and that's all we need to know (male, 75 years, lives with wife).

... when they told me I had a tumour I just went blank .... When I came away I thought 'I should have asked this' 'I should have asked that' ... I didn't even ask him if it was cancerous, that's one of the things I should have asked him (female, 71 years, lives with husband).

Well it might be interesting to know [what services are available]. In hospital I was talking to a lady, she gets the full amount of Attendance Allowance, all her rates paid, a mobility allowance ... (female, 77 years, lives with husband).

Interviews with Professionals

Contrasting with service users, professionals made more comments regarding information provision about services than about medical condition. All professionals (100%) reported the provision of some level of both verbal and written information to service users who they came into contact with or who were provided for by the particular service with which they were involved.

Many individual services and departments produced their own written information which would be available to service users.

There are a number of leaflets that we have produced. There's one which describes community care and the assessment process ... there's a leaflet on appealing against not receiving services, there's one on making your own residential care arrangements and one on making your own home support arrangements (Acting Assistant Director, Older People and Hospitals, Social Services).

They've got all sorts of booklets on the ward. They give them booklets on any benefits they could get, Social Services that sort of thing, any financial help. Plus all the home help, and support and meals on wheels, etc. (Business Development Manager, Medicine, NHS Trust).

> We've got information leaflets from all our specialist services, that we give to the clients, we've got it for district nursing, we've got it around our home loans, our wheelchair services, speech therapy, chiropody the lot. They are available to them (Director of Community Services, Community Trust).

> Verbal information, the social worker will tell them what are the facilities available when he or she goes home like home help or other services ... These things are thoroughly discussed with the patient (Consultant Physician in Elderly Medicine, NHS Trust).

> There are leaflets for district nurses, health visitors and what's involved in having that service (Discharge Planning Co-ordinator, NHS Trust).

Two other types of information referred to were the provision of contact names with telephone numbers for specific services and the distribution of information packs detailing Social Services accredited agencies. Although useful, it is arguable the extent to which these can be deemed informative as they stand.

This raises important issues surrounding how information is conveyed. Strengths and limitations of both written and verbal information were cited by professionals and reinforcing written information with verbal explanations was generally believed to be an effective method of dissemination. Overall there appeared a commitment to providing necessary details in an appropriate manner.

> I do think there is quite a bit of written information that we can give out ... we talk through everything that we're doing with the patients, until we've provided a service and reviewed it (Senior Practitioner, Social Work Department, NHS Trust).

> Everything's verbal but the patients do have their notes, they can read them, they are there for them to see so anything that's discussed is written down, recorded somewhere (Manager, night services and specialist nurses, Community Trust).

> I think often word of mouth is better although of course it can all be forgotten but at least there's a chance to ask questions. So perhaps it needs to be verbal information backed up with written (Community Staff nurse).

In many cases the crucial role of the social worker was identified in providing information relating to discharge including services which may be available. There was also a role for informal channels, with some professionals acknowledging that a lot of valuable information regarding services was distributed via word of mouth between elderly people themselves.

It appeared overall that information was provided about individual services often at the expense of details regarding eligibility. Indeed, determined by individual circumstances, information about services or medical condition was only provided to users in receipt of those particular services or with the particular condition.

There was no generic information given as a matter of course relating to hospital discharge. This is perhaps a positive measure given that a number of professionals (24%) expressed reservations about 'too much' information being provided. The reasons for this were twofold: an excess of information could either not be heeded due to lack of relevance or could incite demands for care where no 'need' existed or where availability was limited. Some examples are given below.

> ... the trouble is you can give people too much and it doesn't go in. So long as they know the important bits and follow it up with it written down ... You can see them sitting there listening and they're really not tuned in (District nurse).

> We don't have a specific package that we give discharge patients, because I get a bit worried about information because it can sometimes set up confusion and it can set up an expectation when there isn't a need (Director of Community Services, Community Trust).

> [social services] probably don't want demand to increase too much. If people got all this information, we look fools then if we turn round and say 'you can't have it'. What are you giving information for? (Senior Home Care Assistant).

> There's a concern in this hospital about information overload. How much of the stuff is actually read? (Executive Director, NHS Trust).

One professional highlighted the difficulty faced by medical personnel in giving information both in deciding which users to inform and what information to impart.

I think the doctors are in a very bad situation here because they've got to choose who they tell and who they don't and if they don't tell someone who then happens to be someone who wanted to know, they can get into real trouble and if they tell someone who didn't want to know, they're equally in trouble (Chief Officer, Community Health Council).

A further concern related to whether information was appropriate to peoples' requirements.

We are looking all the time to ask 'does it need to be in bigger print?' 'is it easily readable?' 'do you easily understand it?' and that's maybe an area for when we talk to the consumers 'were you given any leaflets?' 'do you feel there's any way they could be improved?' It's an ongoing process, we keep reviewing them and updating them (Business Development Manager, Medicine, NHS Trust).

... information on services which are available is a lot more widespread now than it was before ... but of all the information that we have, what is it that people want? ... What information do varying client groups need and want, do we give them the wrong information? (Director of Community Care, Health Authority)

About four years ago we very quickly brought service information leaflets off the ground ... I think they need to be reviewed to make sure they're pitched at a level that a wide range of consumers will understand and that they're not jargonised (Director of Community Services, Community Trust).

Such comments provide useful indicators for future developments in the provision of information, in particular the need for continually updating existing literature.

The information we give out is good but it needs updating. Sometimes by the time we receive it it's almost out of date, then you spend half of the time trying to explain to people the changes (Senior Practitioner, Social Work Department, NHS Trust).

Redress

Experiences and attitudes surrounding the complaints procedure were explored as an element of *redress*. Interestingly, service users and service providers appeared to view the idea of complaints from very different perspectives.

User Responses

No distinction was made between NHS and Social Services care on the questionnaire with regard to complaints. Both a general idea of users' views towards expressing a grievance about care services and their knowledge of how to do so were sought.

Sixty percent (n = 157) of questionnaire respondents stated that they would make a formal complaint if they were dissatisfied with care received from the NHS and Social Services whilst 48% (124) felt that they would know how to do so. There was a highly significant association (p < 0.01) between the answers to the two questions; 40% (105) of respondents felt that they would both make a formal complaint if dissatisfied and would know how to do so, whilst only 7% (19) of respondents would neither make a formal complaint nor know how to do so.

Significant differences were apparent by selected characteristics in terms of knowledge of how to make a complaint. On the basis of adjusted standardised residuals, questionnaire respondents living with others were more likely to claim to know how to do so than those living alone (+/-1.9); respondents receiving an occupational or private pension were more likely to claim to know how to do so than those with no such provision (+/-2.1); males were more likely to report knowing how to do so than females (+/- 2.1) and respondents of 78 years and above were more likely to report knowing how to do so than the younger age group (+/-2.0). These findings are shown in Table 15. Interestingly, no significant differences were found by these variables in terms of respondents reporting whether or not they would actually make a complaint if dissatisfied.

At interview, a distinction was attempted between health care and social care in terms of making a complaint if dissatisfied. In addition, interviewees were able to clarify the circumstances under which they would express grievances formally and were also able to explain any reservations they would have about doing so.

Table 15:   Knowledge of How to Make a Complaint by Selected Characteristics, Questionnaire Respondents (n=260)

	'I KNOW HOW TO MAKE A COMPLAINT ABOUT THE CARE I RECEIVE FROM THE NHS AND SOCIAL SERVICES'		
	No	Yes	Unsure
LIVES ALONE	25 (45%)	42 (34%)	36 (47%)
LIVES WITH OTHERS	31 (55%)	80 (66%)	41 (53%)

(Pearson Chi-Square value = 3.52; degrees of freedom = 2; p = 0.17)

NO PRIVATE/OCC. PENSION	32 (58%)	53 (45%)	44 (57%)
PRIVATE/OCCUPATIONAL PENSION	23 (42%)	66 (55%)	33 (43%)

(Pearson Chi-Square value = 4.27; degrees of freedom = 2; p = 0.12)

MALE	20 (35%)	68 (55%)	37 (47%)
FEMALE	37 (65%)	56 (45%)	42 (53%)

(Pearson Chi-Square value = 6.17; degrees of freedom = 2; p< 0.05)

70-77 YEARS	29 (51%)	55 (44%)	47 (60%)
78 YEARS AND ABOVE	28 (49%)	69 (56%)	32 (40%)

(Pearson Chi-Square value = 4.43; degrees of freedom = 2; p = 0.11)
totals vary slightly due to missing data

Similar results to those gained via questionnaires were obtained at interview: 53% of interviewees reported that they would make a complaint if they were dissatisfied with the health care that they received and, of those also in receipt of care provided by the Social Services, 63% reported that they would make a complaint if dissatisfied. The findings were consistent across the two sectors with interviewees reporting that they would make a complaint about health care also reporting that they would make a complaint about social care, if applicable. However, these figures must be viewed with caution. Even by questioning separately about care provided by the NHS and that provided by the Social Services, many interviewees found it difficult to provide a definitive answer to whether they would make a formal complaint if dissatisfied; their action would be contingent upon specific circumstances. This may account for the high percentage of questionnaire respondents being 'unsure' about whether they would make a complaint and 'unsure' of how to do so.

The following were obtained from interviewees in response to questioning about making a complaint about welfare:

> I don't think we'd complain unless it was really very drastic, we wouldn't (male, 75 years, lives with wife).

> I think if I could isolate it ... and if I could see that there was a point in making a complaint ... I think the nature of the incident would decide (male, 75 years, lives with friend).

> Yes if you thought you were being mistreated or whatever or you weren't getting what they said they were going to supply (male, 70 years, lives with wife).

> They'd have to be, you know, serious complaints (female, 77 years, lives with husband).

> Not unless it was very serious, not for frivolous things like having to wait and so on (female, 87 years, lives alone).

Of interviewees who stated with certainty that they would make a complaint if dissatisfied, 75% were in receipt of a pension other than the state retirement pension and 88% rated their health positively. The interview sample was such that nobody had experienced care which they felt warranted a complaint.

A small number of interviewees (17%) believed that if they were to make a complaint, it could also benefit other people as illustrated by the following:

> Oh yes [I would complain] if I thought it was necessary, especially if I thought it was something that was rife and would affect other people, because some people can't complain. If it was something I thought was wrong or needed looking at then I'd complain (female, 72 years, lives alone).

> Oh I would yes [make a complaint], not necessarily for myself but for others, improve the service (male, 82 years, lives with wife).

> And if I thought it was worthwhile [to complain] it would not only be beneficial to me but beneficial to other people (male, 72 years, lives with wife).

A number of reservations expressed about making a formal complaint were concerned with not wishing to create problems for staff, some examples of which are given below.

> I think it would hit back at the nurses and they probably can't help it if they're short staffed, so I feel that wouldn't be very fair to them to put a complaint in. It's hard on the girls (female, 90 years, lives alone).

> No I don't bother complaining, it doesn't do any good, it only gets people into trouble and what have you gained by it? No, it wouldn't do any good, there's none of us perfect (female, 80 years, lives alone).

> Yes I'd think about it quite deeply because the nurses are doing their best aren't they? They've a lot of patients and some patients grumble for nothing ... (female, 75 years, lives alone).

This high regard for front line workers and health professionals in general was manifest in expressed praise and gratitude for the care received. Praise for health professionals was explicitly expressed by 87% of interviewees. Interestingly, two of the interviewees who did not express praise instead told of their gratitude for the care received. Such feelings obviously have major implications for people expressing any dissatisfaction; that is, they may be more reluctant to do so.

In general, people felt positive in their ability to make any complaint known. Whilst just under half of interviewees (47%) professed definite knowledge of how to make a complaint, most others were confident that they could find out should the need arise. Indeed a small number stated that they had seen posters and leaflets informing them of the procedure to follow in the event of dissatisfaction and what to expect as a result. Others spoke of how they would '*see the person in charge of that particular department*', '*I'd tell them there and then*' or '*I'd send it to the hospital admin.* (sic.) *and they'd send it to the right department*'. Knowledge of how to register dissatisfaction can be seen alongside contact points and sources of information about care in general explored earlier. Indeed, a minority of interviewees (13%) identified their GP as their point of contact to ascertain the procedure to follow.

Interviews with Professionals

There was no consensus amongst professionals as to whether service users would make a complaint if dissatisfied with the care provided and, as with service users, many found it difficult to provide a definite answer. Thirty three percent of professionals believed that elderly users of their service would make a complaint if they were dissatisfied, 33% did not believe this to be the case whilst 33% appeared contradictory in their replies. Some difficulties presented by this questioning are illustrated below.

> It's difficult to measure. There are complaints that do come in but on the whole they're probably very minimal in number to the number of referrals we deal with (Senior Practitioner, Social Work Department, NHS Trust).

> We do get complaints ... complaints I believe are only touching the tip of the iceberg, that a lot of patients even though they may have had an unsatisfactory experience still do not complain (Executive Director, NHS Trust).

From those who felt that service users would make a complaint if dissatisfied, the following are typical comments.

> Oh yes, there's always complaints, it's on the increase, not just in our department, everywhere (Consultant Physician in Elderly Medicine, NHS Trust).

> I think we have more complaints than we used to, a lot of which is to do with patients' expectations ... We don't get a lot about services not being available ... The type of complaints we get tend to be smaller complaints, like the nurses attitude (General Manager, Medicine, NHS Trust).

> I feel they're [complaints] more frequent now than they ever were, people are more aware that they can complain (Manager, night services and specialist services, Community Trust).

And from those who felt that service users would not make a complaint:

> They tend not to complain, they tend not to make any definite complaint. They may have a moan but they tend not to take it any further (Health visitor).

> I think a lot of complaints aren't reported because they're sorted out at the very informal stage (Acting Assistant Director, Older People and Hospitals, Social Services).

> ... you don't often get complaints about the service. It's more likely to be us complaining because we don't feel they're getting the care that's needed (Senior Home Care Assistant).

Quite a stark distinction was apparent between front line workers' and managers' experience of service users making their grievances known; front line workers tended to hear dissatisfaction in an informal way whereas managers were generally only aware of complaints which had entered the system through the formal channels. Front line workers hearing dissatisfaction informally overwhelmingly reported informing the person of the formal complaints procedure.

The reasons cited indicating why this specific age group of people may not complain were pretty consistent: through fear of the consequences for either themselves or care professionals or through feelings of gratitude. Examples of each of these concerns are given below. Although these may also be issues in other age groups, many professionals felt that reservations about complaining were exacerbated with age.

> ... They'll make verbal complaints and you ask if they want to take it further, 'oh no, I don't want to get any body into trouble' ... and then they say 'well it really wasn't that bad' and I think they've convinced

themselves by that time that it really wasn't worth going through with it (Community Social Worker).

You're always bothered about any repercussions in your own care, many people will not say anything until they're well clear of hospitals, nurses, doctors, for fear of how they will then be treated ... you're extremely vulnerable if you are in a so-called professionals hands and then you start complaining about them (Occupational Therapist, NHS Trust).

I think older people are reluctant to complain about welfare state provision. Because they value it so highly and it's better than what was before (Director of Community Care, Health Authority).

I just think they see the NHS as this wonderful thing and they don't feel they have a duty or a right to say that something is not as it should be (Team Manager, Health Visiting).

Conversely to service users, professionals tended to view complaints positively and as something to be welcomed, if not positively encouraged, having the potential to improve future service provision. All professionals (100%) made comments demonstrating their support of service users making complaints, a selection of which are given below.

I think patients should complain if they are not satisfied with the service ... they have that right and they should make it and it should be properly investigated (Team Leader, Social Work Department, NHS Trust).

I think everybody's got a right, if you've got a genuine fault ... Everyone's entitled to make a complaint, we don't live in an ideal world (Senior Home Care Assistant).

... it's the only way the service is going to get any better. The complaints are actually investigated ... It's the only way they're going to find out they're doing something wrong (District Nurse).

If we're doing something and we think we're right and somebody doesn't like it, unless they tell us how can we change it? So you've got to use complaints in a positive, meaningful way. We do try to take action on complaints and improve our services (Business Development Manager, Medicine, NHS Trust).

> You don't improve services if you don't know what the shortfalls are (Discharge Planning Co-ordinator, NHS Trust).

> You're not going to have change if people aren't complaining. Possibly it makes people more on their toes, you have to think a bit more ... (Named nurse, NHS Trust).

Although extolling the value of complaints, a number of professionals acknowledged that resource limitations were often the root cause of the dissatisfaction expressed, thereby eliminating the potential for immediate redress.

Fifty seven percent of professionals believed service users to be knowledgeable of how to make a formal complaint, mainly mentioning the proliferation of leaflets and posters as well as 'The Patients Charter', all available for information.

Most professionals were quite knowledgeable of the provision made by their service in the event of a complaint being registered, all feeling competent to inform service users of how to go about expressing a grievance and what to expect. Most complaints were dealt with 'in house' although an important role for the Community Health Council was given in supporting people or advocating on their behalf in the event of a complaint. In practice however very few are administered through this channel.

> For people to reach the CHC with any complaint about anything it's usually either such a minor one that everybody else has dismissed it or it is a very major one that's a real problem ... We pick up complaints where people have already gone through the complaints system and have been dissatisfied, so they've then come to us and we start again or pick up where they left off (Chief Officer, Community Health Council).

Summary

A summary of the main findings, with regard to the five principles presented here is included after the 'Introduction' in Chapter 7 in order to provide a context for the ensuing 'Discussion'. With regard to demographic and social characteristics and associations with user behaviour and attitude, the main trends are given in the 'Introduction' to Chapter 8, again to provide a context for the ensuing 'Discussion'.

7 Discussion I: Barriers and Enablers in the Use of Health and Social Care

Introduction

Selected findings from the empirical inquiry were presented in Chapter 6 to highlight the main themes to emerge from the data. This largely comprised statistical frequencies and unadorned descriptive information. To consider what the quantitative and qualitative data actually reveals this chapter discusses how the findings can be interpreted and explained in terms of the specific aims of the study. This discussion also locates the findings within the analytical background explored in Chapters 2 to 4 as well as within a broader theoretical context. As such, it is an attempt to progress understanding of the experience and behaviour of elderly people in the use of health and social care services and to determine areas for further research.

Essentially there are two related components of the successful implementation of user-oriented health and social care services which it is necessary to explore to address the aims of this study. These can be equated respectively with the *rights* of service users and their *obligations*. The first is a commitment by service providers to introducing user-oriented policy initiatives (those outlined in Chapter 3); the second being the ability and willingness of service users to adopt an active role in order to reap the benefits of user-oriented services. Both of these are addressed in this chapter.

This chapter begins with a summary of the main findings in relation to the criteria indicating user influence or control which were used to structure the findings in Chapter 6. This provides a context for the discussion of these findings throughout the rest of the chapter which is structured according to the key issues which emerged.

As appropriate the findings in Chapter 6 were presented in relation to various inter-related demographic and social variables: gender, household composition, age group, socio-economic group and self-reported health status.   In order to render the discussion more straightforward for the reader, these associations and various interpretations and explanations are the subject of the following chapter.

Summary of Main Finding

'*Participation (and Representation)*' were explored as central to users assuming an active role in the use of health and social care. The majority of service users felt that they had been involved in decision making about their discharge from hospital. An important role for family members and friends was also revealed. Only a small number of interviewees felt that they had initiated the discharge process, out of a desire to return home yet service users indisputably upheld the role of the 'expert' in the discharge process. In terms of communication, the majority of respondents reported an ability to express their wishes to health and social care professionals.

Most professionals both welcomed opportunities for user participation in decision making regarding care and reported that consultation took place. Many acknowledged however that in practice the relative influence of users may be limited by resource constraints. Concerns were also raised that encouraging participation may raise expectations as to subsequent service provision.

'*Access*' The majority of questionnaire respondents felt that they were in receipt of sufficient care. Fundamentally, health services were deemed more accessible than social services both in relation to knowing whom to contact, in which instances, and how to do so. However, in terms of accessing services independently of statutory providers, doing so for 'social' needs was found to be more straightforward.

The major access theme identified by professionals was a difficulty in users obtaining services, mainly stemming from a lack of resources and from the distinction between care provided by the NHS and that provided by Social Services. The distinction was also acknowledged between users paying for their own (social) care and those reliant upon statutory provision.

The main way in which '*choice*' was apparent for service users was between whether to receive services being offered or not with those not assessed as needing care having no opportunities for such choice. Respondents paying directly for social care or otherwise with additional sources of care were revealed as in the strongest position in relation to exercising choice over service delivery. These issues surrounding choice arose with service providers also but professionals, in general, felt that greater opportunities existed for exercising choice than were perceived by service users and were more confident that choices offered would be honoured. Levels of choice were shown to follow similar trends to levels of access to care. In turn, choice was also found to be closely linked to 'information'.

It was revealed that most respondents had been provided with *'information'* regarding their care. General satisfaction was apparent amongst questionnaire respondents with the level of information provided along with fairly widespread knowledge of where to access further information. Service users reported more information provided about health conditions than about available services, the former of which was generally viewed positively or 'useful', whilst the latter was generally viewed more negatively or as less 'useful'. Closely linked to 'access', information seeking behaviour was apparent amongst just over half of the interviewees. Indeed sources of additional information were in most cases similar to access points to further care.

Professionals were confident of a high level of information being provided, some even expressing concern that 'too much' may be of detriment whilst others acknowledged that printed information soon becomes out-of-date. Professionals reported that the majority of information provided was about services available rather than medical condition.

'Redress', was investigated by examining procedures for complaints. Complaining was viewed negatively by service users although the majority of questionnaire respondents stated that they would make a complaint if dissatisfied whilst almost a half felt that they would know how to do so. Professionals on the other hand viewed the receipt of complaints more positively, although many still felt that service users would be reluctant to make a formal complaint. Both groups of interviewees cited gratitude, praise and 'not wishing to cause trouble' as reasons why this age group in particular may not complain.

These findings provide definite evidence of both a user-oriented approach to the delivery of health and social care and a willingness and ability amongst service users to assume an active role. However, they also demonstrate clearly that there remain a number of areas in which it does not appear practicable to give priority to the wishes of service users or for them to become involved in aspects of their care.   An important observation is that some of the policy initiatives advocating an active user role appear both more straightforward to implement in practice and more readily embraced by service users than others. This was often manifest in a distinction between care provided by the NHS and that provided by the Social Services department.

Practical barriers to the existence of both user-oriented services and an active user role, such as finance and organisational boundaries were identified in addition to less tangible barriers such as the expectations and past experience of service users.

The present chapter considers the findings in the light of policy change, the analysis of which formed the basis of a key research question, seeking to compare the expressed rhetoric with the actual reality. The discussion forming this chapter is structured according to six themes emerging from the analytical background and the empirical study, viz.: *participation; agency and advocacy; entry, exit and voice; seamless provision; paternalism versus consumerism* and *the decision-making process.*

Participation

Participation was explored as the key concept in this study in elderly people playing an active role in the use of health and social care services. Most participation issues however have direct relevance and are very closely linked to the other principles explored in this study. Participation of others acting in the direct interests of the final user (as *representation*) was also explored. It is mentioned here but mainly explored as an element of 'social support' in Chapter 8.

The policy documentation analysed in Chapter 3 displayed huge diversity in advocating the participation of service users and their representatives. Service users and their carers were to be both consulted and informed about decisions regarding their discharge and 'at the centre of the planning process'. Assessments for care and the devising of care plans were to include the active participation of the individual service user and their carer. Intentions were also expressed to consult service users and incorporate their wishes into future planning decisions. This study used a relatively narrow definition of participation: individuals (or their representatives) playing an active role in their own care on an individual basis for their personal benefit.

It was found that most service users felt that they had participated in decisions about their discharge from hospital although interview data revealed that in some instances this may have simply amounted to being informed of what would happen or indeed had happened. The majority had been 'consulted'. For those with family and friends, an important role was revealed for them in participating in discussions regarding the discharge of the respondent.

Interviews revealed how a number of respondents, having been offered the opportunity to participate, allowed professionals to act on their behalf. This is similar to the findings of Haug and Lavin (1983), Strull *et al.* (1984), Beisecker (1988) and Avis (1994). This may be interpreted as due to a lack of specialised knowledge, due to a difficulty in making the link between 'need' and appropriate care (Leavey *et al.*, 1989), through fear of making the 'wrong' decision (Shackley and Ryan, 1994), as a function of health state (Winkler, 1987; Jones, 1996) or related to the esteem with which professionals are held. All of these factors appeared related to participation in this study. This demonstrates how not all users viewed participation as a positive measure to be welcomed, which was suggested in Chapter 2 would probably be the case.

At the extreme, this finding could be interpreted as a wish by users for paternalistic care. Indeed, although the majority of service users felt that they had been involved in decision making, all perceived an important role for professional input in such processes, a feature of both 'paternalistic' and 'consumerist' care as detailed below. Such situations are of particular relevance to this study as they demonstrate a reluctance by some service users to play an active role. This may also be interpreted in the light of Cumming and Henry's *disengagement* theory (1961) whereby people are portrayed as gradually and willingly withdrawing from roles and responsibilities as they become older.

For service users who wished to play an active role in their use of welfare services, participation in decision making was found to be closely related to *choice* about service delivery. Essentially, this study revealed the existence of three types of people particularly in relation to participation and choice: those who expressed their views or stated their preferences when invited to do so, those who accepted the decisions that were made and those who wished to play a greater role than was offered.

It can be suggested that the latter, although the most willing to play an active role, may ultimately be the least satisfied with care provision through lack of influence.

Opportunities for participation were obviously dependent upon individual requirements. As such, those with no formally assessed need for care may be provided with few opportunities to participate, other than possibly over the timing of their discharge, whilst those in need of a high level of care to be met by the statutory services may be presented with the most opportunities. Whilst this may be the case, the findings of this study suggest that due to resource limitations people with a high level of need may be those who ultimately have the least *influence* in decisions regarding their discharge.

Most professionals interviewed expressed support for service users participating in decisions regarding their care and many provided examples of encouraging or enabling them to do so. However many also openly acknowledged that resource limitations are making it increasingly unlikely that service users possess influence in the final decisions. This therefore draws into question the whole issue of service users effectively participating or exercising choice. Importantly however it appeared that there was a commitment by welfare professionals to providing opportunities for participation where possible and to attempting to respect user wishes. Such a commitment constitutes a major component of the successful introduction of user-oriented services and encouraging an active user role. However it can also be interpreted as a simple implementation of the policy rhetoric (see Chapter 3).

This finding appears more positive than previous studies. Cahill (1998), in a comprehensive review of empirical studies addressing patient participation since 1980, found that findings from the practitioner's perspective were not consistent. The key themes revealed were that many practitioners saw patient participation as a threat to their position and independence or as a cost-cutting exercise.

A general consensus amongst professionals in this study was that gaining an assessment of needs was relatively straightforward compared to securing the delivery of services to meet those needs. This suggests that user participation in assessing needs may be a possibility. Again, respondents having no formally assessed needs on discharge would have been presented with little or no opportunity for participation. Most evidence was of respondents participating in decision making regarding service use once 'need' was established.

A number of the 'rungs' of Arnstein's ladder of citizen participation (Arnstein, 1969) are relevant to the provision of welfare and were evident in this study, particularly those in the middle range, denoted 'degrees of tokenism' that *allow the have-nots to hear and to have a voice*' (p.217). These 'tokens' are 'informing', 'consultation' and 'placation'. They are not the only mechanisms through which the 'have-nots' will hear and have a voice, the complaints procedure being an important forum explored in this study. In addition, these 'tokens' all suggest a *passive* role for the 'participant' in being *informed*, *consulted* or *placated* whereas this study also ascertained the degree to which service users actively seek to participate. Only through consultation, which was apparent in this study, do the 'degrees of tokenism' imply any opportunity for activity on the part of the service user. This is also compatible with the definition given by Brownlea (1987) of being involved in a decision making process and being consulted on an issue or matter. Examples of service users being *informed* were also evident in this study; this is explored further under 'Agency and Advocacy' and 'The Decision-Making Process'.

The top rungs in Arnstein's model: 'partnership', 'delegated power' and 'citizen control', collectively denoted 'degrees of citizen control', suggest a much greater shift in the balance of power towards service users than any 'degrees of tokenism'. It could be argued that such a shift is not relevant to the provision of statutory welfare, even given the policy initiatives outlined in Chapter 3. 'Partnership' is perhaps the most realistic to apply given these initiatives, a notion also discussed by Winkler (1987) as a possible model of 'consumerism' in health care. It could be argued that if individual service users 'participate' in any way in decision making surrounding their discharge, they have been a *partner* in the process. This is consistent with Arnstein's belief that partnership is apparent when citizens '*negotiate and engage in trade-offs with traditional powerholders*' (p.217). Whilst it would perhaps be unreasonable to expect this to be an equal partnership, the evidence of participation with service providers revealed by this study suggests that 'partnership' is a possibility. This also relates to Richardson's (1979) definition of participation as an activity undertaken by service users in conjunction with individuals who were previously the sole players in the decision making process.

Arnstein also includes mechanisms for participation actually classified as 'non-participation': therapy and manipulation. These are defined as methods employed by those in authority, under the guise of enhancing participation, but which actually have the opposite effect. In a similar vein, a possible outcome of encouraging participation (and choice) is that it may ultimately *disempower* service users by appearing to offer a wide range of services and then being unable to meet those which are requested through lack of resources. Offering users opportunities for participation and choice where there is little hope of honouring expressed wishes is undesirable, not least because of raising expectations, as acknowledged by professionals in this study. It would perhaps be understandable therefore if professionals displayed a reluctance to provide such opportunities. Indeed a pragmatic approach, in evidence in this study, is for providers to offer fewer, yet realistic, opportunities for both participation and choice for service users and to not inform them of the full range of services. These are all possible ways in which 'manipulation' may be used to restrict demand in order to address resource limitations and can be related to the arguments of participation as a mechanism for social control.

Richardson (1983) contrasts *participation* to *apathy* which would include people 'being concerned' about issues whether or not they take any action. Whilst this was deemed insufficient for this study, and a definition was used instead of an *active* role being assumed, it would be reasonable to assume that people are concerned about their discharge from hospital and the care they will receive. This could also be extended to *representation*, that is, family and friends of the elderly person being discharged from hospital can also be assumed to be concerned about these issues.

McEwen *et al.* (1983) and Saunders (1995) believe that individuals must be active to be defined as *participating*. McEwen *et al.* contrast this to the traditional passive role in health care. There were examples found in this study of service users not wishing to play an active role in decisions surrounding discharge and care delivery and instead assuming passivity. This was in the knowledge that 'professionals' would take the necessary action on their behalf and out of a desire to take advantage of the input of 'experts'. These individuals accepted the care that was offered to them. Given McEwen *et al.*'s and Saunders' definitions, they could not be classed as participating.

Importantly however most questionnaire respondents and interviewees had been offered the opportunity to participate along with their family and friends. This is compatible with participation being interpreted as the right of people to make representations and express their wishes given by Boaden *et al.* (1982). Boaden *et al.* suggest that 'taking part' may involve shifting the balance of power towards the individual user. This suggests that they would have influence in any decisions taken.

Most professionals felt that user influence in decision-making was desirable but also mentioned other considerations, usually resources, similar to the findings of Higgins (1992). Booth (1993), in relation to care management, identified *resources* as the main obstacle to user participation and how assessments of need and decisions regarding service delivery continue to be supply-led. Data from professionals in this study suggested the same.

Agency and Advocacy

One of the major differences between conventional markets and 'quasi' markets for the delivery of statutory health and social care is the distinction between the purchaser and the final user. One of the main implications of this is that the final user does not have direct access to services and has to obtain it via a third party. This is largely due to the nature of funding of statutory services. In no cases in this study were users paying privately for *health* care although, in a number of cases, users of *social* care were also the purchasers through arranging and paying for private provision. In market terms, it has been suggested that the purchaser of the service must be the same, or barely distinct from, the user (Neuberger, 1990).

The asymmetry of information and knowledge between users of health care and purchasers is also an important issue (Mooney and Ryan, 1993; Shackley and Ryan, 1994). This may be exacerbated by the less than optimum health state of the (potential) user, the increasing sophistication of medicine (Winkler, 1987) and the infrequent nature of the user role. These all contribute to the 'uncertainty of demand' for health care (Lees, 1965; Titmuss, 1969; Le Grand and Robinson, 1984) whereby users may require a professional to confirm that a need does/does not exist or to compel a person to receive care and collectively place the service user in a relatively weak position for playing an active role in decision making.

In addition, it is assumed that it is the outcome rather than the process of health care that is desired by users (Williams, 1988; Mooney and Ryan, 1993; Shackley and Ryan, 1994) and although the user is probably the best judge of improvements in health status, it is not a commodity that can be demanded (Leavey *et al.*, 1989).   As such, an 'agent' is required to make the link between health care and health status.

At its simplest, an agent can be defined as an informed individual who acts on behalf of the user/principal who is an ill-informed individual (Mooney and Ryan, 1993).   Whilst in economic terms, it is assumed that both agent and principal pursue their own interests, it is recognised that health care 'agents' act, to some extent, in the principal's interests (Ryan, 1994).   The agent can fulfil their role either by providing information to enable the principal to make their own decisions (termed the 'perfect agency relationship' (Williams, 1988)) or by making decisions on their behalf (Culyer, 1989).   The relationship between 'agent' and 'principal' therefore has direct implications in terms of *participation, access, choice* and *information* for the service user.   The relationship established may also affect the likelihood of the user making a complaint if dissatisfied.

Literature on agency in health care focuses on this asymmetry of information between users and purchasers.   The availability of *information* can be seen as essential if the other four components examined by this study (*participation (*and *representation), access, choice* and *redress*) are to be meaningful (Hogg, 1990; Winkler, 1990).   Although it is rarely the case that users of goods and services have complete information with which to make decisions (Nelson, 1970), information imperfections are most apparent in the markets for products which are obtained infrequently, exhibit a high rate of technological change and whose performance characteristics are not immediately apparent (Aaker and Day, 1974; Wistow *et al.*, 1994).   These are all attributes of health care with some application to social care.

Professionals identified by service users in this study as points of access to welfare services or as sources of information and explanation about medical condition, services available or about how to make a complaint can be argued as central to users assuming an active role. Individuals filling these roles could feasibly be classed as 'agents' of the final user.   If an active role for service users is deemed desirable, communication with such professionals assumes crucial importance.

Although compatible with the definition of an agent as an informed individual acting on behalf of the health care user, this study goes beyond existing literature by considering a role beyond the provision of information in addition to considering agents in the provision of 'social' care.   Indeed the *provision* of information, which is user-orientation, was not necessarily by a specific 'agent'.   However it is suggested here that identifying a professional as a source of information is indicative of a willingness and ability to assume an active role. The discussion here therefore centres around ways in which users may contact or utilise their agent rather than opportunities their agent may provide to them.

The specific identity of 'agents' in this study was, quite logically, determined by the services required or received. Although most questionnaire respondents indicated that they would know whom to contact about their care and how to access information, no further details were gained. At interview, a distinction was revealed between 'health' and 'social' care in terms of access points and sources of information; respondents were found to be more specific and confident about health-related contacts. This may be interpreted in terms of respondents possibly having greater experience of receiving health care than social care or by the organisation of the NHS whereby the vast majority of people are registered with a general practitioner who, by definition, is the first point of access in receiving health care.

General practitioners were the professional role most commonly mentioned as contact points and sources of information followed by social workers. Professionals in particular highlighted the important role of social workers in the process of hospital discharge. Other professionals identified at interview as points of contact or as sources of information, for example, health visitors, home helps, charity organisations could also feasibly be classed as 'agents'. However, it is debatable the extent to which they would be able to facilitate or authorise service delivery. Although the individual or organisation with financial authority may be the one who ultimately dictates access to services, thereby fulfilling a classic 'gatekeeping' role, there is most certainly a role for other professionals to negotiate on behalf of the service user or to provide support in the process of obtaining care.

'Support' along with 'access' was identified by Croft and Beresford (1990), with specific reference to Social Services provision, as an essential component in the participation of service users. Similarly Bowl (1996), with reference to users of mental health services, highlights the critical role of professionals in supporting users seeking to become involved in their care. 'Support' can be viewed as a component of the agent's role.

This raises questions about the most appropriate role for an agent. One possibility apparent from this discussion would be for service users to establish an on-going relationship with one professional, most probably their GP, who would act in a generic capacity, facilitating access to services as required. A second approach would be for individual users to negotiate access to health and social care in the manner most convenient, utilising relevant professionals as agents, for expertise and advice, as required. The first scenario is the more accurate in relation to the findings of this study although in most instances, contact was not limited to a single professional, largely due to the multi-disciplinary process under study. This perhaps suggests a desire amongst respondents for 'seamless' provision (see later discussion). There was no evidence revealed of service users assuming the active role to the extent suggested by the latter of these scenarios.

Further advantage could be possible if the final user enjoys an established relationship with the agent(s) acting on their behalf, in evidence amongst selected respondents in this study. That is, most respondents identified the same professional as a point of contact for information and for access to services. The greater possibility of such a relationship being in evidence with health professionals as opposed to social care professionals can be interpreted in terms of probable greater experience of health care.

This study found evidence of uncertainty amongst service users of the roles and remits of different professionals. If ignorance of the identity of professionals and their respective roles and responsibilities is apparent, this would effectively exclude service users from initiating obtaining services directly from the provider or from maximising the potential of utilising appropriate professionals as agents. This could be a further reason for such importance being given to a single identified professional as agent, with whom the service user has had previous contact. Such problems of identity can only be exacerbated by the multi-disciplinary nature of hospital discharge and indeed by the introduction of 'markets' which encourage many different providers in order to create competition (see Chapter 3).

If services users are to assume an active role, communication and ease with agents must be seen as fundamental. If people are not at ease with providers of care, the environment cannot be deemed conducive to service users assuming an active role; they are likely to be inhibited in participating, exercising choice, attempting to access information and services and in seeking redress. Indeed on the part of professionals, although their skills are central to them fulfilling their role, interpersonal skills are also fundamental (Johnson, 1972).

This study revealed that the majority of questionnaire respondents felt able to express their wishes to care professionals. At interview, however, a distinction was shown between hospital doctors or consultants and all other staff in terms of ease of communication. This suggests the traditional doctor-patient roles when encountering hospital doctors yet a more equal relationship with other health and social care professionals. Possible reasons for this could include less experience of communicating with hospital doctors, the high esteem with which such professionals are viewed or the heightened power difference between users and professionals in the hospital setting. This study revealed however that the majority of respondents felt able to express their wishes whilst in hospital, suggesting that the hospital setting itself has little effect on communication.

It appeared that in the case of care provided in the community setting, service users were at ease with all professionals. This finding is important and positive given the intention in the policy documentation to provide an increasing amount of care outside the hospital setting and explicitly to promote the primary care sector. The increasing emphasis on health promotion and illness prevention may further heighten communication in that people have contact with care professionals when not suffering from ill health. This may be linked to a move away from the traditional medical view of health which focuses on disease and as such justifies the power of the medical professional and lack of user involvement (Hogg, 1990).

It must also be considered that the functioning of the agency relationship is not necessarily straightforward nor guaranteed to promote the interests of the final user. A possible clash of priorities may be experienced in that the agent must reconcile a 'rationing' of resources with acting to secure the user's best interests. Skelcher (1996) believes the agent to be in the paradoxical position of both welcoming and controlling the public. Evidence of this was provided by the professionals included in this study. For example, professionals reported that the *choice* offered to users was deliberately limited and there were concerns that encouraging *participation* and providing *information* may raise expectations or increase demand. Agents in welfare provision must also reconcile the interests of the patient along with their own, those of other clients and the wider society (Scrivens, 1992; Ryan, 1994; Myers and MacDonald, 1996). It is therefore debatable the extent to which agents act as true representatives of the user.

Haug and Lavin (1983) even apply the idea of mistrust to the patient-physician relationship examining in particular the possible power dynamics between the two parties whilst Moros (1993) identifies a potential for conflict in this complex relationship. Moros, commenting on the expectations and duties of doctors and patients, believes that doctors have a moral requirement to act for their patients yet acknowledges the occasional need for paternalism.

Clashes of priorities within the agency relationship suggest that points of contact in order to access care and information, although central, may not be sufficient in bestowing an active role upon service users or in ensuring that their interests are represented.

An alternative to users views being represented by an agent, who is also a purchaser or a provider of care, may be for representation to be via *advocates*. Winkler (1987) stresses how advocates who are independent and separate from the provision of care yet know how the system works may alter the balance of power between the provider and user. She discusses how advocates may offer users help and support in negotiations with providers about their care and how their key function would be to help patients to make informed choices. Phillipson (1993) discusses the issue with particular relation to vulnerable older people. He discusses this in terms of an unequal balance of power and an attempt to increase the *representation* or *participation* of older service users.

Advocates clearly fulfil a different role for service users than agents, who tend to be welfare professionals and may have other priorities in addition to representing the interests of the service user. An important role was also revealed by this study for family and friends of the service user in representing their interests. Whilst these individuals can be assumed to be acting in the best interests of the final service user, their influence and knowledge may be insufficient to effectively fulfil the role of agent or advocate. The availability of 'social support' is discussed in Chapter 8 as affecting the extent to which users assume an active role.

Entry, Exit and Voice

A further distinction between conventional markets and 'quasi' markets for health and social care is that access in the latter is not based on an ability and willingness to pay. Whilst this remains true for statutory care, users in this study who were accessing care privately faced a quite different situation in their influence over the services used.

Access can broadly be defined as gaining 'entry' to the receipt of services. It can be assumed that such access is ultimately determined by individual 'needs', which are assessed by a professional, although assessments and decision-making regarding care increasingly involve service users. Such is the basis of this study. Possible ways in which user influence and access may be restricted, namely lack of resources, have already been discussed.

This study found examples of users both attempting to gain access to care (*entry*) and declining to receive care that was offered (*exit*) as well as users accepting the care that was offered to them. Respondents willing and able to access care privately faced a different situation than those dependent upon statutory provision. In addition there were important distinctions in this area between social care and health care ('Seamless Care' below). This was in terms of both making the link between perceived need and appropriate service delivery and in securing services independently of the statutory sector.

In terms of seeking to access services, some interviewees felt that it was their responsibility to initiate gaining access, and had indeed tried, whilst others felt that this lay within the remit of professionals. Whilst perceived need can obviously determine people 'demanding' services, social and demographic characteristics were also found to have an influence and are discussed in the following chapter.

Over half of interviewees in this study were making use of private resources to access care, mainly domestic help, in response to perceived need. The main reasons for this were either that statutory care was not available or that a charge would have been made for statutory care. Such respondents had heightened choice as well as access to such services in that they could decide when to receive care and what care to receive, a finding also revealed by Allen *et al.* (1992) in their study of elderly people. Questionnaire responses in this study revealed fairly low levels of choice given to service users.

Respondents with the least need or wish for care in this study were found to be in the strongest position in terms of choice. They were able to refuse services, that is, *choose* not to receive them. This was both elderly people who had alternative sources of provision, whether private or informal, and those who declined to accept care or aids, or indeed did not attempt to access them, out of a desire to retain independence. Allen *et al.*

(1992) concluded that refusing services was the best way of exercising choice although acknowledged that this was related to health status. The Citizen's Charter (HMSO, 1991), in relation to public services in general, stated a similar notion: '*Whenever the client can exercise a choice, the most effective form of redress is the right of exit: the decision not to accept the service provided and to go somewhere else*' (p.50).

Choice regarding service provision can be equated with the 'exit' mechanism (Pfeffer and Coote, 1991; Hambleton and Hoggett, 1993) in market provision. That is, a preference for one option could possibly indicate dissatisfaction with other options. However the option of complete exit can be argued as only available to those with minimal care requirements, with alternative sources of provision or able to finance alternative provision. With statutory care debates surrounding access to services, the monopoly provision of health care and the lack of direct purchasing power by users make exit and option not available to many users.

'Exit' may also be an option for carers or family members of service users in that they may refuse to provide informal care (Myers and MacDonald, 1996). Whilst carers were not included in the empirical phase of this study, professionals reported how disagreements may be experienced between carers and service users and it was suggested that this may be due to caring responsibilities. This is explored further as an aspect of 'social support' in the following chapter. Myers and MacDonald claim that in such situations, carers may have greater bargaining power than users.

The way in which dissatisfaction was approached in this study was through exploring perceptions regarding making a complaint or expressing 'voice' (as an indicator of *redress*). This is the democratic approach to expressing dissatisfaction. 'Exit and voice' are discussed as options in signalling dissatisfaction by Hirschman (1970) in his seminal work.

For an analysis of user-oriented services and the willingness and ability of users to assume an active role, attitude towards making a complaint and knowledge of how to do so were felt to be more important than experience of having done so. Of the five principles relating to user influence or control explored in this study, *redress* can be argued to be the most negative and as such may be less readily adopted than all others. This did not appear to be strictly the case from the findings of this study, although negative feelings were uncovered.

The major theme which emerged from this study was the almost opposite ways in which service users and professionals viewed complaints, which suggests that the true worth of complaints are not being realised. That is, complaints can only fulfil a role in improving services and assuring quality, as envisaged by professionals, if service users make use of mechanisms for feedback. Obviously not all people who experience unsatisfactory care will complain. Professionals suggested as much, relating the few comments received to the overall level of care delivered. Only a minority of service users saw the potential for complaints in improving services; most felt that any such feedback would be unwelcome.

Even though the majority of service users reported that they would make a formal complaint if dissatisfied, general feelings were negative. Of concern is the highly significant association between questionnaire respondents' feelings regarding making a complaint and their knowledge of how to do so. This suggests a causal link but provides no impression of the direction. It could either be that people are more likely to make a complaint because they know how to do so or because they feel that they would make a complaint, they are also confident in how to go about doing so. Similar to the findings for knowledge of contact points and sources of information, interviewees generally expressed confidence in their ability to '*find out*' how to make a complaint should the need arise. This is indicative of a desire and an ability to assume an active role. Alternatively respondents may have been reporting such knowledge as displaying ignorance may be perceived undesirable.

Service users and professionals alike acknowledged the proliferation of leaflets and posters informing service users what to do in the event of experiencing dissatisfaction. This is probably the reason for general confidence expressed in users' knowledge of how to make a complaint. The provision and acknowledgement of such information however does not mean that it has either been read or heeded.

Also of note is the unwillingness of service users to provide a definitive answer to such questioning suggesting that findings must be viewed with caution. If unsatisfactory care had not been experienced their uncertainty may have simply been due to responding to a hypothetical situation. Alternatively, as evidenced by this study, respondents may not wish to commit themselves to a definite answer preferring to consider individual instances of dissatisfaction if and when they arise.

Concerns about creating trouble for staff were the main reservations about making a complaint found by this study. Gratitude and praise for staff, as found by this study, and the likely implications for users expressing dissatisfaction must also be considered as a factor. In addition, people do not like to criticise a service they see as 'free' (Symonds, 1991). This study found no evidence of service users fearing for their future care although this was given by service providers as a possible reason why service users may not make a formal complaint. Peoples' likelihood of complaining must be related to expectations of services which in turn will be related to past experience and is explored in the following chapter.

One consideration in the light of the findings of this study is the actual use of the pejorative term 'complaints'. A term having less negative connotations may be 'suggestions' or even 'dissatisfactions' however this would deviate from official policy documentation and leaflets detailing action to be taken in the event of an unsatisfactory experience. The wording on the questionnaire and the questioning at interview were given special consideration with regard to 'complaints' for these very reasons.

Financial restrictions on service provision, stated explicitly by professionals but more implicitly by service users, aware of such restrictions through lack of service availability, are a further possible explanation for service users' reluctance to complain if services do not meet their satisfaction. They may feel it to be futile. Booth (1993) cites two barriers to older people using complaints procedures in health and social care: the fear of complaining and the need for advocacy. Both of these can be related to their lack of power but also the knowledge that services are scarce. This in turn nurtures low expectations and '*leaves them feeling lucky to have what they are given and wary of feeling ungrateful*' (Booth, 1993: 165). As discussed earlier, the need for advocacy may also have implications for people *participating* and *accessing* services.

A further way for providers to receive feedback, one less dependent upon users being pro-active, would be the distribution of patient satisfaction surveys, examples of which proliferated in the late 1980s (Dixon and Carr-Hill, 1989; Sitzia and Wood, 1997). However the extent to which 'satisfaction' is a valid concept is questionable (Fitzpatrick and Hopkins, 1983; Williams, 1994). Carr-Hill (1992) argues that feedback surveys are unsophisticated and measure 'satisfaction' and 'gratitude' rather than 'quality' or 'need satisfaction' whilst Pollitt (1988) refers to satisfaction surveys as a 'charm school variant of consumerism'. In comparison to 'exit', Hambleton and Hoggett (1993) believe complaints procedures and user satisfaction surveys represent 'more gentle and manageable feedback' (p.108).

People on the whole express high levels of satisfaction (Blaxter, 1995; Sitzia and Wood, 1997) for similar reasons that they are reluctant to complain about care. In addition, elderly people have been found to express higher levels of satisfaction than younger age groups (Symonds, 1991; Carr Hill, 1992; Cohen, 1996; Sitzia and Wood, 1997) although this has not been a consistent finding. It is suggested that older people have lower expectations yet are more dependent upon welfare services.

If fully developed and implemented, complaints mechanisms and feedback surveys could be viewed alongside the excellence approach to ensuring quality and responsiveness in commercial enterprise (Peters and Waterman, 1982).

'Seamless' Provision

The policy analysis in Chapter 3 found no reference to promoting 'seamless' care. Indeed the publication of two distinct White Papers, 'Working for Patients' (Department of Health, 1989a) and 'Caring for People' (Department of Health, 1989b) referring to NHS and Social Services care respectively could even be interpreted as an attempt to specify and maintain separate responsibilities and budgets. Although seamless provision is not a requisite for user-orientation and an active user role, its implications for continuing care, as found by this study, are discussed here.

The differences between accessing care provided by the NHS and that provided by the Social Services, although recognised by both service users and professionals, was reported in different ways. The divide appeared more embedded in the structure of provision to professionals than to service users although this was suspected to be largely political due to the distinct budgets held by providers of health care and providers of social care and the many restrictions placed on service provision. For service users this divide was manifest in difficulties in obtaining statutory services other than strictly health care. This raises important issues surrounding the ways in which resources are allocated, that is, whether restrictions are implicit or explicit. Both health care and social care are 'rationed' but the ways in which this is carried out will be important for the perceptions of service users with explicit 'rationing' being the most apparent to the final user.

The differences between health authorities and local authorities in terms of different processes of needs assessment and decision making; separate budgets; separate managements with different systems of accountability and employee relations (Hudson, 1998) in addition to different priorities, goals and cultures (Langan and Clarke, 1994) indicate how different the two sectors are.

It has been postulated that social care needs are more varied than health care needs as the former are dependent upon an individual's physical and mental state and also on their social and material circumstances (Social Services Committee, 1990: para. 30). However it is argued here that potential service users are more able to assess the social care required to enable them to stay living in their own homes and to go about their daily lives than the health care required from the presence of symptoms.   It can be assumed that there is no difference in the predictability of demand between the two sectors. This may be used to interpret the greater likelihood of service users in this study to report shortfalls in social care provision. That is, through being able to assess the care required, potential service users may be more likely to register when statutory supply falls short of demand. Alternatively, it may indeed be that Social Services are being increasingly restricted, a fact also suggested by care professionals. This is similar to the findings of Thompson *et al.* (1992) who found that users wished to participate in care that did not require medical expertise but had little preference for participation in care that required medical expertise.

The ability of service users to determine the social care required more readily than the health care required can be coupled with the finding of there being a greater possibility of accessing social care independently of the statutory sector, dependent upon ability and willingness to pay, than gaining such access to health care. This is mainly due to the expansion in independent providers of such care (see Chapter 3).   Indeed many respondents were found to be privately resourcing additional help as required.

These complementary factors can be used to explain the relatively low emphasis given to 'agents' in the provision of social care, as shown earlier. That is, an agent is not necessarily needed to assess the social care required or to provide access to that care, as was found to be the case with health care. It must be stressed however that a number of respondents remained dependent upon statutory social care for which an agent would be required. No evidence of independent access to health care was revealed by this study.

As discussed earlier, an important role for agents is in the *provision* of information to enable users to participate and make choices regarding care but also as a *source* of information for those willing and able to seek it out. As such, with agents for health care being more clearly defined it may be expected that potential users of health care would be more able to act independently. The relative lack of emphasis given to social care agents yet the greater ease with which social care users acted independently therefore is surprising. Similarly, the finding of almost equal numbers of service users feeling knowledgeable of entitlement to health care as to social care perhaps suggests equal ease of accessing care from the two sectors.

An ability to determine the required service provision would include making choices as to the most convenient or appropriate way in which services will be delivered. This therefore also goes some way towards explaining the greater choice perceived by those privately resourcing their care than those dependent upon statutory services.

Professionals reported how resource limitations affect the ultimate influence of users in decisions regarding their care. They also reported how resource limitations were more pronounced in the delivery of social care rather than health care. Taken together these two findings suggest that users of statutory social care would have less influence than users of statutory health care. Whilst this certainly appeared to be the case for statutory care, the level of social care acquired independently distorted the finding.

Much of the care secured independently by respondents in this study was with domestic duties, an area identified by professionals where service provision was not meeting demand. This provides strong evidence of service users assuming an active role in response to perceived need. However, it also suggests a situation in which statutory services are supply rather than demand-led. Although fewer shortfalls were perceived in health provision, this is not to suggest that health care is demand as opposed to supply-led rather that potential users are less able to assess their health care requirements.

A further possible distinction between health care and social care was expressed by a number of front line Social Services professionals. This was that health care, with the role of treating illness or disease, could be deemed more *professional* than social care, with the role of maintaining independence and preserving dignity. From this, it could follow that users of social care would be more at ease and so more likely to assume an active role. However, this does not appear consistent with the finding that fewer questionnaire respondents felt able to express their wishes to social workers than felt able to express their wishes whilst in hospital. A percentage of this must be accounted for by the fact that not all respondents will have seen a social worker. Again, this is obviously a factor closely related to individual need.

The shifting health-social care boundary towards care provided in the community (Roberts *et al.*, 1995; Wistow, 1995) would appear welcome given the perceived greater access to social care, for those willing and able to pay, and the greater potential to assume an active role. However, an important factor, mentioned by only one professional in this study, is the associated shift in cost towards the service user, as means testing, and to individual responsibility for provision (Vickridge, 1995; Wistow, 1995). Payment for care as a distinction between health and social care was, surprisingly, not mentioned by service users in this study.

If service users have an established point of access into 'the system', most probably in the guise of an agent, an assessment of need and a referral should ensue with no need for service users to assess for themselves the precise services required or indeed whether they would be provided by the NHS or Social Services. This is not a new idea: '*From the point of view of the person receiving it, there should not be health care, and social care but simply care*' (Social Services Committee, 1990: paras. 33-34). Such would be the nature of a truly 'seamless' service. Overall, there was little evidence of such a service in operation in this study yet there appeared evidence of support for such a system amongst service users.

These findings perhaps indicate that a 'one-stop shop' to facilitate access would be a positive measure. That is, a single point of access into the health and social care system to secure all the necessary services. Although not an imminent possibility, such an arrangement would certainly address some of the issues surrounding access evident from this study, most notably around the health-social care divide. It could be argued that knowledge of professional identities and roles or sources of information about various services would be of little significance, indeed would be of no importance, if a 'one stop shop' were a reality.

Such provision however is not in accordance with the concept of user-orientation and an active user role and could even be argued to entail notions of the traditional paternalistic doctor-patient relationship where the latter is in a sub-ordinate position and guided by the former (Parsons, 1951). This represents the opposite to service users guiding themselves through the system, utilising information and professionals as appropriate in order to obtain the required services. Paternalism and consumerism have been posed as the two extremes of possibility for the medical encounter (Beisecker and Beisecker, 1993; Hogg, 1994) each respectively suggesting very different values, roles and responsibilities for each party concerned.

Paternalism versus Consumerism

Paternalism and consumerism as two extremes have very different connotations for the role of the welfare user. As with the agency relationship, most literature focuses on the health as opposed to the social care sector.

Beisecker and Beisecker (1993) analyse the respective roles of professionals and service users implied by the use of the terms *paternalism* and *consumerism* with respect to health care delivery and highlight the implications for the doctor-patient relationship. They see the paternalistic model of care as one in which the doctor is in a position of dominance, is obliged to put the needs as opposed to the wishes of the patient first and the patient is obliged to co-operate with the professional who controls information, determines access and is solely responsible for decision-making. Similarly, Hogg (1994) denotes paternalistic care as characterised by the medical professional in the dominant position; an overriding concern with the patient's health by both doctor and patient; an emphasis on doctors' obligations and patients' needs and the doctor having sole responsibility for decision making. Childress and Siegler (1984) analyse paternalism as centring on care rather than respect; needs rather than rights and professional discretion rather than patient autonomy with the professional as the locus of decision making.

These analyses are all in line with the traditional doctor-patient relationship first discussed by Parsons (1951). He saw the relationship as reciprocal but governed by 'expected' social roles which included both rights and obligations for both participants. Patients were obliged to present themselves to the doctor when ill and comply with the recommended action from the doctor in return for being temporarily relieved of their roles and responsibilities. The doctor is obliged to act in the interests of the patient but has the right to act as s/he feels appropriate.

Such definitions effectively rule out any role for service users in accessing services, participating in decisions, exercising choice, seeking out information or indeed making a complaint; these would all be subsumed under the role of the doctor in the way deemed most suitable. Whilst there are definite parallels with the agency relationship discussed above, a major difference is the level of trust which may be assumed between the participants. Agency may imply an element of distrust whereas a paternalistic relationship is based on trust and the professional can be assumed to be acting in the interests of the patient. As such, there would be no place for third parties as advocates or otherwise.

Komrad (1983) believes paternalism to be reciprocal with autonomy that is, where autonomy is eroded, paternalism advances. He suggests that the knowledge gap between doctor and patient (central to both agency and advocacy) can be used to justify paternalism. Further, as with the agency relationship, he argues that illness represents a state of diminished autonomy and that patients may even welcome paternalism. Ill health was specifically cited by a small number of respondents as a reason for them not wishing to assume an active role. Jones (1996) however, regarding autonomy as a 'desirable attribute', believes the autonomy model in health care to be gaining prominence. The greatest example of autonomous behaviour revealed by this study was in service users independently accessing domestic help as required.

The belief of 'doctor/nurse knows best' has been classed as the most quoted definition of paternalism (Jones, 1996). Although this study found most service users confident of communicating with professionals and feeling that they had participated in decisions regarding their care, this notion of the professional 'knows best' was evident to a significant degree. This was both in terms of not wishing to participate in decisions, but instead leaving them to be made by professionals, and in accepting the care that was provided. Similar feelings were apparent amongst interviewees who did not feel it was their responsibility to attempt to access services and did not feel it was necessary to be aware of the services they were entitled to. The notion of patients co-operating with professionals can therefore be assumed but was also in evidence in this study. This is similar to the findings of Beisecker (1988) who concluded that elderly people (60 years and above) were more inclined than younger people to wish the health professional to assume a dominant role.

There was evidence of feeling that the professional knows best amongst health and social care professionals, particularly with regard to clinical aspects of care. However there also appeared a commitment to providing information to service users as relevant and encouraging users to participate in their care. The fact that many users were dependent upon being provided with such opportunities is also indicative of paternalism. This was particularly the case with regard to the range of 'choice' offered which some professionals acknowledged as being limited before being offered to users. In the case of true paternalism however, users would be provided with no opportunities to assume an active role.

Coupled with the notion of placing complete faith in professionals is the high esteem in which service users hold care providers. Although not a perfect proxy, an indicator of such esteem was widely evidenced in this study through both expressed gratitude and praise for professionals. This is hardly a perception conducive to service users embracing an active role in their encounters with them. It is further suggested that the differences in communication found between service users and doctors or consultants and service users and other front-line workers is indicative of the higher esteem with which doctors and consultants are held.

Komrad (1983) concludes that it would be undesirable to dispose entirely of paternalism in medicine. He believes that 'limited paternalism' is most appropriate to the clinical setting which involves the doctor maximising the capacity of the patient to be autonomous. It would be reasonable to suggest that in some instances paternalism may be assumed by default, particularly given that this is the 'traditional' model. Chapter 8 discusses this as an element of 'health experience'.

The consumerist model of care given by Beisecker and Beisecker (1993) emphasised a more equal relationship between doctor and patient, who are both motivated by self-interest, in which patients' rights dominate, the doctor provides information and the patient is responsible for decision-making. Similarly, Hogg (1994) does not rule out a powerful role for the doctor in her analysis of consumerism instead advocating a more equal and dynamic relationship between doctors and their patients and so a more active role for the service user. The doctor still determines the 'need' for medical treatment but the values of the patient dominate; efficiency and effectiveness are important considerations and market principles, notably competition, are often apparent; decisions are made by the patient on the basis of information and advice from the doctor and patients have explicit rights. Again there are parallels with the agency relationship.

In terms of the relative dominance of users' needs implied by the models of paternalism and consumerism given above, a number of interpretations are possible. Resource constraints and an increasing concern with economic factors as found by this study raise questions regarding the extent to which professionals are able to *paternalistically* consider users' needs as the overriding concern. This can also be related to possible conflicts identified earlier in the role of the agent who must reconcile their own interests with pursuing those of the patient whilst possibly also assuming a gatekeeping role.

Other possibilities for the doctor-patient relationship have previously been given by Szasz and Hollender (1956) who identify three possible models: the activity-passivity model, the guidance-co-operation model and the mutual participation model. Prototypes are respectively given as the parent-infant, parent-child (adolescent) and adult-adult relationships whilst clinical applications of such relationships are respectively illustrated as the patient being in a coma, as suffering from an acute infection or in the management of long-term chronic disease. Komrad (1983) sees these models as points along the spectrum between paternalism and autonomy.

The first two of Szasz and Hollender's models were evident to some degree in this study, from the perspective of both service users and care professionals. That is, some respondents did not wish for an active role in their encounters with welfare services whilst some assumed a degree of activity with advice and guidance from professionals as appropriate. There was no evidence of the third arrangement in the provision of statutory care, which assumes that the participants have approximately equal power, are mutually interdependent and engage in activity that will be in some way satisfying to both (Szasz and Hollender, 1956). Childress and Siegler (1984) refer to this last model as 'partnership', a concept discussed under 'participation' earlier.

These models can also be used to examine the attitude of potential service users towards accessing care. That is, whether they felt that it was their responsibility to seek access to care or the role of professionals to negotiate access on their behalf. All three models are interpreted as present in this study. That is, some respondents remained passive, appearing to not have considered the possibility of initiating access to care, some respondents attempted to access care but upheld the knowledge and authority of professionals whilst some had independently accessed care, which appears to go beyond the mutual participation model. The last of these scenarios was evident in relation to social care only.

A major criticism levelled against the consumerist model is that it erodes trust, to be replaced by accountability as all parties are concerned with their own interests. A further limitation, at the extreme, is that it risks under-utilising the expertise of the health professional (Stewart and Roter, 1989). There was no evidence of this found by this study as users sought the expert input of both health and social care professionals, which went beyond legitimization of their illness, even when desiring their own participation in decisions.

Even in conventional markets where users of goods and services, backed by the ability and willingness to pay, are able to assume all roles of the decision making process (see discussion below) unaided, there is still a role for 'expert' input. Due to the highly specialised nature of health and social care, it is perhaps unrealistic to imagine a situation in which 'the expert' did not have a role to play either in assessing the need for welfare or in securing its delivery. Neither Beisecker and Beisecker (1993) nor Hogg (1994) advocate such a situation in their analysis of consumerism as applied to the medical encounter. Both authors however envisage an element of 'participation' by the final user of services.

The Decision-Making Process

One of the main areas this study addressed was ways in which users may have been provided with opportunities to assume an active role or otherwise sought to do so in the *decision-making process* surrounding discharge and subsequent care provision. The findings of this study are now explored using a model of consumer behaviour (Engel *et al.*, 1990) and also the notion of 'rational' behaviour (Katona, 1960). As these models are derived from conventional markets in the private sector, the characteristics of quasi markets again become apparent, of which the distinction between purchaser and final user (for statutory care) is the most relevant.

Engel *et al.* (1990) identify five roles in the consumption process: *initiator, influencer, decider, buyer* and *user* whilst rational behaviour encompasses the process of *need recognition, information search, alternative evaluation* and *choice* (Katona, 1960). Also of relevance are both the *rights* and *responsibilities* of service users.   That is, the opportunities presented to assume an active role but also ways in which users are able and willing to take advantage of such opportunities in addition to possibly creating further opportunities.

The *initiator* recognises the existence of need, so starting the (discharge) decision making process. In this study, preparation for hospital discharge presented the requirement for decision making. This role was usually filled by either ward staff or a social worker in that they were the person who broached the subject of discharge.   A small number of interviewees felt that they had initiated the discharge process by asking when they could expect to return home or expressing a desire to do so. However, all rated their health positively and so it can be assumed that they had minimal requirements for continuing care and so had possibly recognised a need or desire to return home rather than the existence of a care need.   In addition all sought 'approval' of their desire from a professional rather than simply leaving inpatient care.

Moving away from hospital discharge, respondents expressing an ability to seek information or contact professionals as required can feasibly be defined as fulfilling an 'initiating' role, in recognising a need and acting accordingly.   For those wishing to obtain provision from the statutory sector however there is still a requirement for legitimation of need from a professional who must be consulted in order for the process to begin; such is the nature of a gatekept service.   This study revealed how, when perceiving shortfalls in service, some respondents felt that it was their role to initiate gaining access to services whilst others felt that this was definitely the responsibility of a professional. Perceptions such as this are central in determining the role assumed when in need of care. Respondents willing and able to secure care privately can be interpreted as fulfilling the role of 'initiator' and indeed all subsequent stages of the decision-making process.

The role of *initiator* can also be filled by a third party acting in the interests of the final user. There was evidence provided by this study of family and friends assuming this role.

The *influencer* is the person(s) whose opinions weigh heavily in the options evaluated and chosen. Given policy advocating the provision of *participation, choice* and *information* (Chapter 3) and the fact that the *influencer 'does not make any decisions'* (Engel *et al.*, 1990: 28), a role for service users could be expected. A number of professionals stated how they would wish service users to have a degree of influence once their need for care was established however, resource limitations make this increasingly unlikely.

The fact that the *influencer* evaluates and chooses options suggests that they can make the link between perceived need and appropriate service delivery. This was found to be a greater possibility in the receipt of social care than in the receipt of strictly health care (see 'Entry, Exit and Voice' and 'Seamless Provision'). Also central to the evaluation and choice of options must be the availability of *information*. As such, this relates to the *information search* and *alternative evaluation* of rational behaviour.

Most questionnaire respondents in this study appeared satisfied with the level of information they had received about their care. Professionals reported providing more information than users reported receiving. This must be explained by the fact that users are only provided with information regarding the services they are receiving or the conditions they have. This is indicative of *paternalism*, with professionals providing services also determining the type and level of information supplied, and can be argued to limit the scope of users in accessing further care. This is similar to users being dependent upon the provision of opportunities by professionals to *participate* and to exercise *choice*.

In this study, users reported that the majority of information provided was regarding medical condition, with less being provided about available services. Users also expressed a desire for more information. Furnishing potential users with information about all services provided by the NHS and Social Services department would be the most effective way of enabling them to play an active role (Hogg, 1990; Winkler, 1990). Allen *et al.* (1992) identified the major gap in the provision of information to elderly people to be the lack of comprehensive information detailing the services that might be available. An unwelcome outcome of providing such information, mentioned by a number of professionals in this study, may be users demanding services that they have not formally been assessed as needing. A study by the Social Services Inspectorate (1991) found staff reluctant to give too much information through fear of creating a demand which they could not guarantee to deliver.

Griffiths (1988b) and Pollitt (1988) go beyond this, concluding that whilst such information about public services is useful, it is evaluative data about the effectiveness and quality of alternatives which is necessary to empower service users. Moreover Winkler (1987), in relation to health, believes that user information ought to provide details of service availability, delivery, accessibility and above all be compiled independently of NHS management.   There was no evidence in this study of information being provided and distributed *independently* of service providers.   Professionals reported information being produced 'in house' whilst service users reported being provided with information by service providers and mentioned health and social care personnel as sources of further information.

Solely providing information relating to actual condition or services received may mean that people receiving a shortfall in their care are provided with no explanation as to why this is the case.   Eligibility criteria for care services assumes particular importance in the light of the uncertain health-social care boundary.   However this must be balanced with concerns about providing 'too much' information, expressed by some professionals in this study.   This study found no information provided routinely on discharge from hospital, which is not inconsistent with a study showing how not all Trusts provide discharge information as a matter of course (National Consumer Council, 1997).

With regard to seeking out information, most questionnaire respondents reported that they would know how to do so whilst over half of interviewees reported having done so.   These are both indicative of a willingness to assume an active role.   This varied by the social and economic characteristics of respondents explored in this study and is discussed further in the following chapter.

The definition of the *decider* as the person or organisation with financial authority or power to dictate the final choice inextricably links decision making power with financial power.   As such, it appears to exclude users of statutory care services from final decisions due to lack of financial authority.   There was little evidence from this study of service users wishing to, or indeed being given the opportunity to, make final decisions.   The users who were found to be in the strongest position in making final choices in this study were those who had the least need for care and had declined that which was offered and those who were purchasing private (social) care (see 'Entry, Exit and Voice').   Only the latter of these is truly accurate given the definition linking decision making with financial authority.   Those found to be in the least strong position in terms of *deciding* were those who perceived a shortfall in their care.   That is, their needs were not formally consolidated and they were unable to access care privately.

With regard to statutory care, the role of the *decider*, as linked to financial authority, seems almost synonymous with that of gatekeeper due to the provision of care free at the point of delivery and on the basis of professionally defined need. It is probable that a gatekeeper will have criteria upon which to base such decisions although individual purchaser units have increasing discretion in the allocation of resources. Again perhaps this suggests a close relationship with one designated agent or advocate, who can provide both information and authority, may be the most effective way of users assuming an active role.

The way in which welfare services are financed and the distinction between purchaser and user in quasi markets, categorically exclude service users from the role of *buyer* when seeking statutory care. Purchasers, largely distinct from providers, since the advent of quasi markets in the delivery of welfare, can be health authorities, Social Services departments, general practitioners or individual care managers. Only in the case of the latter two are users likely to have direct contact with the professional purchasing care on their behalf.

Not all users receive services free of charge as means tests are implemented for many aspects of social care. In this study, this was mainly for 'home help' services. The payments are not made directly to the provider nor are they made at the point of delivery and as such are unlikely to confer any advantage compared to people not making such payments. This study found how users paying for *private* 'home help' services were in a stronger position in terms of deciding when to receive the care and what would be provided than those receiving means tested statutory 'home helps'. Opportunities do exist for those willing and able to pay to determine aspects of care provision; for example, supplements may be paid to upgrade social care (Department of Health, 1989b), whilst inpatients may pay extra for certain facilities or for a private room (Department of Health, 1989a). Importantly, such opportunities are only available once care is being provided and not during the decision-making process.

If the role of the *buyer* is simply to 'make the purchase', it could be deemed relatively less important than the other roles in terms of playing an active role in decision making regarding use of care services. Similarly with the role of *user* which it can be safely assumed will be filled by the respondent.

This discussion has shown a definite role for the service user in the decision-making process yet also how the service user sought and valued professional input which was available.

Summary

This chapter has considered the findings of this research in relation to the broad aims of the study. The main issues and themes which emerged as pertinent to the level of user-orientation and an active user role in the discharge process have been discussed. Interpretations of the findings showed different ways in which 'participation' could be interpreted and applied, the importance of the relationship between services users and providers of care, specifically an 'agent', and the possible application of models to the user – provider relationship, namely *paternalism* and *consumerism*. Differences in accessing care were revealed between people meeting the cost of their care and those dependent upon statutory provision and also distinctions between accessing social care as opposed to health care.

In relation to the policy directives analysed in Chapter 3, this study provides overall evidence of user-orientation in the use of care by elderly people on discharge from hospital. This was mainly in terms of being provided with opportunities to participate in decisions and being provided with information about their health condition. However opportunities for service users to adopt an active role in relation to all five principles indicating user influence or control were revealed to some extent by this study. As such, there were definite possibilities for most service users who wished to assume an active role to do so. Experience and behaviour by sub-groups of the sample are discussed in the following chapter.

8 Discussion II: Social Differentiation and the Use of Health and Social Care

Introduction

Chapter 7 comprised a discussion of the findings of this study according to the key themes which emerged from the data and in relation to the stipulated policies for service delivery detailed in Chapter 3. No consensus was apparent amongst service users of the extent to which they assumed an active role in using health and social care including their expressed ability and willingness to do so. This study defined elderly people (70 years and over) as forming a 'critical case' by suggesting that they may be the least likely age group to be able and willing to assume an active role; however no assumptions were made about them forming a homogeneous group. Indeed Chapter 4 demonstrated the diversity of this age group.

The analysis carried out for selected demographic, social and health-related characteristics of respondents revealed a number of notable results and important associations with their experience and behaviour. The general nature of social differentiation mainly in terms of gender, socio-economic grouping and age, on which there is an abundance of literature, is instrumental in interpreting many of these findings.

The main trends from this study appeared to be that the least likely to assume an active role amongst the sample were also the most vulnerable and dependent members of society in terms of low income, poor health and lack of social support. That is, females, respondents in the lower socio-economic groups, respondents reporting a negative health state and respondents living alone. Few consistent findings were revealed on the basis of age, that is, between 'young elderly' people (70-77 years) and 'old elderly' people (78 years and above). These trends were in relation to both experiences of using health and social care and ability and willingness to assume an active user role.   These variables are interrelated to a large degree which is acknowledged in interpreting the findings and which confounds attempts to draw any firm conclusions regarding the relative influence of each of the variables. All factors are obviously located within the wider experience of a person's life and so cannot be divorced from their present situation nor their past experience. In recognising this, the interpretation of these findings takes place under four main headings: *health experience; employment experience, social support* and *the life course approach.*

Health Experience

The age group under study was deliberately chosen as the one with the longest experience of using health and social care services prior to the 1990 reform of welfare, a factor which must underlie and influence their current attitudes and interpretation of events.   This includes experience before the welfare state was established in 1948. Taken to the extreme the situation in 1948, at the inception of the NHS and the situation in the 1990s, following the introduction of market principles, could theoretically be interpreted as examples of *paternalism* and *consumerism* respectively. Although neither of these extremes can be argued as wholly realistic, it is useful to employ these crude analogies in order to provide possible interpretations of the actions of this sample of people (see Chapter 7). Expectations arising from past experience by gender and socio-economic grouping are now considered as important factors in interpreting reported experience and behaviour.

Firstly however ways in which interviewees' self-reported health status at the time of the study was related to user experience and behaviour is discussed.

Self-reported Health Status

This study simply asked interviewees to rate their health either positively or negatively to gain a snap shot of their health at the time of the study.

The subjectivity of self-reporting was not felt to pose any threats to validity as observations made by the interviewer were able to verify respondents' health assessments. In addition, the General Household Survey uses subjective measures of peoples' perceptions of their health (OPCS, 1992).

As far as was revealed by this work, a negative health rating appeared to be producing a downward effect on users assuming an active role. This was apparent in not wishing to participate in decisions regarding discharge, in not expressing an opinion to professionals if asked and in feeling unable to communicate with doctors or consultants. Abramson (1988), with specific reference to discharge planning, similarly found low participation amongst service users suffering from poor mental and physical health whilst in a small scale study by Biley (1992) 'being too ill' was given as a reason for not participating in decision making regarding nursing care. In addition, ill health has been highlighted as a strong threat to autonomy (Komrad, 1983) and as lowering resistance to paternalism (Jones, 1996). In comparison to younger people, Cornwell (1993) cited ill health as a reason for elderly people being less willing to adopt an active role in their care.

It is understandable how a specific illness, disability or an overall negative health rating could feasibly have a downward effect on an individual's willingness and ability to assume an avtive role. By definition (potential) users of health and social care are in a less than optimum state of health and therefore not in an ideal position for articulating needs and desires to create effective demand or indeed wishing to do so. It is also feasible that ill health may preclude service users from being presented with opportunities to assume an active role; out of concern for the recipient of care, service providers may act paternalistically. Whilst no such evidence was found in this study, such situations could be redressed to a degree by the presence of a third party, acting as either agent or advocate for the service user. When filled by a family member or friend at the wish of the service user, such a relationship can be classed as *representation* or 'social support'; the latter is explored later in this chapter as a factor associated with user experience and behaviour.

Of those interviewees who stated with certainty that they would make a complaint if dissatisfied, the vast majority (88%) reported a positive health state. This may also be related to the effect of ill health on ability or willingness to play an active role. A further explanation is that respondents with a negative health rating may feel more dependent and grateful for care received and indeed upon providers of care and as a result may feel less likely to make a formal complaint. This is a particular possibility given the praise and gratitude expressed, regardless of health state, in this study which may be indicative of gratitude. It must be remembered that feelings regarding making a complaint are not necessarily related to experience of unsatisfactory care delivery.

Respondents rating their health positively had the least need for care which was found to enhance their position for playing an active role in a number of ways. Firstly, all interviewees who felt that they had initiated the discharge process, by expressing a desire to return home, rated their health positively. It can be assumed that they had minimal continuing care requirements. Secondly, those not perceiving a need for additional care were ironically found to be in the strongest position in terms of exercising choice over services in that they were able to refuse what was offered. Although these two trends were also related to the levels of informal care available, the amount of care purchased privately and a desire for independence, the need for care must initially stem from health state.

There appeared to be a definite association between perceptions of the quality of information about both medical condition and services available and interviewees' self-reported health status. All interviewees (100%) rating the provision of information very highly rated their health positively, compared to a smaller amount of those feeling 'satisfied' with the provision of information and even less of those feeling dissatisfied with the provision. One interpretation of this is that respondents with poor health may feel that they require additional information about either their condition or services available due to their high level of dependency or possible desire for a higher level of service provision. They may be unable or unwilling to seek this out because of their health condition. Conversely, respondents with a positive health rating are likely to have a lower need for information about both medical condition and services available. As discussed in Chapter 7, it is to be expected that different levels of information would be provided to those experiencing differing health conditions and using different levels of services as relevant to their situation. This was interpreted as an example of *paternalistic* care and of *manipulation.*

Satisfaction with information may alternatively be seen as a function of general satisfaction with welfare provision. However this was not investigated by this study. Previous work in the hospital sector has revealed no direct association between health status and general satisfaction (Cohen, 1996). This is surprising given the number of studies which demonstrate how older people, who may be assumed to have poorer health status, are less dissatisfied than younger people with health care ('Entry, Exit and Voice', Chapter 7).

It can be expected that there will be an association between age and health status which will have implications for levels of required care (see also Chapter 4). Although this study found no association between age group and self-reported health status, there was evidence of interviewees in the older age group (78 years and above) requiring a higher level of care than those in the younger group (70-77 years). Blaxter's finding of a tendency for elderly people to be increasingly optimistic about their health (Blaxter, 1990) is an important consideration in interpreting such a trend. The requirement of the younger age group for a lower level of care may be used to explain the finding that all interviewees who expressed a desire to return home from hospital were aged 70-77 years. Minimal care requirements can be assumed.

By solely considering health status at the time of interview, no account was taken of whether the illness or disability was long-standing or whether it was permanent. Socio-demographic characteristics may be of use in discussing more long-term health trends and any possible influence on experience and behaviour in using health and social care. There did not appear to be any association between self-reported health status at the time of the study with either gender or socio-economic status. However, expected trends in the use of services throughout life by such sub-groups are now considered.

Past Experience

In addition to the reported health state of the respondent at the time of study, past experience is an important consideration. However, this is unlikely to be uniform across the sample. This is particularly important in terms of expectations regarding care delivery and the appropriate user role.

Statistics (see Chapter 4) and previous research reveal an apparent gender bias in the distribution of ill health which extends into later life (Arber and Ginn, 1993a). Although at all ages, mortality for males is higher than that for females, the pattern is reversed with regard to morbidity (Lonsdale, 1990). The Health and Lifestyle Survey found how women tend to rate their health less positively than men (Cox *et al.*, 1987; Blaxter, 1990); similarly, the General Household Survey shows how women have higher perceived morbidity throughout life than men (Office for National Statistics, 1997b). Differences in experience of illness and disability between the genders coupled with higher life expectancy for women (Office for National Statistics, 1997a), inevitably mean differing levels and frequency of contact with welfare providers. Women tend to be higher users of welfare services than men are at all ages (Roberts, 1990; Foster, 1995; Office for National Statistics, 1997b). However, debates exist surrounding differences between the genders in reporting and acting upon symptoms (for example, Doyal and Elston, 1986; Kane, 1991; Popay, 1992) in that true differences in morbidity may be distorted.

It may be seen as a paradox that women tend both to live longer than men do *and* make greater use of welfare services throughout their lives. From women's greater longevity it may be expected that they are healthier throughout life than men and so use health care less. However, medical needs associated with advancing years and the reproductive capacity of women in addition to female roles in negotiating access to care for family members and fulfilling the role of both formal and informal care providers all serve to increase the contact between women and providers of welfare (Doyal and Elston, 1986).

The well-documented inequalities in both mortality and morbidity by socio-economic group (Hart, 1971; Townsend and Davidson, 1982; Whitehead, 1987; Blane *et al.*, 1996; Wilkinson, 1996) which persist into later life are also important in this debate. Those in lower socio-economic groups persistently suffer worse health at all ages than those in the higher groups. Blaxter (1990) found consistent differences in self-assessed health by all measures of social disadvantage including low income, unemployment and area of residence. In addition to providing an indicator of likely levels of income, an individual's socio-economic grouping also allows assumptions to be made regarding their status both within employment and society more generally, their working conditions, their lifestyle and so on. Interestingly, Blaxter (1990) also revealed how the tendency for those in lower socio-economic groups to rate their health as 'fair' or 'poor', was particularly prevalent in the older age groups.

As a result of these trends it can be assumed that females and people in lower socio-economic groups have a greater number of contacts with providers of health and social care, are in contact with a greater number of providers and have greater knowledge of welfare provision than males and people in higher socio-economic groups. The same could also be suggested of 'old elderly' as higher users of services than 'young elderly' people.

It may be expected therefore that these groups would assume the most active roles in the use of health and social care. Such advantages would be achieved for example, through having established relationships with service providers, knowledge and experience of services that are available and how to access both them and any relevant information. Such advantages would be further enhanced for females by some of this contact being at times not necessitated by ill health, for example, when seeking care for family members or throughout the stages of pregnancy and birth. It is surprising therefore that women appear less able and willing than males to assume an active role, less knowledgeable of their entitlement to care and less knowledgeable of how to make a complaint. Similarly with those dependent upon the state retirement pension, as indicative of low socio-economic grouping, in terms of knowing where to access information and in knowing how to make a complaint if dissatisfied.

A further factor relating to levels of morbidity with a potential influence on user experience and behaviour is the regularity of demand for services. It could be hypothesised that those experiencing poorer states of health may find themselves in a stronger position for assuming an active role due to experience of ill health being more predictable and regular. For neither females nor member of lower socio-economic groups did such advantages seem apparent. Similarly with chronic illness in that experience and knowledge would be gained in managing the condition.

Respondents aged 78 years and above, regardless of gender or socio-economic group, were found by this study to feel more knowledgeable of where to obtain information about their care and to report knowing how to make a complaint than their younger counterparts. These findings could be related to levels of contact with care services and professionals due to higher levels of service use or indeed due to greater regularity or certainty of demand for care, all of which may heighten the potential for them to assume an active role. However, this must also be considered as inconsistent with other findings throughout this study showing how those with a need for high levels of care are least likely to assume an active role.

As already shown by this study, respondents with less need for statutory care were in a strong position in terms of choice of services, through being able to refuse them. As a result of increasingly limited resources, it is suggested that it may be easier to fulfil the wishes of users with lower levels of need than those with complex needs or who are otherwise 'resource intensive'. This may explain the higher levels of choice perceived by males and respondents in receipt of a private or occupational pension. However perceived choice of what services to receive and of who to deliver them suggests that services are being used and not that a choice was made to decline to receive them. The possible lower need for care by males due to trends in morbidity by gender may go some way to explaining why males were more likely to feel in receipt of sufficient care than females although the level of informal care available (see 'Social Support') is also likely to be an issue.

The general links between life expectancy, morbidity and socio-economic grouping could mean that those who have survived, particularly in the older age groups, are likely to belong to higher socio-economic groups – the 'Darwinist' effect. It is therefore possible that the sample may be skewed towards those from higher socio-economic groups, particularly in the higher age groups. Such a possibility may be used to explain the inconsistency in findings on splitting the sample into age groups. Those in lower socio-economic groups who have survived and were included in this study may be expected to have higher morbidity and so be more vulnerable and less likely to assume an active role, which certainly appeared to be the case.

An alternative explanation for high use of services yet passive behaviour is that by nature of seeking care, people are necessarily vulnerable and dependent upon those providing care, a situation which can only be exacerbated by the inherent power difference between users and providers of care. Donaldson *et al.* (1991) believed the vulnerability and dependency of older people caused them to play less of an active role in the use of health care than younger people.

In addition, a long experience of receiving care and interacting with care professionals by females, people in lower socio-economic groups and 'old elderly', rather than nurturing an active role may instead be interpreted as long experience of *paternalistic* care. It would follow therefore that those with most experience of the welfare sector would be in the least strong position in terms of assuming an active role, finding it more difficult to adopt an active role where once passivity and compliance were expected. Similarly, for these people it may be that paternalistic care occurred through default; that is, they did not *expect* to play an active role or to be provided with opportunities to do so due to long experience of a passive role and not being expected to act otherwise.

Similarly with service providers, the prevailing culture when they received training may affect both how they deliver care (Jones, 1996) and perceptions of the appropriate user role (Haug and Ory, 1987). That is, if they have a long experience of delivering *paternalistic* care it may be that they would be more inclined to report service users playing an active role and the provision of opportunities for them to do so in contemporary service provision. This did not prove to be the case. If anything providers with greater experience were more likely to be aware of how resource limitations were restricting provision and so making an active role for service users and influence in decision-making less likely.

This section has shown how females and those in the higher socio-economic groups have the highest life expectancy. Yet an anomaly is introduced into this association by the concentration of females in the lower socio-economic groups.

Employment Experience

The links between gender, socio-economic grouping and health experience and possible implications for user experience and behaviour detailed above are now shown to be inter-related to a greater degree and so more complex due to trends in former employment.

Economic Grouping and Gender

The variable 'pension' was used as an indicator of socio-economic grouping due to the significant association of whether respondents received a pension other than the state retirement pension with former occupational grouping and housing tenure (see Tables 4 and 5). This demonstrates how inequalities in access to resources in retirement are simply a continuation of those experienced throughout life (Victor, 1989; Taylor and Ford, 1993; Wilson, 1993). Indeed such inequalities may be exacerbated rather than alleviated on retirement as intimated by the findings of this study.

A number of associations between socio-economic grouping and user experience and behaviour, as related to health state, have already been revealed in this chapter. However, it is important to keep findings relating to socio-economic group in the context of gender. Males who were found to be more willing and able to assume and active role than females, are also more likely to be located in the higher socio-economic groups (Office for National Statistics, 1997b). As highlighted, this appears inconsistent with associations between gender, life expectancy and socio-economic grouping.

The well-documented nature of gender inequality is instrumental in interpreting the different behaviour by gender towards assuming an active role in aspects of the discharge process and subsequent care use. The findings for males and females in this study reinforce literature reporting gender inequality (for example, Millar and Glendinning, 1989; Arber and Ginn, 1991; Payne, 1991), particularly marked amongst elderly women (Walker, 1992). This is a function of life-long low access to resources, extending into retirement and the socially constructed relationship between gender and the labour market, including informal and domestic work. As such, participation in paid employment, remuneration levels for such employment and entitlement to an occupational or private pension are major ways in which men and women have widely different experiences (Groves, 1992; Lonsdale, 1992; Walker, 1992; Siltanen, 1994). The gendered division of labour is such that females tend to be concentrated in the lower socio-economic groups to the extent that they can be seen as a 'reserve army of labour' (Payne, 1991; Alcock, 1993). This can be seen to stem largely from the gendered division of labour within the domestic environment with women traditionally undertaking most household and child rearing responsibilities. Taken in conjunction with Phillipson's (1982) analysis of elderly people as a 'reserve army of labour' this further suggests that women experience double discrimination in later life.

Such differences can be expected to be particularly marked in the age group under study due to women's widespread participation in paid employment outside the home and their entitlement to pensions other than the state retirement pension in their own right being relatively new phenomena (Office for National Statistics, 1997a). These are two of the major contributors to the 'gendered distribution of poverty' (Alcock, 1993).

Pension Entitlement

Respondents in receipt of a private or occupational pension were found to be most likely to feel at ease with care professionals; all interviewees (100%) who felt able to communicate with doctors or consultants were in receipt of an occupational or private pension (see Table 10). Type of job formerly held must be an important factor here, determining whether people are used to articulating their views, expecting to influence outcomes, being involved in decision making and so on. That is, whether they are used to being active or more passive in formal encounters. It would follow therefore that those formerly employed in lower socio-economic posts doing manual work will have fewer expectations of being involved in decisions and expecting to influence outcomes. From the above trends relating to socio-economic groups and gender, an active role can be expected from males more readily than from females, providing a further insight into the differences by gender found in this study.

Respondents in receipt of a private or occupational pension appeared more consumer oriented in feeling knowledgeable of where to obtain information and of how to make a complaint than those with no such pension provision. They also reported being more likely to actually make a complaint if dissatisfied. These are all indicators of a positive attitude towards assuming an active role suggesting confidence and self-assertion in achieving desired outcomes. Again, this may be related to former employment experience, expectations and willingness in voicing an opinion. This may also be of use in interpreting the finding that males were more likely to engage in information-seeking behaviour than females and were more knowledgeable of how to make a complaint if dissatisfied than females. The probable different health states by socio-economic group and gender must also be borne in mind.

Employment experience provides a possible explanation of the ability and willingness of service users in assuming an active role but does not itself provide any insight into the extent to which professionals encourage or provide opportunities for communication.

It has previously been shown how doctors provide more information and explantions to people in higher socio-economic groups than those in lower socio-economic groups (Brody, 1980; Pendleton and Bochner, 1980; Street, 1991). Brody (1980) terms this the 'social gap' and believes it is compounded by the fact that people in lower socio-economic groups often feel intimidated by their physicians. Pendleton and Bochner,

(1980) explain their findings in the primary care sector in terms of the GP's ability to communicate with the different social groups and the GP's assumptions about people's ability to understand. Haug and Ory (1987) give 'class-based' language differences as obstacles to communication and as contributing to understanding why patients may interact more readily with nurses than with doctors. Street (1991) also found that younger patients received more information from doctors than older patients and interprets this finding, and that related to socio-economic group, as a result of the communicative styles of patients and doctors' perceptions of patient's ability to understand. These explanations are also useful in interpreting the expressed ease of male interviewees and those in receipt of a private or occupational pension in communicating with doctors or consultants.

The majority of interviewees (65%) paying privately for additional services or having purchased aids or adaptations were in receipt of a private or occupational pension. These respondents were found to be in a relatively stronger position in terms of assuming an active role mainly due to being able to directly access a higher level of services than respondents with no such pensions. The services most often received in this way were shown to be domestic help. A greater level of choice was also exercised by respondents paying privately for care in that they could determine the timing of services and what duties would be performed. A number of interviewees who had declined to receive services did so due to the availability of privately financed sources of help, again mainly for domestic cleaning; this choice was most common amongst those in receipt of a private or occupational pension. These findings demonstrate how users of welfare services with the financial backing to do so have greater opportunities and ability to assume an active role. Professionals were also plainly aware of how access was greater for those able and willing to pay for care. The greater ease of people in higher socio-economic groups in communicating with professionals and in knowing how to access information may also be relevant for independently accessing care. Wilson (1994) in a study of people aged 75 years and over found how paying for care, from the private and voluntary sector, was more common amongst middle class than working class people and how lack of money constrained elderly people from using private care.

A small percentage of interviewees (18%) in this study who were accessing private services or aids or had adapted their homes in some way were in receipt of Attendance Allowance. Entitlement to this benefit is based on professionally assessed need but was also found to be related to interviewees' self-reported health status. This demonstrates a limited way in which a small number of interviewees in poor health were able and willing to assume an active role. However most were in receipt of a private or occupational pension and therefore gaining the other advantages highlighted in this section.

Social Support

The position of respondents with family or friends available to either provide care directly or to provide assistance in accessing care or information was found to differ quite markedly from those with no such support. Related to the variable 'household composition' this section goes beyond solely considering respondents with co-residents by also taking into account friends and family resident elsewhere. Questionnaires provided data relating to the involvement of 'family and friends' in decision making in addition to recording 'number of people in household' whilst interview data was able to differentiate between help received from co-residents and from those resident elsewhere. Social support or *'help and assistance, or other evidence of caring, provided through a person's social relationships'* (Qureshi, 1990: 32), of which co-residents must form an important component, was found to be related to many aspects of user experience and behaviour. If the third party plays an active role, acting directly in the interests of the service user, such support can be classed as *representation*, an element in enhancing the position of the service user explored by this study, or as an example of an agent or advocate. These were shown in Chapter 7 to be central to users being provided with opportunities to assume an active role and in being willing and able to assume such a role.

Gender, age and ill health are variables related to living arrangements (see Chapter 4) as an indicator of levels of social support. Blaxter (1990) found that people living alone tended to experience worse health than those living with others. In terms of 'social support' more generally, it has been shown how social isolation has a downward effect on health (Blaxter, 1990; Wenger *et al.*, 1996). An alternative explanation is that health is the causal variable with those experiencing poor health no longer able to participate in social activities (Jerrome, 1991). Introducing the variables age and gender however and the associations with both living alone and health state demonstrates the complexity of the relationship.

Amongst questionnaire respondents, a significant association was found in this study between gender and household composition, with females much more likely to live alone than males. Therefore a number of explanations relating to the situation of respondents living alone may also contribute to interpreting the extent to which females are provided with opportunities to assume an active role and are able and willing to assume the role. However, in terms of social support more generally, females have been shown to both provide and receive better support than males (Vaux, 1985) due to the different characteristics of female compared to male relationships. This demonstrates how isolation and loneliness are not synonymous (Wenger *et al.*, 1996).

Respondents with sources of social support were found to be in a stronger position on a number of aspects of their hospital discharge and subsequent use of services in terms of both experience and behaviour than those with no such support. Whilst this may have been anticipated to a degree due to third parties acting as advocates or otherwise representing the service user, other interpretations are possible.

For interviewees with informal care available, particularly in the form of a co-resident, there appeared to be greater flexibility over the timing of discharge. All interviewees had been keen to return home from hospital and so those living with others were shown to be in an advantageous position. This was recognised by both service users and professionals who spoke of fabrication of the level of care available in order to expedite discharge.

A definite role was revealed for family and friends in negotiating on behalf of, or along with, service users regarding the discharge process and subsequent use of servcies. Questionnaire respondents who lived with others reported having a greater role in needs assessment than those living alone whilst qualitative comments suggested an important role for family members in all aspects of participation and negotiation. The assumption was that service users view the involvement of third parties positively.

Respondents living with others and males were more likely to feel in receipt of sufficient care than those living alone. This is probably due to the role of co-residents in providing informal care, which may feasibly be in direct response to perceived shortfalls in statutory provision. Alternatively, it could be that informal carers have negotiated on behalf of the service user to access the required care or acted to provide support in the process of seeking and receiving care. All of these factors were apparent in the findings of this study. Interviewees living with others felt more able to communicate with doctors and consultants than interviewees living alone suggesting ease and confidence in negotiations regarding their care and possibly little requirement for representation. Alternatively it could simply be that family and friends have provided support in such communication. Beisecker (1988) found how older people were more likely than younger people to take a companion when consulting a doctor and that older people's companions were more likely to wish to be involved in decisions.

These roles for co-residents may also be cited in the greater degree of choice for respondents living with others compared to those living alone. Similarly, this may be interpreted as either due to a role for co-residents in negotiations or supporting users in negotiations or as representing an alternative source of care provision. In terms of exercising choice, this study found ironically that people in the strongest position were those who chose to decline the statutory care offered. One of the reasons for declining care, acknowledged by service users and professionals alike, was the availability of informal care. This of course assumes that informal care is always the preferred option. Respondents with family and friends to provide care yet who do not wish their care needs to be met informally, may therefore find themselves in a weaker position in terms of choice. However no evidence of this was provided by this study.

Respondents in receipt of an occupational or private pension also reported having choice regarding service provsion. Whilst this may mainly relate to private care provision (see 'Pension Entitlement'), research also suggests that the informal care networks of middle class people are quite different from those of working class people (Arber and Ginn, 1993b). Firstly, middle class people may require care at a later age than their working class counterparts, increasing the likelihood of their informal carers having left the labour force. In addition, although they are more likely to have access to resources (material, financial and cultural) to enable them to heighten autonomy in their own home, members of their informal networks are also likely to have resources (for example, higher income, private transport) to fulfil the caring role comprehensively. As such choice, along with other indicators of an active role for service users, may be enhanced.

It may follow therefore that a possibility for the future, particularly in the face of increasingly limited resources, could be for those with family or friends available to have fewer opportunities for exercising choice regarding statutory care delivery due to an obvious source of help. This would also have implications for being provided with opportunities for participating and being provided with information regarding statutory care. A possible outcome of this may be that the position of people living alone, or those with no family or friends, would be greater in terms of being offered choice, information and opportunities to participate. Resource limitations on the provision of statutory care however again appear likely to present a barrier. Associations have been found between household size and use of both statutory health and statutory social services in that those living alone use more services (Morgan, 1980; Arber *et al.*, 1988; Bowling *et al.*, 1991; Boniface and Denham, 1997). This may suggest either that people living alone were given priority in service allocation or that they have no informal care available, are unable to afford private care or have higher levels of need.

Other possibilities for people living alone are that professionals delivering services, aware of an individual's circumstances, may take greater care to ensure that they are aware of their service entitlement and that they receive the required care. However, there is no obligation for professionals to act in this way, unless having explicitly assumed an advocacy role. In terms of the delivery of care provided to peoples' homes, in this study it appeared that service providers were more flexible in undertaking tasks for those living alone quite feasibly due to knowledge of the lack of alternative provision. Those living with others can be assumed to have help with household tasks. This demonstrates an element of choice for people living alone once services are in place yet not in the decision-making process.

The involvement of third parties in negotiations regarding discharge could be equated, at least partially, with the role of the agent or advocate as discussed in Chapter 7. This is applicable due to a role in assisting to secure welfare. Although they might not be fully informed individuals, nor able to authorise access to statutory care, it can be assumed that a family member or friend will not be suffering from ill health or otherwise be vulnerable as the service user may be. As such, they may be more able to engage in 'rational' decision making. In terms of defining access points into the NHS and Social Services, actually contacting service providers, seeking out necessary information or explanations and knowing how to make a complaint, a representative in 'normal' health could also prove invaluable. The advantageous position of users with family or friends can be related to a number of these processes from the findings of this study.

The availability of family and friends to become involved in negotiations surrounding discharge and the delivery of services however was not always viewed positively. A number of professionals revealed how there was not always agreement between the service user and their representative regarding the required care. As such it could be that the service user may not reveal their true opinion or desires mindful of the wishes of those on whom caring responsibilities will fall. This would particularly be a possibility if discussions take place with service users whilst their representatives are present. In such an instance therefore the service user with representatives to either negotiate on their behalf or provide informal care may find themselves in a weaker position, for expressing an opinion or otherwise participating in decision making or exercising choice, than those with no such representative(s). As with professionals acting as agents (Chapter 7), it cannot always be assumed that there is a consensus of opinion between agent and principal or that the agent will reflect the true opinion of the principal. Service users living alone and with no representatives can be assumed to be providing a true opinion of their needs and perceived requirements, not having to be concerned with placing demands on informal carers. No such issues were raised with service users in this study.

Myers and MacDonald (1996) reported counselling both user and carer to enable them to understand each other's position and needs in the event of a disagreement arising between them and how this is particularly important given the increasing reliance upon informal care. This demonstrates how the presence of a third party may do little to facilitate the decision-making process. Indeed the very input of three (or more) rather than two interests can be argued to complicate decision-making and a triad can easily dissolve into a dyad causing one person's views to be marginalised (Haug and Ory, 1987). Alternatively the two interest with similar views may pressure the other participant to adopt their wishes.

This again raises the possible need for advocates who, if employed specifically to do so, could be assumed to be acting in the best interests of the final service user. There was no mention of any need for such provision by service users, although this must be viewed in the light of expectations. Also, if this is not a possibility that users are aware of, they are unlikely to raise it as a possibility. Independent advocates may assume a more effective role for service users than family or friends in that they would be specifically charged with representing the interests of the service user and would have no personal interest to protect.

Qureshi (1990) discusses the diversity of social support in terms of mechanisms and roles in relation to the particular needs of elderly people. Jerrome (1990) distinguishes between 'friends' and 'family' discussing how there is a role for the family in meeting the needs of its dependents and how it is likely to be family members called upon for support in times of need. In the case of elderly people who are still married, the role of caring and providing support falls upon the spouse. This study revealed a role for family members rather than friends or neighbours in relation to providing care and support.

Jerrome further discusses the value of peer relationships concluding that good friends or neighbours are more important than family in increasing satisfaction with life. In addition, Taylor (1988) showed how elderly people living alone have fewer close relationships than those living with others but due to the compensatory effect of many friends experience similar levels of psychological functioning. Also, although the frequency of visiting family and friends declines with age, there is little variation in the likelihood of being visited by such acquaintances (Freer, 1988; OPCS, 1996). These perhaps suggest that living alone is not necessarily the risk factor that may be expected and informal networks have greater potential than were witnessed or investigated by this study. 'Disengagement' (Cumming and Henry, 1961) from social activities and roles due to age as analysed in Chapter 4 may not therefore be apparent in the case of personal relationships. That was not explored by this study.

The Life Course Approach

Previous studies have concluded that elderly people may be less likely than younger age groups to assume an active role when using or seeking to use health and social care services (Haug and Lavin, 1983; Hibbard and Weeks, 1987; Abramson, 1988; Beisecker, 1988; Donaldson *et al.*, 1991). This study used such an assumption in its rationale; the sample population is utilised as a 'critical case' due to factors analysed in Chapter 4. These include trends in illness and disability and in the use of health and social care along with expectations arising from past experience. That is, people of 70 years and over were argued as the *least* likely age group to assume an active role in the use of health and social care.

Analysis of the data from this study by age group, distinguishing between young elderly people (70-77 years) and old elderly people (78 years and above) revealed a number of apparent differences which have been highlighted and interpreted throughout this chapter as related to health state, gender and levels of social support. Overall however there were few consistent findings on splitting the sample by age. In addition, age was not felt to be a useful characteristic on which to place too much emphasis as related to user experience and behaviour due to the huge range of respondents who would be clustered together and analysed on the basis of a chronologically determined variable. Such an approach could also be classed as 'ageist' (see Chapter 4) on the basis of making general assumptions about the homogeneity of an age group (Victor, 1994). Similarly, notions of 'burden' and a 'dependent' status (Chapter 4) can plainly not be applied to the whole population of elderly people due to the huge diversity in characteristics demonstrated and the complexity of the relationships between different variables.

The relationships between age and the other socio-demographic and health-related variables analysed demonstrate the difficulties in isolating any one variable as an influence on user experience and behaviour. It has also been demonstrated how, as a result of demographic, social and health-related factors, people have different experiences throughout their lives, which continue into old age (Taylor and Ford, 1983; Walker, 1992). Such an approach can be interpreted as a 'life course approach' (Arber and Evandrou, 1993) emphasising links between the different phases of life rather than seeing each in isolation.

The research considered the possible association between various socio-demographic variables *at the time of study* with users' experience and behaviour in using health and social care services. The life course approach considers experience and behaviour in old age to be determined by experiences, values and interests *throughout life* (Arber and Evandrou, 1993). Gender can be taken as fixed and socio-economic status can be assumed to be long-standing whereas the duration of living arrangements and health status, as reported at the time of study, were not determined. Assumptions were made instead from the well-established trends reported in Chapter 4 as to the experience of these factors throughout life and on making the transition to different life phases, namely old age and very old age.

This study found how females, respondents reporting a negative health state, respondents in lower socio-economic groups and respondents living alone were least likely to be both provided with opportunities to assume an active role in the use of health and social care and be willing and able to do so. The analysis in Chapter 4 and in the preceding sections in this chapter demonstrate how these respondents can be deemed the most vulnerable and dependent in terms of health, income and social support (also Arber and Ginn, 1991). In comparison to men, women can be assumed to suffer from worse health, be more likely to live alone and be less likely to be in receipt of an occupational or private pension. Similarly, in comparison to those in higher socio-economic groups, respondents in low socio-economic groups can be assumed to suffer from worse health, have lower levels of social support and be less likely to be in receipt of an occupational or private pension.

Whilst comparing younger (under 70 years of age) and older age groups in terms of experience and behaviour in using health and social care was beyond the remit of this study, the analysis on the basis of health, income and social support within one age group were shown to be more valuable. All of these however can be expected to be inversely related to age. Although a number of differences were revealed in experience and behaviour on splitting the age group into two there were no consistent findings. Indeed, this would appear to concur further with the life course approach which suggest that *'chronological age is less important than the social status occupied by individuals'* (Arber and Evandrou, 1993:12).

Summary

This chapter has analysed ways in which the experience and behaviour of service users differed across the sample studied. Such findings have been interpreted in terms of self-reported health status, gender, socio-economic group and levels of social support. However, it has been argued here that it is more realistic to locate these differences within a wider context rather than simply interpreting them as a function of the demographic or social characteristics to which they relate. As such, the life course approach is discussed. In order to encompass the wider life experience of the respondents, health experience, both current health status and experience throughout life, employment experience and levels of social support have been explored in this chapter as possible ways of interpreting the findings of this study. Interpretations of the findings are given in the light of existing research, demographic and social trends and the analytical framework employed.

9   Summary and Evaluation

Introduction

The findings of this study and the subsequent discussion detailed in the previous chapters have illustrated the ways in which the empirical work addressed the aims of the study within the context of the analytical framework. These chapters also progressed beyond this framework. This final section serves to provide both a tentative evaluation of the study in the light of the original aims, including the analytical framework devised and the research approach and design employed, and a summary of the main conclusions regarding the extent to which users were found to assume an active role in using health and social care. The convention of suggesting areas for further research is also observed.

The Analytical Framework

The analytical framework developed for this study and within which the research took place proved fairly comprehensive and was utilised effectively in designing and executing the empirical work and in interpreting the findings.

The enquiry maintained a very focused approach through considering a specific phase in the care of a relatively narrowly defined group of service users. That is, people of 70 years and over on discharge from inpatient care to their own homes. In exploring this phase of care however a number of issues indicative of a strengthening of the position of service users in relation to service providers, were explored. In addition to the key theme of *participation*, the issues of *representation, access, choice, information* and *redress* were explored. Examples of the promotion of each of these in the delivery of health and social care were apparent in the policy documentation issued during the period upon which this study was based. The different definitions of *participation* were returned to in analysing the findings in addition to considering the extent to which all the other issues were apparent in the use of care by the respondents to this study.   This also facilitated a consideration of how the experiences of service users compared with stipulated policies for service delivery.

The vast literature interpreting the policy implemented during the 1989-1997 period was drawn upon in formulating the analytical framework to provide a greater depth of understanding of the initiatives and their possible implications for care delivery.   This was mainly focused on the initiatives relevant to users discharged from hospital with the possibility of requiring continuing care.   Whilst this mainly related to user-orientation and ways in which the position of the service user may be enhanced, other possible and actual consequences were also discussed.   Differences between 'quasi' markets and conventional markets, most notably the distinction between purchaser and final user, were also considered when analysing the findings.

The increasing prominence of the older age groups in contemporary society, particularly as users of health and social care, was illustrated. Although a fairly narrow age group of people were sampled in this study, it was not expected that uniform experience or behaviour would be revealed.   Indeed the disparate nature of the population aged 70 years and above in terms of demographic, social and health circumstances was illustrated.   It is plain such that any attempt to classify them as homogeneous is quite unrealistic. These differentials were then utilised in the research design and analysis to consider and interpret differences in user experience and behaviour.

There was a paucity of research reports of studies exploring similar issues. Of those that do exist however the general conclusion was that elderly people appeared less likely than younger people to assume an active role in the use of care services. Whilst these previous studies were of limited use in interpreting the findings of the present study due to their relatively limited scope, they provide support for the application of the 'critical case' rationale in this study.

The discussion of the findings went beyond the framework constructed demonstrating ways in which the research was original in addition to building upon and contributing to existing knowledge. This was particularly evident in the analysis of the increasingly crucial divide which persists between health and social care, in the analysis of the complexity of the user-provider relationship and in the analysis of such a wide variety of social differentiation and inequality. The significance of these issues for users being provided with opportunities to assume an active role and in being willing and able to assume such a role had not been addressed in formulating the analytical background.

The Research Approach

The research approach utilised was effective in that it yielded a variety of sources and types of data which were consolidated and compared during analysis and interpretation.

Both a quantitative and a qualitative approach were employed with service users whilst solely a qualitative approach was employed with health and social care professionals. The large sample size of service users sought in terms of general experience and behaviour regarding hospital discharge meant that a quantitative approach was suitable. More modest samples in terms of seeking to explore and understand the complex process of hospital discharge, with respect to users being provided with opportunities to assume an active role and being able and willing to do so, allowed an in-depth qualitative approach to be used with service users and health and social care professionals.

The necessarily modest sample of service users that were included in the in-depth phase of the study yielded data of arguably greater value in understanding the complex process under investigation than that from the postal survey. Such was the intention. Questionnaire data was able to provide an impression of overall trends and a general overview of user experience and behaviour. Qualitative data was then used to provide additional evidence to support (or contradict) these general findings and to provide explanations and greater understanding of them.

Use of these three approaches was interpreted as a form of triangulation in that different methods and approaches were used with both the same and with different groups of informants so generating a variety of data. In addition, the different approaches with the different informants addressed both the same as well as different aspects of the discharge process. Some issues were only suitable for exploration via a face to face approach. 'Triangulation' ensured that the research aims were comprehensively addressed as well as providing different perspectives on the process under study. As such, confidence can be expressed that the research approach and design adopted served to enhance both the reliability and the validity of the findings.

Lack of control over the sample of service users to whom to administer the postal questionnaire, and the subsequent adoption of a convenience sample, resulted in a very diverse sample in terms of social, demographic and health related variables. Purposively sampling the interviewees on the basis of demographic characteristics of questionnaire respondents (age, gender and household composition) therefore also produced a very diverse sample. A degree of heterogeneity had been anticipated and even built into the research design such that age, gender, household composition and socio-economic group were to be explored for possible associations with user experience and behaviour. In terms of health state, it had originally been envisaged that all respondents would have continuing care needs but this information was not available to define the sample. Any difference in self-assessed health state (which was only ascertained at interview) however provided an additional dimension to the analysis as a possible association with user experience and behaviour.

The snowball method of sampling health and social care professionals was used exhaustively. That is until no new job titles, a representative of which would have a bearing on or knowledge of the discharge process of elderly people, were emerging. As such, confidence can be expressed that the professionals interviewed represented all those (and their line managers) that elderly people may come into contact with regarding their discharge from hospital and in the period shortly afterwards.

The data from the three sources were compared and consolidated thoroughly during the analysis phase of this study in order to comprehensively meet the research aims. The variety of sources and types of data meant that the experience and behaviour of service users during the processes of hospital discharge could be reported as well as possible explanations provided. The findings were discussed in relation to the key themes to emerge. This demonstrates a commitment to allowing the data to form the framework for discussing the overall implications of the research in addition to building upon the analytical framework to demonstrate an original contribution to knowledge.

Main Conclusions

The findings of this study and the subsequent discussion provide convincing evidence of a variety of ways in which elderly users of health and social care assumed an active role during and in the short period after discharge from inpatient care. There was evidence of both a user-oriented approach to the delivery of care and of service users being able and willing to assume an active role. That is, opportunities were being provided for service users to assume an active role in aspects relating to their discharge and subsequent care delivery and service users were taking these opportunities in addition to creating additional opportunities. Fundamentally, the diversity of the elderly population was apparent in both of these aspects with some respondents appearing to be both provided with greater opportunities to assume an active role and more willing and able to assume such a role.

The study revealed three broad categories of people: people who did not wish to receive statutory care, including those who declined that which was offered; people who accepted the services that were offered, not wishing to play an active role and people who wished for a higher level of care but were unable to obtain it. Important differences were revealed between these three categories in terms of participation in decision making, access to services and choice of services. The first group were found to be in the strongest position in these aspects although this was sometimes by default. The reasons for declining to receive care were due to other sources of care being available (both private and informal) and out of a desire for independence. It was suggested that these respondents had exercised their right to 'exit' although not necessarily as a result of dissatisfaction with statutory care. Respondents with private sources of care available were mainly in receipt of a pension other than the state retirement pension whilst those with informal care available mainly lived with others. Males were shown to be over-represented compared to females on both of these factors.

The group which accepted the services that were offered were the most passive and displayed a desire for paternalistic care. Although some of these respondents were found to accept the opportunities for participation and choice that were offered to them and the information that was offered to them, they wished professionals to make any decisions. In addition, this group of people displayed no desire to create opportunities to assume an active role.

It may be that the group who wished for a higher level of care could be the most willing and able to assume an active role in that they recognised there was scope for their situation to be improved. However they were ultimately the least likely to have any influence and were likely to be the least satisfied with care delivery demonstrating how users are still dependent upon service providers for their wishes to be fulfilled.

Discussion of the findings suggested that there was a key role for professional agents in health and social care in both providing service users with opportunities to play an active role and in supporting them in assuming such a role. Amongst service users there appeared a desire for a single contact point across both health and social care, usually a GP or social worker, for attempting to access services, to obtain information and to ascertain the complaints procedure. Whilst such a situation was not always apparent, it suggests a desire for seamless care which in turn entails notions of paternalistic care. It was also suggested that agents may have other loyalties to consider and financial motives were found to be a factor determining the extent to which they represent users' views. It was proposed that there may be a role for independent advocates to represent users' interests to service providers.

A role was highlighted for informal carers or contacts in representing service users or otherwise supporting them in the process of hospital discharge including identifying professional contact points or sources of information. Whilst such people may fulfil an advocacy or even an agency role, their knowledge of available services may be insufficient to be effective in actually securing care.

The persisting divide between health and social care was apparent in a number of aspects of users assuming an active role. It was suggested that it is easier for lay people to assess their own needs for social care and determine appropriate service delivery than is the case for health care. In addition services to meet 'social' needs appeared easier to access independently of the statutory sector than purely medical services. These factors are also given as reasons for less emphasis being placed on the identity of agents of social care compared to health care. Users independently accessing social care (mainly domestic cleaning) was the clearest example in this study of users actively seeking to secure services in response to perceived need.

Past experience of receiving care must also be seen as a factor in clarity of contact points, sources of information and so on and it was suggested that probable greater experience of receiving health services explained the differences in emphasis between agents in health compared to social care. Past experience can also be discussed in terms of social inequality in that women and people in lower socio-economic groups suffer higher levels of morbidity at all ages and so have greater contact with providers of care services than males and members of higher socio-economic groups. However they were found to be the least likely groups both to be provided with opportunities to play an active role and to be willing and able to do so. Possible explanations for this include that past experience has been of mainly paternalistic care which has formed their expectations for playing a passive role and that ill health has affected their ability and willingness to become involved. Ill health was in fact found to have a downward effect on users being involved in decisions about their care.

Paternalism and consumerism were discussed as the two extremes of the user-provider relationship and whilst neither was wholly apparent, there were elements of each in evidence. This was mainly in the extent to which service users and providers perceived opportunities for users to have input into decision making, ways in which users perceived responsibilities for determining and securing appropriate service provision and ways in which users sought out information.

Application of a model of decision making derived from the private sector focused on the identification of need and then the evaluation and choice of options to satisfy need. Information was central to this process, both the extent to which it was provided by professionals and how far users actively sought it out. This model was discussed in relation to the ranges of experience and behaviour revealed from users not wishing to play an active role to those securing care independently of service providers.

The Critical Case Approach

The sample of service users in this study was defined in the analytical framework as a 'critical case'. That is, by virtue of their age (70 years and over) and assumptions regarding health state, dependency and income they were assumed the *least* likely to adopt an active role in their care. Following this assumption to its conclusion, the evidence revealed of user-oriented services and users assuming an active role therefore suggests there are good grounds for assuming an even wider application within the general population. That is, in those areas in which service users played an active role, this could be extrapolated with some certainty to sections of the wider population. On aspects of care in which no evidence was revealed of service users playing an active role, no conclusions could be drawn about the wider population.

Discussion of the findings however interpreted social status and social inequality as the most powerful determinants of users playing an active role, including being provided with opportunities to do so. It is perhaps more meaningful therefore to view elderly people as simply a section of society containing all the same differences and values as any other age group due to differing experiences throughout life. Indeed it is possible that with the age group under study, these differences and values are more pronounced due to experience over a greater number of years. In addition, values relating to the traditional role of females in the home and in the workplace are more likely to be prevalent in this age group. Such values were interpreted in this study as impacting upon the ability and willingness of females to assume an active role. With changing employment patterns and domestic roles for males and females, such 'traditional' values are less likely to be held by younger age groups.

The inconsistency of findings on distinguishing between 'young elderly' people and 'old elderly' people further supports these interpretations and conclusions as to the relative insignificance of 'age'. Social differentiation in terms of gender, socio-economic grouping, self-reported health state and household circumstances were found to be significantly associated with different aspects of user experience and behaviour. However it was also recognised that these factors are related to such a degree that it is difficult to separate them and draw definite conclusions as to which is producing the largest effect. The life course approach was therefore advocated as taking into account the continuity and change experienced throughout life rather than viewing 'old age' as a static phase to be experienced uniformly regardless of gender and socio-economic group. Returning to the idea of a critical case, it would follow that any extrapolation to other age groups would be most accurate on the basis of social status.

Reconsideration of Aims

The broad aim of this study was exploratory. It sought to investigate service utilisation and participation during and in the short period after discharge from inpatient care among a sample of people aged 70 years and over. This was to be explored using six criteria indicating user influence or control and from the perspective of both service users and health and social care professionals. The two key elements explored were the extent to which service users were provided with opportunities to play an active role in using health and social care and the extent to which they were willing and able to adopt such a role. Barriers to both or either of these elements were also explored.

The research approach adopted enabled these areas to be explored both quantitatively and qualitatively to the extent that the aims were comprehensively addressed and met (see 'The Research Approach' above). The nature of the postal quantitative survey distributed to service users meant that initial themes were explored and determined within a framework defined by the researcher. The semi-structured qualitative approach however permitted more flexibility in comprehensively exploring the issues and in determining themes from the point of view of respondents (both service users and professionals).

The six criteria were explored thoroughly in all aspects of decision-making around hospital discharge and subsequent service use with both service users and with health and social care professionals. No consensus was reached however as to the experience of service use by this age group or to the extent to which opportunities were provided for users to assume an active role. This was due to both differences in the level of service use, as a result of health state, and differences in social status across the sample. As such, although evidence was certainly revealed of services being provided in a user-oriented way as stipulated in the policy guidelines, and with all six criteria apparent to some extent, there was no uniformity across the sample.

In the exploration of service users' attitude towards assuming an active role and their subsequent behaviour in using health and social care, a range of examples was again revealed such that no consensus was apparent. This was partially explained as related to health experience determining the level of service use. More importantly however, differences in social status appeared to govern both the ability and willingness of users to assume an active role.

In exploring both of these areas, barriers to both the implementation of user-oriented services and the adoption of an active role by service users were revealed such that the final aim was addressed. This was explicitly addressed with health and social care professionals and more implicitly with service users.

Areas for Further Study

This study explored the extent to which elderly people were provided with opportunities to assume an active role in the use of health and social care during and in the short period after discharge from inpatient care. It also explored how far users were able and willing to assume such a role. It was presented in the analytical framework that such outcomes may be encouraged and facilitated by the policy initiatives introduced mainly in the later part of the 1979-1997 period of Conservative governance. At the time of completion of this work, the 'internal market' in health care has been abolished by the new Labour government which took office in May 1997 (Department of Health, 1997a). Changing policy means that whilst services that are responsive and accessible to those who seek to use them remains an important aim, future research on the outcomes of policy must take place within the framework of specific policy initiatives. Given the passage of legislation promoting collaboration between NHS and Social Services departments and enabling the pooling of budgets, joint assessments and increasingly 'seamless' care is now a more distinct reality. This scenario makes it easier for service users, at least in theory, to become pro-active since they will interface with smaller numbers of health and social care professionals, arguably increasing their sense of control.

This study demonstrated clearly the importance of all of the six principles and the associations with various characteristics of respondents which were explored. Broadly there is the potential for further research into any one of the six principles. A further focus, given the continuing government rhetoric about the prominence of the service user in care delivery, could be the inter-relationships between these principles, for example, information and choice or participation and choice. In any future study which considers social status and differentiation, changing demographic and socio-economic trends must also be borne in mind. These include women's employment patterns and entitlement to occupational or private pensions in their own right.

Alternatively, more specific categories of discharge could be used to compile the sample, for example, people discharged from specific wards or having undergone specific procedures. Whilst this may ensure a more homogeneous group, most probably in terms of health state, scope for considering social and economic differentials may be maintained. Indeed, as a number of associations between self-reported health state and user experience and behaviour were apparent in this study, the impact of health state on assuming an active role warrants further investigation. This study only ascertained self reports of health state at the time of study and then only from interviewees. Any further study could ascertain such reports from all respondents thus permitting greater analysis around the impact of health state on user experience and behaviour. Health state could also be explored in terms of whether the illness or disability was long-standing or of a more acute nature.

Related to health state must be the level and frequency of contact with individual providers of health and social care. The discussion of this study made a number of assumptions regarding an individual's contact with providers of care on the basis of gender, socio-economic group and self-reported health state. This was then interpreted as having implications for users' familiarity with service providers and systems of service provision which may affect their ability to assume an active role. Future studies could record such variables as actual contact with health and social care services, frequency of contact and length of time in hospital to consider possible associations with user experience and behaviour. Any likely future health related trends, for example, any increase in long-standing illness must also therefore be relevant to future studies.

Addressing the House of Commons on the day that the new Health and Social Care Bill was published, Health Minister John Denham stated that this Bill:

> ... will put patients at the very heart of the NHS, giving them a voice at every level, and ensuring that they are involved in decisions made about their local health services. The NHS Plan signalled the way forward for greater patient involvement in the modern NHS – this Bill is about making that happen (Department of Health Press Release 2000/0752; 21/12/2000).

There is no doubt that the New Labour government which was returned to power in May 1997 views public involvement and participation in health and social care as an important component of 'modernisation'. The message from this particular empirical study is that whilst the foundations for greater participation have been considerably strengthened, the great cultural transformation envisaged is likely to take decades before it approaches realisation.

Bibliography

Aaker, D.A. and Day, G.S. (eds.) (1974). *Consumerism: Search for the Consumer Interest.* New York: The Free Press.

Abramson, J.S. (1988). Participation of Elderly Patients in Discharge Planning: Is Self-Determination a Reality? *Social Work*, Sept-Oct, 443-48.

Adams, R. (1996). *The Personal Social Services.* London: Longman.

Alcock, P. (1993). *Understanding Poverty.* Basingstoke: Macmillan.

Allen, I. (ed.) (1990). *Care Managers and Care Management.* London: Policy Studies Institute.

Allen, I., Hogg, D. and Peace, S. (1992). *Elderly People: Choice, Participation and Satisfaction.* London: Policy Studies Institute.

Allsop, J. (1989). Health. *In* M. McCarthy (ed.) (1989), *The New Politics of Welfare: An Agenda for the 1990s?* London: Macmillan.

Allsop, J. (1995). *Health Policy and the NHS: Towards 2000.* London: Longman.

Arber, S. (1996). Is Living Longer Cause for Celebration? *Health Service Journal*, July 18, 28-31.

Arber, S. and Evandrou, M. (1993). Mapping the Territory: Ageing, Independence and the Life Course. *In* S. Arber and M. Evandrou (eds.) (1993), *Ageing, Independence and the Life Course.* London: Jessica Kingsley Publishers Ltd.

Arber, S. and Ginn, J. (1991). *Gender and Later Life.* London: Sage Publications.

Arber, S. and Ginn, J. (1993a). Gender and Inequalities in Later Life, *Social Science and Medicine*, 36, 33-46.

Arber, S. and Ginn, J. (1993b). Class, Caring and the Life Course. *In* S. Arber and M. Evandrou (eds.) (1993), *Ageing, Independence and the Life Course.* London: Jessica Kingsley Publishers Ltd.

Arber, S., Gilbert, G.N. and Evandrou, M. (1988). Gender, household composition and receipt of domiciliary services by elderly disabled people, *Journal of Social Policy*, 17 (2), 153-175.

Armitage, S.K. and Kavanagh, K.M. (1998). Consumer-oriented outcomes in discharge planning: a pilot study, *Journal of Clinical Nursing*, 7, 67-74.

Arnstein, S.R. (1969). Ladder of Citizen Participation, *Journal of the American Institute of Planners*, 35, 216-24.

Ashton, J. and Seymour, H. (1988). *The New Public Health.* Milton Keynes: Open University Press.

Askham, J., Barry, C., Grundy, E., Hancock, R. and Tinker, A. (1992). *Life After 60: A Profile of Britain's Older People.* London: Gerontology Data Service, Age Concern Institute of Gerontology, King's College.

Audit Commission (1992). *Community Care: Managing the Cascade of Change.* London: HMSO.

Avis, M. (1994). Choice cuts: an exploratory study of patients views about participation in decision-making in a day case surgery, *International Journal of Nursing Studies*, 31 (3), 289-298.

Bailey, R. and Brake, M. (eds.) (1975). *Radical Social Work.* London: Edward Arnold.

Barker, P.J. (1991). Interview. *In* DFS. Cormack (ed.) (1991), *The Research Process in Nursing.* London: Blackwell Scientific Publications.

Barnes, M. and Cormie, J. (1995). On the Panel, *Health Service Journal* (March 2), 30-31.

Barnes, M. and Wistow, G. (1992a). Understanding User Involvement. *In* M. Barnes and G. Wistow (eds.) (1992), *Researching User Involvement.* Leeds: Nuffield Institute for Health Services Studies.

Barnes, M. and Wistow, G. (1992b). Researching User Involvement: Contributions to Learning and Methods. *In* M. Barnes and G. Wistow (eds.) (1992), *Researching User Involvement.* Leeds: Nuffield Institute for Health Services Studies.

Barnes, M., Prior, D. and Thomas, N. (1990). Social Services. *In* N. Deakin and A. Wright (eds.) (1990), *Consuming Public Services.* London: Routledge.

Barr, N., Glennerster, H. and Le Grand, J. (1989). Working for Patients? The Right Approach? *Social Policy and Administration*, 23 (2), 117-127.

Bartlett, W. and Le Grand, J. (1993). The Performance of Trusts. *In* R. Robinson and J. Le Grand (eds.) (1993), *Evaluating the NHS Reforms.* London: King's Fund Institute.

Bartlett, W., Propper, C., Wilson, D. and Le Grand, J. (eds.) (1994). *Quasi-Markets in the Welfare State: The Emerging Findings.* Bristol: School for Advanced Urban Studies.

Bates, E. (1983). *Health Systems and Public Scrutiny: Australia, Britain and the United States.* Beckenham: Croom Helm Ltd.

Beisecker, A.E. (1988). Aging and the Desire for Information and Input in Medical Decisions: Patient Consumerism in Medical Encounters, *The Gerontologist*, 28, 330-35.

Beisecker, A. and Beisecker, T. (1993). Using Metaphors to Characterize Doctor-Patient Relationships: Paternalism versus Consumerism, *Health Communication*, 5, 41-58.

Bellamy, R. and Greenaway, J. (1995). The New Right Conception of Citizenship and the Citizen's Charter, *Government and Opposition*, 30 (4), 469-491.

Beveridge, W. (1942). *Report on Social Insurance and Allied Services.* London: HMSO.

Biley, F.C. (1992). Some determinants that affect patient participation in decision-making about nursing care, *Journal of Advanced Nursing*, 17 (4), 414-421.

Black, D. (1984). A Medical View. *In* R. Maxwell and N. Weaver (eds.) (1984), *Public Participation in Health.* London: King's Fund.

Blane, D., Brunner, E. and Wilkinson, R. (eds.) (1996). *Health and Social Organisations*. London: Routledge.

Blaxter, M. (1990). *Health and Lifestyles*. London: Tavistock/Routledge.

Blaxter, M. (1995). *Consumer Issues Within the NHS*. Leeds: Department of Health.

Bloor, M. (1997). Techniques of Validation in Qualitative Research: A Critical Commentary. *In* G. Miller and R. Dingwall (eds.) (1997), *Context and Method in Qualitative Research*. London: Sage Publications.

Boaden, N., Goldsmith, M., Hampton, W. and Stringer, P. (1982). *Participation in Local Services*. Harlow: Longman.

Bond, J. and Coleman, P. (eds.) (1990). *Ageing in Society: An Introduction to Social Gerontology*. London: Sage Publications.

Boniface, D.R. and Denham, M.J. (1997). Factors Influencing the Use of Community Health and Social Services By Those Aged 65 and Over, *Health and Social Care in the Community*, 5 (1), 48-54.

Booth, C. (1889). *Life and Labour of the People of London*. London: Macmillan.

Booth, T. (1993). Obstacles to the development of user-centred services. *In* J. Johnson and R. Slater (eds.) (1993), *Ageing and Later Life*. London: Sage Publications.

Boufford, J.I. (1994). *Shifting the Balance from Acute to Community Health Care*. London: Kings Fund College.

Bowl, R. (1996). Involving Service Users in Mental Health Services: Social Services Departments and the NHS and Community Care Act 1990, *Journal of Mental Health*, 5, 287-303.

Bowling, A., Farquhar, M. and Browne, P. (1991). Use of Services in Old Age: Data from Three Surveys of Elderly People, *Social Science and Medicine*, 33 (6), 689-700.

Bowsher, J., Bramlett, M., Burnside, I.M. and Gueldner, S.H. (1993). Methodological Considerations in the Study of Frail Elderly People, *Journal of Advanced Nursing*, 18, 873-79.

Brake, M. and Bailey, R. (eds.) (1980). *Radical Social Work and Practice*. London: Edward Arnold.

Brannen, J. (1992a). Introduction. *In* J. Brannen (ed.) (1992), *Mixing Methods: Qualitative and Quantitative Research*. Aldershot: Avebury.

Brannen, J. (ed.) (1992). *Mixing Methods: Qualitative and Quantitative Research*. Aldershot: Avebury.

Brearley, S. (1990). *Patient Participation: the literature*. Harrow: Scutari Press.

Breemharr, B., Visser, A. and Kleijnen, J.G.V.M. (1990). Perceptions and behaviour among elderly hospital patients: Description and explanation of age differences in satisfaction, knowledge, emotions and behaviour, *Social Science and Medicine*, 31 (12), 1377-1385.

Brewer, J. and Hunter, A. (1989). *Multimethod Research: A Synthesis of Styles*. London: Sage Publications.

Brody, D.S. (1980). The Patient's Role in Clinical Decision-Making, *Annals of Internal Medicine*, 93, 718-722.

Brownlea, A. (1987). Participation: Myths, Realities and Prognosis, *Social Science and Medicine*, 25 (6), 605-614.

Bryman, A. (1988). *Quantity and Quality in Social Research*. London: Routledge.

Bryman, A. and Cramer, D. (1997). *Quantitative Data Analysis With SPSS for Windows*. London: Routledge.

Burgess, RG. (1984). *In the Field: An Introduction to Fieldwork*. London: Allen and Unwin.

Bury, M. (1988). Arguments About Ageing: Long Life and Its Consequences. *In* N. Wells and C. Freer (eds.) (1988), *The Ageing Population: Burden or Challenge?* London: The Macmillan Press Limited.

Bury, M. and Macnicol, J. (1990a). Introduction. *In* M. Bury and J. Macnicol (eds.) (1988), *Aspects of Ageing: Essays On Social Policy and Old Age*. Egham, Surrey: Department of Social Policy and Social Science, Royal Holloway and Bedford New College.

Bury, M. and Macnicol, J. (eds.) (1990). *Aspects of Ageing: Essays on Social Policy and Old Age*. Egham, Surrey: Department of Social Policy and Social Science, Royal Holloway and Bedford New College.

Buskirk, R.H. and Rothe, J.T. (1970). Consumerism – An Interpretation, *Journal of Marketing*, 34, (October), 61-65.

Butcher, T. (1995). *Delivering Welfare: The Governance of the Social Services in the 1990s*. Buckingham: Open University Press.

Butler, A. (1990). Research Ethics and Older People. *In* S.M. Peace (ed.) (1990), *Researching Social Gerontology: Concepts, Methods and Issues*. London: Sage Publications.

Butler, J. (1992). *Patients, Policies and Politics: Before and After Working for Patients*. Buckingham: Open University Press.

Butler, J. (1994). Origins and early development. *In* R. Robinson and J. Le Grand (eds.) (1994), *Evaluating the NHS Reforms*. London: King's Fund.

Butler, R.N. (1969). Age-Ism: Another Form of Bigotry, *The Gerontologist*, 9, 243-46.

Butler, R.N. (1987). Ageism. *In Encyclopedia of Ageing*. New York: Springer.

Bynoe, I. (1996). *Beyond the Citizen's Charter: New Directions for Social Rights*. London: Institute of Public Policy Research.

Bytheway, B. (1995). *Ageism*. Buckingham: Open University Press.

Bytheway, B. and Johnson, J. (1990). On Defining Ageism, *Critical Social Policy*, 10, 27-39.

Cahill, J. (1998). Patient Participation – a review of the literature, *Journal of Clinical Nursing*, 7, 119-128.

Calnan, M. and Gabe, J. (1991). Recent developments in general practice: a sociological analysis. *In* J. Gabe, M. Calnan and M. Bury (eds.) (1991), *The Sociology of the Health Service*. London: Routledge.

Carnegie UK Trust (1993). *Life, Work and Livelihood in the Third Age.* Dunfermline, Fife: Carnegie UK Trust.

Carr-Hill, R.A. (1992). The Measurement of Patient Satisfaction, *Journal of Public Health Medicine*, 14, 236-49.

Cervi, B. (1996). Collision Course, *Health Service Journal* (October 24), 14-15.

Chandler, J. (1997). The Citizen's Charter: Empowering Users or Providers? A Rejoinder, *Review of Policy Issues*, 3(4), 35-39.

Chapman, T. and Jack, B. (1996). The discharge of elderly patients from hospital, *Reviews in Clinical Gerontology*, 6, 241-247.

Chapman, T. and Johnson, A. (1995). *Growing Old and Needing Care.* Aldershot: Avebury.

Charny, M., Klein, R., Lewis, P.A. and Tipping, G.K. (1990). Britain's New Market Model of General Practice: Do Consumers Know Enough to Make It Work? *Health Policy*, 14, 243-52.

Childress, J.F and Siegler, M. (1984). Metaphors and Models in Doctor-Patient Relationships: Their Implications for Autonomy, *Theoretical Medicine*, 5, 17-30.

Clarke, J. and Langan, M. (1993). Restructuring Welfare: The British Welfare Regime in the 1980s. *In* A. Cochrane and J. Clarke (eds.) (1993), *Comparing Welfare States: Britain in International Context.* London: Sage Publiations.

Clarke, J. and Newman, J. (1997). *The Managerial State.* London: Sage Publications.

Clarke, J., Cochrane, A. and McLoughlin, E. (1994). *Managing Social Policy.* London: Sage.

Clayton, S. (1988). Patient Participation: an underdeveloped concept, *Journal of the Royal Society of Health*, 2, 55-56.

Cohen, G. (1996). Age and Health Status in a Patient Satisfaction Survey, *Social Science and Medicine*, 42, 1085-93.

Colebatch, H.K. (1998). *Policy.* Buckingham: Open University Press.

Coleman, P. and Bond, J. (1990). Ageing in the Twentieth Century. *In* J. Bond and P. Coleman (eds.) (1990), *Ageing in Society: An Introduction to Social Gerontology.* London: Sage Publications.

Connolly, M., McKeown, P. and Milligan-Byrne, G. (1994). Making the Public Sector More User Friendly? A Critical Examination of the Citizen's Charter, *Parliamentary Affairs*, 47 (1), 23-26.

Conservative Party (1979). *The Conservative Manifesto 1979.* London: Conservative Central Office.

Corner, J. (1991). In Search of More Complete Answers to Research Questions. Quantitative Versus Qualitative Research Methods: Is There a Way Forward? *Journal of Advanced Nursing*, 16, 718-27.

Cornwell, J. (1993). *The Consumer's View: Elderly People and Community Health Services.* London: King's Fund Centre.

Cowgill, D.O. and Holmes, L.D. (1972). *Ageing and Modernisation.* New York: Appleton-Century-Crofts.

Cox, B., Blaxter, D.M., Buckle, A.L.J., Fenner, N.P., Golding, J.F., Gore, M., Huppert, F.A., Nickson, J., Roth, M., Stark, J., Wadsworth, M.E.J. and Whichelow, M. (1987). *The Health and Lifestyle Survey: Preliminary Report.* London: The Health Promotion Research Trust.

Cramer, D. (1994). *Introducing Statistics for Social Research.* London: Routledge.

Croft, S. and Beresford, P. (1989). User-involvement, citizenship and social policy, *Critical Social Policy,* 26, 5-18.

Croft, S. and Beresford, P. (1990). *From Paternalism to Participation: Involving People in Social Services.* London: Open Services Project and Joseph Rowntree Foundation.

Croft, S. and Beresford, P. (1992). The Politics of Participation, *Critical Social Policy,* 35, 20-44.

Culyer, A.J. (1989). The normative economics of health care finance and provision, *Oxford Review of Economic Policy,* 5, 34-58.

Cumming, E. and Henry, W.E. (1961). *Growing Old: The Process of Disengagement.* New York: Basic Books.

Dahl, R.A. (1956). *A Preface to Democratic Theory.* Chicago: University of Chicago Press.

Deakin, N. (1994). *The Politics of Welfare: continuities and change.* New York: Harvester Wheatsheaf.

Deakin, N. and Wright, A. (1990). Introduction. *In* N. Deakin and A. Wright (eds.) (1990), *Consuming Public Services.* London: Routledge.

Dempsey, P.A. and Dempsey, A.D. (1992). *Nursing Research With Basic Statistical Applications.* Boston: Jones and Bartlett Publishers.

Denzin, N.K. (1989). *The Research Act.* London: Prentice Hall.

Department of Health (1986). *Primary Care: An Agenda for Discussion.* London: HMSO.

Department of Health (1987). *Promoting Better Health.* London: HMSO.

Department of Health (1989a). *Working for Patients.* London: HMSO.

Department of Health (1989b). *Caring for People.* London: HMSO.

Department of Health (1989c). *HC (89) 5 Discharge of Patients from Hospital.* London: HMSO.

Department of Health (1989d). *Discharge of Patients from Hospital.* London: HMSO.

Department of Health (1990). *National Health Service and Community Care Act 1990.* London: HMSO.

Department of Health (1991). *The Patient's Charter.* London: HMSO.

Department of Health (1994a). *A Framework for Local Community Care Charters in England.* London: Department of Health.

Department of Health (1994b). *Hospital Discharge Workbook: A Manual of Hospital Discharge Practice.* London: Department of Health.

Department of Health (1995a). *The Patient's Charter and You.* London: HMSO.

Department of Health (1995b). *HSG (95) 8 NHS Responsibilities for Meeting Continuing Care Needs.* London: HMSO.

Department of Health (1995c). *HSG (95) 39 NHS Responsibilities for Meeting Health Care Needs. Discharge from NHS Inpatient Care of People With Continuing Health or Social Care Needs: Arrangements for Reviewing Decisions On Eligibility for NHS Continuing Inpatient Care.* London: HMSO.

Department of Health (1995d). *Community Care (Direct Payments) Bill.* London: HMSO.

Department of Health (1996a). *Choice and Opportunity. Primary Care: The Future.* London: HMSO.

Department of Health (1996b). *Health and Personal Social Services Statistics for England.* London: Government Statistical Service.

Department of Health (1997a). *The New NHS: Modern, Dependable.* London: HMSO.

Department of Health (1997b). *Press Release: 8th Wave Fundholding Deferred.* London: Department of Health.

Department of Health and Social Security (1981). *Growing Older.* London: HMSO.

Department of Health and Social Security Welsh Office (1979). *Patients First: Consultative Paper on the Structure and Management of the NHS in England and Wales.* London: HMSO.

Dixon, P. and Carr-Hill, R.A. (1989). *Consumer Satisfaction Surveys: A Review. The NHS and Its Customers.* York: Centre for Health Economics.

Doern, G.B. (1993). The UK Citizen's Charter: Origins and Implementation in Three Agencies, *Policy and Politics*, 21, 17-29.

Domarad, B.R. and Buschmann, M.T. (1995). Interviewing Older Adults: Increasing the Credibility of Interview Data, *Journal of Gerontological Nursing*, September, 14-20.

Donaldson, C., Lloyd, P. and Lupton, D. (1991). Primary Health Care Consumerism Amongst Elderly Australians, *Age and Ageing*, 20, 280-86.

Dowse, R.E. and Hughes, J.A. (1986). *Political Sociology.* 2nd edition. Chichester: John Wiley and Sons Ltd.

Doyal, L. (1994). Changing Medicine? Gender and the Politics of Health Care. *In* J. Gabe, D. Kelleher and G. Williams (eds.) (1994), *Challenging Medicine.* London: Routledge.

Doyal, L. and Elston, M.A. (1986). Women, Health and Medicine. *In* V. Beechey and E. Whitelegg (eds.) (1986), *Women in Britain Today.* Milton Keynes: Open University Press.

Drewry, G. (1993). Mr Major's Charter: empowering the consumer, *Public Law*, Summer, 248-256.

Ehrenreich, J. (1978). *The Cultural Crisis of Modern Medicine.* Monthly Review Press.

Elston, M.A. (1991). The Politics of Professional Power: Medicine in a Changing Health Service. *In* J. Gabe, M. Calnan and M. Bury (eds.) (1991), *The Sociology of the Health Service*. London: Routledge.

Engel, J.F., Blackwell, R.D. and Miniard, P.W. (1990). *Consumer Behaviour*. Florida, USA: The Dryden Press.

England, H. (1986). *Social Work as Art: Making Sense for Good Practice*. London: Allen and Unwin.

Estes, C.L., Swan, J.S. and Gerard, L.E. (1982). Dominant and competing paradigms in Gerontology: Towards a Political Economy of Ageing, *Ageing and Society*, 2, 151-164.

Evans, J.G. (1996). Rewriting the Rules of the Ageing Game, *Economics, Medicines and Health*, Spring, 28-29.

Evans, J.G. (1997). The Rationing Debate. Rationing Health Care by Age: the case against, *British Medical Journal*, 314, 820-822.

Falconer, P., Ross, K. and Conner, M.H. (1997). The Citizen's Charter: Empowering Users or Providers? *Review of Policy Issues*, 3(3), 79-95.

Farnham, D. and Horton, S. (eds.) (1993). *Managing the New Public Services*. Basingstoke: The Macmillan Press.

Fawcett, J. and Downs, F.S. (1986). *The Relationship of Theory and Research*. Norwalk, Connecticut: Prentice Hall Inc.

Fennell, G., Phillipson, C. and Evers, H. (1988). *The Sociology of Old Age*. Milton Keynes: Open University Press.

Ferlie, E. (1994). The Evolution of Quasi-Markets in the NHS: Early Evidence. *In* W. Bartlett, C. Propper, D. Wilson and J. Le Grand (eds.) (1994), *Quasi-Markets in the Welfare State*. Bristol: School for Advanced Urban Studies.

Fielding, N.G. and Fielding, J.L. (1986). *Linking Data*. London: Sage Publications.

Fitzpatrick, R. and Hopkins, A. (1983). Problems in the Conceptual Framework of Patient Satisfaction Research: An Empirical Exploration, *Sociology of Health and Illness*, 5, 297-311.

Fletcher, D. (1996). Ageing Trend as Population Grows Older, *The Telegraph*, (February 16).

Flynn, F. (1990). *Public Sector Management*. Hemel Hempstead: Harvester Wheatsheaf.

Flynn, N. and Common, R. (1990). *Contracts for Community Care*. London: London Business School.

Forder, J., Knapp, M. and Wistow, G. (1996). Competition in the Mixed Economy of Care, *Journal of Social Policy*, 25, 201-21.

Foster, P. (1995). *Women and the Health Care Industry: An Unhealthy Relationship?* Buckingham: Open University Press.

Freer, C. (1988). Old Myths: Frequent Misconceptions about the Elderly. *In* N. Wells and C. Freer (eds.) (1988), *The Ageing Population: Burden or Challenge?* London: The Macmillan Press Ltd.

Freidson, E. (1970). *The Profession of Medicine: a study of the Sociology of Applied Knowledge*. New York: Harper and Row.

Fries, J.E. (1980). Ageing, natural death and the compression of morbidity, *New England Journal of Medicine*, 303, 3, 130-135.

Gabe, J., Calnan, M. and Bury, M. (1991). Introduction. *In* J. Gabe, M. Calnan and M. Bury (eds.) (1991), *The Sociology of the Health Service*. London: Routledge.

Gabe, J., Kelleher, D. and Williams, G. (eds.) (1994). *Challenging Medicine*. London: Routledge.

Gamble, A. (1987). *The Free Economy and the Strong State*. London: Pluto.

George, V. and Wilding, P. (1994). *Welfare and Ideology*. Harvester Wheatsheaf.

Giddens, A. (1984). *The Constitution of Society*. Cambridge: Polity Press.

Giddens, A. (1989). *Sociology*. Cambridge: Polity Press.

Glennerster, H. (1992). *British Medical Journal*, 304, 276.

Glennerster, H., Matsaganis, M., Owens, P. and Hancock, S. (1994). *Implementing GP Fundholding: Wild Card or Winning Hand?* Buckingham: Open University Press.

Goldsmith, W. and Clutterbuck, D. (1984). *The winning streak: Britain's top companies reveal their formulas for success*. London: Penguin Books.

Goldthorpe, J.H., Lockwood, D., Bechhafer, F. and Platt, J. (1971). *The Affluent Worker in the Class Structure*. Cambridge: Cambridge University Press.

Gough, M. (1990). The Economics of Ageing. *In* M. Bury and J. Macnicol (eds.) (1990), *Aspects of Ageing. Essays on Social Policy and Old Age*. Egham, Surrey: Department of Social Policy and Social Science, Royal Holloway and Bedford New College.

Green, D.G. (1987). *The New Right: The Counter-Revolution in Political, Economic and Social Thought*. Hemel Hempstead: Wheatsheaf Books.

Green, D. (1992). The NHS Reforms: From Ration-Book Collectivism to Market Socialism, *Economic Affairs*, 12, 12-17.

Greene, M., Adelman, G.R., Charon, R. and Hoffman, S. (1986). Ageism in the Medical Encounter: An Exploratory Study of the Doctor-Elderly Patient Relationship, *Language and Communication*, 6, 113-24.

Griffiths, R. (1983). *NHS Management Inquiry Report*. London: DHSS.

Griffiths, R. (1988a). *Community Care: Agenda for Action*. London: HMSO.

Griffiths, R. (1988b). Does the Public Service Serve? The Consumer Dimension, *Public Administration*, Summer, 66 (2).

Griffiths, R. (1990). Foreword. *In* S. Croft and P. Beresford (1990), *From Paternalism to Participation. Involving People in Social Services*. London: Open Services Project and Joseph Rowntree Foundation.

Groves, D. (1992) Occupational Pension Provision and Women's Poverty in Old Age. *In* C. Glendinning and J. Millar (eds.) (1992), *Women and Poverty in Britain: the 1990s*. London: Harvester Wheatsheaf.

Habermas, J. (1981). New Social Movements, *Telos*, 49, 33-37.

Hadley, R. and Hatch, S. (1981). *Social Welfare and the Failure of the State: Centralised Social Services and Participatory Alternatives*. London: George Allen and Unwin.

Hakim, C. (1987). *Research Design: Strategies and Choices in the Design of Social Research*. London: Unwin Hyman.

Ham, C. (1992). *Health Policy in Britain: The Politics and Organisation of the National Health Service*. Basingstoke: The Macmillan Press Ltd.

Ham, C. (1993). Power in Health Services. *In* M. Hill (ed.) (1993), *The Policy Process: A Reader*. Hemel Hempstead: Harvester Wheatsheaf.

Ham, C. (1994). *Management and Competition in the New NHS*. Oxford: Radcliffe Medical Press Ltd.

Ham, C. and Hill, M. (1993). *The Policy Process in the Modern Capitalist State*. 2nd edition. Hemel Hempstead: Harvester Wheatsheaf.

Hambleton, R. and Hoggett, P. (1987). Beyond Bureaucratic Paternalism. *In* P. Hoggett and R. Hambleton (eds.) (1987), *Decentralisation and Democracy: Localising Public Services*. Bristol: School for Advanced Urban Studies.

Hambleton, R. and Hoggett, P. (1993). Rethinking Consumerism in Public Services, *Consumer Policy Review*, 3 (2), 103-11.

Hambleton, R., Hoggett, P. and Toal, P. (1989). The Decentralisation of Public Services, *Local Government Studies*, 15, 1, 39-56.

Hampton, W. (1990). Planning. *In* N. Deakin and A. Wright (eds.) (1990), *Consuming Public Services*. London: Routledge.

Harris, D.K. (1990). *Sociology of Ageing*. New York: Harper Row.

Harrison, S. (1995). Clinical autonomy and planned markets: The British case. *In* R.B Saltman and C. von Otter (eds.) (1995), *Implementing Planned Markets in Health Care. Balancing Social and Economic Responsibility*. Buckingham: Open University Press.

Hart, J.T. (1971). The Inverse Care Law, *The Lancet*, 27 February, 1, 405-412.

Hart, N. (1985). *The Sociology of Health and Medicine*. Ormskirk: Causeway Press Ltd.

Hatch, S. (1984). Participation in Health. *In* R. Maxwell and N. Weaver (eds.) (1984), *Public Participation in Health*. London: King's Fund.

Haug, M. and Lavin, B. (1983). *Consumerism in Medicine: Challenging Physician Authority*. Beverly Hills: Sage Publications.

Haug, M.R. and Ory, M.G. (1987). Issues in Elderly Patient-Provider Interactions, *Research on Ageing*, 9 (1), 3-44.

Hayes, C. (1991). The White Paper and the Consumer, *Senior Nurse*, 11, 11-13.

Healthcare 2000 (1995). *UK Health and Healthcare Services: Challenges and policy options*. London: Healthcare 2000.

Held, D. (1987). *Models of Democracy*. Cambridge: Polity Press.

Held, D. and Pollitt, C. (1986). *New Forms of Democracy*. London: Sage.

Henwood, M. and Wistow, G. (1993). *Hospital discharge and community care: early days*. Nuffield Institute for Health: University of Leeds.

Hibbard, J.H. and Weeks, E.C. (1987). Consumerism in Health Care, *Medical Care*, 25, 1019-32.

Higgins, J. (1983). *Government and Urban Poverty: Inside the Policy-Making Process*. Oxford: Basil Blackwell.

Higgins, R. (1992). Consumerism and Participation, *Senior Nurse*, 12, 5, 3-4.

Higgs, P. (1995). Citizenship and Old Age: The End of the Road? *Ageing and Society*, 15, 535-50.

Hill, M. and Bramley, G. (1986). *Analysing Social Policy*. Oxford: Basil Blackwell Ltd.

Hirschman, A. (1970). *Exit, Voice and Loyalty: Responses to decline in firms, organisations and states*. Cambridge, Massachusetts: Harvard University Press.

HMSO (1991). *The Citizens Charter*. London: HMSO.

Hogg, C. (1990). Health. *In* N. Deakin and A. Wright (eds.) (1990), *Consuming Public Services*. London: Routledge.

Hogg, C. (1994). *Beyond the Patient's Charter: Working With Users*. London: Health Rights Ltd.

Hogwood, B.H. and Gunn, L.A. (1984). *Policy Analysis for the Real World*. Oxford: Oxford University Press.

Hood, C. (1991). A Public Management for All Seasons? *Public Administration*, 69, Spring, 3-19.

Horton, R. (1984). *Buyer Behaviour: A Decision-Making Approach*. Ohio: Charles E. Merrill Publishing Co.

Hudson, B. (1992). Quasi-Markets in Health and Social Care in Britain: Can the Public Sector Respond? *Policy and Politics*, 20, 131-42.

Hudson, B. (1994). *Making Sense of Quasi Markets in Health and Social Care*. Sunderland: Business Education Publishers Limited.

Hudson, B. (1998). Circumstances Change Cases: Local Government and the NHS, *Social Policy and Administration*, 32, 1, 71-86.

Hughes, B. (1995). *Older People and Community Care: Critical Theory and Practice*. Oxford: Oxford University Press.

Hunt, G. (1990). "Patient Choice" and the National Health Service Review, *Journal of Social Welfare Law*, 4, 245-55.

Hunter, D.J. (1989). First define your terms, *Health Service Journal*, 99, 1475.

Hunter, D.J. (1994). From tribalism to corporatism: the managerial challenge to medical dominance. *In* J. Gabe, D. Kelleher and G. Williams (eds.) (1994), *Challenging Medicine*. London: Routledge.

IHSM (1996). *IHSM Health and Social Services Yearbook 1996/97*. London: The Institute of Health Services Management.

Jefferys, M. (ed.) (1991). *Growing Old in the Twentieth Century*. London: Routledge.

Jefferys, M. and Thane, P. (1991). Introduction: An Ageing Society and Ageing People. *In* M. Jefferys (ed.) (1991), *Growing Old in the Twentieth Century*. London: Routledge.

Jenkins, B. (1993). Policy analysis: models and approaches. *In* M. Hill (ed.) (1993), *The Policy Process: A Reader*. Hemel Hempstead: Harvester Wheatsheaf.

Jennings, K. (1993). Rationing and Older People, *Critical Public Health*, 4 (1), 33-35.

Jerrome, D. (1990). Intimate Relationships. *In* J. Bond and P. Coleman (eds.) (1990), *Ageing in Society: An Introduction to Social Gerontology*. London: Sage Publications.

Jerrome, D. (1991). Loneliness: possibilities for intervention, *Journal of Ageing Studies*, 5 (2), 195-208.

Jessop, B. (1994). The Transition to post-Fordism and the Schumpterian workfare state. *In* R. Burrows and B. Loader (eds.) (1994), *Towards a Post-Fordist Welfare State?* London: Routledge.

Jobling, R. (1989). Health Care. *In* P. Brown and R. Sparks (eds.) (1989), *Beyond Thatcherism: Social Policy, Politics and Society*. Milton Keynes: Open University Press.

Johnson, M. (1990). Dependency and Interdependency. *In* J. Bond and P. Coleman (eds.) (1990), *Ageing in Society: An Introduction to Social Gerontology*. London: Sage Publications.

Johnson, N. (1989). The Privatisation of Welfare, *Social Policy and Administration*, 23 (1), 17-30.

Johnson, N. (1993). Welfare Pluralism: Opportunities and Risks. *In* A. Evers and I. Svetlik (eds.) (1993), *Balancing Pluralism: New Welfare Mixes in Care for the Elderly*. Aldershot: Avebury.

Johnson, P. (1987). *The Structured Dependency of the Elderly: A Critical Note*. London: Centre for Economic Policy Research.

Johnson, P. (1991). The Structured Dependency of the Elderly: A Critical Note. *In* M. Jefferys (ed.) (1991), *Growing Old in the Twentieth Century*. London: Routledge.

Johnson, P. and Falkingham, J. (1992). *Ageing and Economic Welfare*. London: Sage Publications.

Johnson, T.J. (1972). *Professions and Power*. London and Basingstoke: The Macmillan Press Ltd.

Johnson, T.J. (1977). The professions in a class structure. *In* R. Scase (ed.) (1977), *Industrial Society: Class, Cleavage and Control*. London: Allen Unwin.

Johnston, H., Larana, E. and Gusfield, J.R. (1994). Identities, Grievances and New Social Movements. *In* H. Johnston, E. Larana and J.R. Gusfield (1994), *New Social Movements: From Ideology to Identity*. Philadelphia: Temple University Press.

Jones, H. (1996). Autonomy and Paternalism: Partners or Rivals? *British Journal of Nursing*, 5 (6), 378-81.

Jones, K., Brown, J. and Bradshaw, J. (1978). *Issues in Social Policy*. London: Routledge and Kegan Paul.

Jones, R. (1994). The Citizen's Charter Programme: An Evaluation, Using Hirschman's Concepts of 'Exit' and 'Voice', *Review of Policy Issues*, 1(1), 43-55.

Kane, P. (1991). *Women's Health: From Womb to Tomb*. Basingstoke: The Macmillan Press Ltd.

Katona, G. (1960). *The Powerful Consumer*. London: McGraw-Hill Book Co Inc.

Keat, R. (1991). Introduction: Starship Britain or Universal Enterprise. *In* R. Keat and N. Abercrombie (eds.) (1991), *Enterprise Culture*. London: Routledge.

Kellaher, L., Peace, S. and Willcocks, D. (1990). Triangulating Data. *In* S.M. Peace (ed.) (1990), *Researching Social Gerontology: Concepts, Methods and Issues*. London: Sage Publications.

Kelleher, D. (1994). Self-help groups and their relationship to medicine. *In* J. Gabe, D. Kelleher and G. Wilkins (eds.) (1994), *Challenging Medicine*. London: Routledge.

Kennedy, D. (1996). NHS Internal Market an Illusion, Says Watchdog, *The Times*, 21/10/96.

Key, T. (1988). Contracting out auxiliary services. *In* R. Maxwell (ed.) (1988), *Reshaping the National Health Service*. London: Policy Journals.

King, D.S. (1987). *The New Right: Politics, Markets and Citizenship*. London: Macmillan.

Kirkpatrick, I. and Lucio, M.M. (eds.) (1995). *The Politics of Quality in the Public Sector; the Management of Change*. London: Routledge.

Klein, R. (1983). *The Politics of the National Health Service*. London: Longman.

Klein, R. (1984). The Politics of Participation. *In* R. Maxwell and N. Weaver (eds.) (1984), *Public Participation in Health*. London: King's Fund.

Klein, R. and Lewis, J. (1976). *The Politics of Consumer Representation: a study of CHCs*. London: Centre for Studies in Social Policy.

Komrad, M.S. (1983). A defence of medical paternalism: maximising patients' autonomy, *Journal of Medical Ethics*, 9, 38-44.

Laczko, F. and Phillipson, C. (1990). Defending the Right to Work: Age Discrimination in Employment. *In* E. McEwan (ed.) (1990), *Age: The Unrecognised Discrimination*. London: Age Concern.

Laing, W. and Hall, M. (1991). *The Challenges of Ageing*. London: Association of the British Pharmaceutical Industry.

Langan, M. and Clarke, J. (1994). Managing in the Mixed Economy of Care. *In* J. Clarke, A. Cochrane and E. McLoughlin (eds.) (1994), *Managing Social Policy*. London: Sage.

Langan, M. and Lee, P. (1989). Whatever Happened to Radical Social Work? *In* M. Langan and P. Lee (eds.) (1989), *Radical Social Work Today*. London: Unwin Hyman.

Laslett, P. (1987). The Emergence of the Third Age, *Ageing and Society*, 7, 133-60.

Le Grand, J. (1990). *Quasi Markets and Social Policy. Studies in Decentralisation and Quasi Markets No.1.* University of Bristol: School of Advanced Urban Studies.

Le Grand, J. (1991). Quasi markets and social policy, *The Economic Journal*, 101, 1256-1276.

Le Grand, J. (1993). *Quasi Markets and Community Care. Studies in Decentralisation and Quasi Markets No.17.* University of Bristol: School of Advanced Urban Studies.

Le Grand, J. and Robinson, R. (1984). *The Economics of Social Problems: The Market Versus the State.* Basingstoke: Macmillan.

Leat, D. (1990). Overcoming Voluntary Failure: Strategies for Change. *In* I. Sinclair, R. Parker, D. Leat and J. Williams (eds.) (1990), *The Kaleidoscope of Care: A Review of Research on Welfare Provision for Elderly People.* London: HMSO.

Leavey, R., Wilkin, D. and Metcalfe, D.H.H. (1989). Consumerism and General Practice, *British Medical Journal*, 298, 737-9.

Lees, D.S. (1965). Health through Choice: An Economic Study of the British National Health Service. *In* R. Harris (ed.) (1965), *Freedom or Free-For-All.* London: The Institute of Economic Affairs.

Leneman, L., Jones, L. and Maclean, U. (1986). *Consumer Feedback for the NHS: a literature review.* Department of Community Medicine: University of Edinburgh.

Levenson, R. (1992). Patients and the Market in Health Care, *Critical Public Health*, 3(1), 26-34.

Levitt, R. (1984). Health or health services: professional and public choices. *In* R. Maxwell and N. Weaver (eds.) (1984), *Public Participation in Health.* London: King's Fund.

Levitt, R., Wall, A. and Appleby, J. (1995). *The Reorganised National Health Service.* 5th ed. London: Chapman and Hall.

Lewis, J., Bernstock, P., Bovell, V. and Wookey, F. (1996). The Purchaser/Provider Split in Social Care: Is It Working? *Social Policy and Administration*, 30 (1), 1-19.

Lewis, N. (1993). The Citizen's Charter and Next Steps: A New Way of Governing? *The Political Quarterly*, 64 (3), 316-326.

Light, D.W. (1992). Equity and Efficiency in Health Care, *Social Science and Medicine*, 35, 465-69.

Lloyd, P. (1991). The Empowerment of Elderly People, *Journal of Aging Studies*, 5 (2), 125-135.

Lloyd, P., Lupton, D. and Donaldson, C. (1991), Consumerism in the Health Care Setting: An Exploratory Study of Factors Underlying the Selection and Evaluation of Primary Medical Services, *Australian Journal of Public Health*, 15, 194-201.

Loader, B. and Burrows, R. (1994). Towards a Post-Fordist Welfare State? The Restructuring of Britain, Social Policy and the Future of Welfare. *In* R. Burrows and B. Loader (eds.) (1994), *Towards a Post-Fordist Welfare State?* London: Routledge.

Lonsdale, S. (1990). *Women and Disability.* Basingstoke: Macmillan.

Lonsdale, S. (1992). Patterns of Paid Work. *In* C. Glendinning and J. Millar (eds.) (1992), *Women and Poverty in Britain: the 1990s.* London: Harvester Wheatsheaf.

Lookinland, S. and Anson, K. (1995). Perpetuation of Ageist Attitudes among Present and Future Health Care Personnel: Implications for Elder Care, *Journal of Advanced Nursing*, 21 (1), 47-56.

Lunt, N., Mannion, R. and Smith, P. (1996). Economic Discourse and the Market: The Case of Community Care, *Public Administration*, 74, 369-91.

Lupton, C., Peckham, S. and Taylor, P. (1998). *Managing Public Involvement in Healthcare Purchasing.* Buckingham: Open University Press.

Lupton, D., Donaldson, C. and Lloyd, P. (1991). Caveat Emptor or Blissful Ignorance? Patients and the Consumerist Ethos, *Social Science and Medicine*, 33, 559-68.

Macnicol, J. (1990). Old Age and Structured Dependency. *In* M. Bury and J. Macnicol (eds.) (1990), *Aspects of Ageing: Essays On Social Policy and Old Age.* Egham, Surrey: Department of Social Policy and Social Science, Royal Holloway and Bedford New College.

Marsh, D. and Rhodes, R.A.W. (1992). Implementing Thatcherism: Policy Change in the 1980s, *Parliamentary Affairs*, 45, 33-50.

Marshall, C. and Rossman, G.B. (1995). *Designing Qualitative Research.* 2nd Edition. London: Sage Publications Inc.

Martin, J., Meltzer, H. and Elliot, D. (1988). *The Prevalence of Disability in Great Britain. OPCS Surveys of Disability in Great Britain, Report 1.* London: HMSO.

Mason, J. (1994). Linking Qualitative and Quantitative data analysis. *In* A. Bryman and R.G. Burgess (eds.) (1994), *Analysing Qualitative Data.* London: Routledge.

Mason, J. (1996). *Qualitative Researching.* London: Sage Publications.

Matsaganis, M. and Glennerster, H. (1994). Cream-Skimming and Fundholding. *In* W. Bartlett, C. Propper, D. Wilson and J. Le Grand (eds.) (1994), *Quasi-Markets in the Welfare State.* Bristol: School for Advanced Urban Studies.

Maxwell, R. and Weaver, N. (1984). Introduction. *In* R. Maxwell and N. Weaver (eds.) (1984), *Public Participation in Health.* London: King's Fund.

McCarthy, M. (1992). Preventive Medicine and Health Promotion. *In* E. Beck, S. Lonsdale, S. Newman and D. Patterson (eds.) (1992), *In the Best of Health? The status and future of health care in the UK.* London: Chapman and Hall.

McCarthy, M. (ed.) (1989). *The New Politics of Welfare.* London: Macmillan.

McEwen, J., Martini, C.J.M. and Wilkins, N. (1983). *Participation in Health.* Beckenham: Croom Helm Ltd.

McKeown, T. (1976). *The Role of Medicine.* London: Nuffield Provincial Hospitals Trust.

Milbrath, L.W. (1965). *Political Participation: How and why do people get involved in politics?* Chicago: Rand McNally.

Miles, M.B. and Huberman, A. (1994). *Qualitative Data Analysis: A Sourcebook of New Methods.* Beverly Hills: Sage.

Millar, J. and Glendinning, C. (1989). Gender and Poverty, *Journal of Social Policy*, 18, 363-81.

Millerson, G.L. (1964). *The Qualifying Associations.* London: Routledge and Kegan Paul.

Milne, R. (1992). Competitive tendering of support services. *In* E. Beck, S. Lonsdale, S. Newman and D. Patterson (eds.) (1992), *In the Best of Health? The status and future of health care in the UK.* London: Chapman and Hall.

Mohan, J. (1991) Privatisation in the British health sector: a challenge to the NHS? *In* J. Gabe, M. Calnan and M. Bury (eds.) (1991), *The Sociology of the Health Service.* London: Routledge.

Moon, G. (1995). Demographic and Epidemiological Change. *In* G. Moon and R. Gillespie (eds.) (1995), *Society and Health: An Introduction to Social Science for Health Professionals.* London: Routledge.

Mooney, G. and Ryan, M. (1993). Agency in Health Care: Getting Beyond First Principles, *Journal of Health Economics*, 12, 125-35.

Morgan, M. (1980). Marital status, health, illness and service use, *Social Science and Medicine*, 14A, 633.

Moros, D.A. (1993). Consumerism Rampant: A Critique of the View of Medicine As a Commercial Enterprise, *Mount Sinai Journal of Medicine*, 60 (1), 15-19.

Mould, A., Vermont, R., Miles, J. and Gregory, J. (eds.) (1996). *Social Services Yearbook 1996.* London: Pitman Publishing London.

MRC (1994). *The Health of the UK's Elderly People.* London: Medical Research Council.

Mullen, P. (1993). Planning and Internal Markets. *In* P. Spurgeon (ed.) (1993), *The New Face of the NHS.* Harlow: Longman Group UK Ltd.

Munro, J. (1996). Working for Nobody, *Health Matters*, 25, 12-13.

Myers, F. and MacDonald, C. (1996). Power to the people? Involving users and carers in needs assessments and care planning – views from the practitioner, *Health and Social Care in the Community*, 4(2), 86-95.

NAHAT (1994). *Close to Home: Healthcare in the 21st century.* Birmingham: NAHAT.

NAHAT (1995a). *Rationing of Health Care.* Birmingham: NAHAT.

NAHAT (1995b). *Reshaping the NHS: strategies, priorities and resource allocation.* Buckingham: NAHAT.

National Consumer Council (1986). *Measuring Up: Consumer Assessment of Local Authority Services.* London: National Consumer Council.

National Consumer Council (1997). *Finding Out About NHS Continuing Care: A Consumer Perspective On Locally Published Information.* London: National Consumer Council.

National Institute of Social Work (1982). *Social Workers: their roles and tasks.* (Chairman PM Barclay). London: Bedford Square Press.

Navarro, V. (1976). *Medicine Under Capitalism.* New York: Prodist.

Navarro, V. (1986). *Crisis, Health and Medicine: A Social Critique.* London: Tavistock Publication.

Nelson, P. (1970). Information and Consumer Behaviour, *Journal of Political Economy*, 78, 311-29.

Neuberger, J. (1990). A Consumer's View. *In* D.G. Green (ed.) (1990), *The NHS Reforms: Whatever Happened to Consumer Choice?* London: The IEA Health and Welfare Unit.

NHS Executive (1994). *Developing NHS Purchasing and GP Fundholding: Towards a Primary Care-Led NHS.* London: Department of Health.

NHS Executive (1997). *NHS Priorities and Planning Guidance 1998/99.* London: Department of Health.

NHS Management Executive (1992). *Local Voices.* London: Department of Health.

O'Donovan, O. and Casey, D. (1995). Converting Patients into Consumers: Consumerism and the Charter of Rights for Hospital Patients, *Irish Journal of Sociology*, 5, 43-66.

Office for National Statistics (1996). *Family Spending: A Report of the 1995-95 Family Expenditure Survey.* London: The Stationery Office.

Office for National Statistics (1997a). *Social Trends 27: 1997 Edition.* London: The Stationery Office.

Office for National Statistics (1997b). *Living in Britain: Results from the 1995 General Household Survey.* London: The Stationery Office.

Oliver, M. (1990). *The Politics of Disablement.* London: Macmillan Education Ltd.

OPCS (1992). *Living in Britain: Results from the 1990 General Household Survey.* London: HMSO.

OPCS (1996). *Living in Britain: Results from the 1994 General Household Survey.* London: HMSO.

Oppenheim, A.N. (1992). *Questionnaire Design, Interviewing and Attitude Measurement.* London: Pinter Publishers.

Parker, R. (1993). Ideology and the Private Sector of Welfare. *In* J. Johnson and R. Slater (eds.) (1993), *Ageing and Later Life.* London: Sage Publications.

Parry, G. and Moyser, G. (1990). A Map of Political Participation in Britain, *Government and Opposition*, 19, 68-92.

Parry, G., Moyser, G. and Day, N. (1992). *Political Participation and Democracy in Britain.* Cambridge: Cambridge University Press.

Parsons, T. (1951). *The Social System.* London: Routledge and Kegan Paul.

Parston, G. (1988). General Management. *In* R. Maxwell (ed.) (1988), *Reshaping the National Health Service.* London: Policy Journals.

Pateman, C. (1970). *Participation and Democratic Theory.* Cambridge: Cambridge University Press.

Paton, C. (1996). *Health Policy and Management: The Health-Care Agenda in a British Political Context.* London: Chapman and Hall.

Paton, C. (1997). Counting the Costs, *Health Service Journal*, August 21, 24-27.

Patton, M.Q. (1990). *Qualitative Evaluation and Research Methods.* 2nd edition. London: Sage Publications.

Payne, S. (1991). *Women, Health and Poverty.* London: Harvester Wheatsheaf.

Pearson, P. (1997). Integrating Qualitative and Quantitative Data Analysis, *Nurse Researcher*, 4 (3), 69-80.

Pendleton, D.A. and Bochner, S. (1980). The Communication of Medical Information in General Practice Consultations as a Function of Patients' Social Class, *Social Science and Medicine*, 14A, 669-73.

Peters, T.J. and Waterman, R.H. (1982). *In Search of Excellence: Lessons from America's Best-Run Companies.* New York: Harper and Row.

Pfeffer, N. and Coote, A. (1991). *Is Quality Good For You?* London: Institute for Public Policy Research.

Phillipson, C. (1982). *Capitalism and the Construction of Old Age.* London: The Macmillan Press Ltd.

Phillipson, C. (1993). Approaches to Advocacy. *In* J. Johnson and R. Slater (eds.) (1993), *Ageing and Later Life.* London: Sage Publications.

Pierre, J. (1995). The Marketization of the State: Citizens, Consumers, and the Emergence of the Public Market. *In* B.G. Peters and D.J. Savoie (eds.) (1995), *Governance in a Changing Environment.* London: McGill Queen's University Press.

Pinker, R. (1992). Making Sense of the Mixed Economy of Welfare, *Social Policy and Administration*, 26 (4), 273-84.

Plamping, D. and Delamothe, T. (1991). The Citizen's Charter and the NHS, *British Medical Journal*, 303 (6796), 203-204.

Polit, D.F. and Hungler, B.P. (1993). *Essentials of Nursing Research: Methods, Appraisal and Utilization.* 3rd ed. Philadelphia: JB Lippincott Company.

Pollitt, C. (1988). Bringing Consumers into Performance Measurement: Concepts, Consequences and Constraints, *Policy and Politics*, 16, 77-87.

Pollitt, C. (1994). The Citizen's Charter: A Preliminary Analysis, *Public Money and Management*, April-June, 9-14.

Popay, J. (1992). 'My Health Is All Right, but I'm Just Tired All the Time': Women's Experience of Ill Health. *In* H. Roberts (ed.) (1992), *Women's Health Matters.* London: Routledge.

Pope, C. and Mays, N. (1995). Researching the parts other methods cannot reach: an introduction to qualitative methods in health and health services research, *British Medical Journal*, 311, 42-45.

Potter, J. (1988). Consumerism and the Public Sector: How Well Does the Coat Fit? *Public Administration*, 66, 149-64.

Pratt, M.W. and Norris, J.E. (1994). *The Social Psychology of Ageing.* Massachusetts, USA: Blackwell.

Qureshi, H. (1990). Social Support. *In* S.M. Peace (ed.) (1990), *Researching Social Gerontology: Concepts, Methods and Issues.* London: Sage Publications.

Ranade, W. (1994). *A Future for the NHS? Health Care in the 1990s.* Harlow: Longman Group UK Ltd.

Ranade, W. and Haywood, S. (1989). Privatising from within: The National Health Service under Thatcher, *Local Government Studies*, 15(4), 19-34.

Reid, I. (1977). *Social Class Differences in Britain.* London: Fontana.

Richardson, A. (1979). Thinking about Participation, *Policy and Politics*, 7 (3), 227-244.

Richardson, A. (1983). *Participation.* London: Routledge and Kegan Paul.

Richardson, A. and Goodman, M. (1983). *Self-help and social care: Mutual Aid Organisations in Practice.* London: Policy Studies Institute.

Roberts, C., Crosby, D., Dunn, R. and Evans, K. (1995). What Do We Mean By Care? *Health Service Journal*, March 30, 21.

Roberts, H. (ed.) (1990). *Women's Health Counts.* London: Routledge.

Robinson, R. (1991). Health Expenditure: Recent Trends and Prospects for the 1990s, *Public Money and Management*, Winter, 19-23.

Robinson, R. and Le Grand, J. (1995). Contracting and the Purchaser-Provider Split. *In* R.B. Saltman and C. von Otter (eds.) (1995), *Implementing Planned Markets in Health Care: Balancing Social and Economic Responsibility.* Buckingham: Open University Press.

Robson, C. (1993). *Real World Research: A Resource for Social Scientists and Practitioner-Researchers.* Oxford: Blackwell.

Rodgers, W.L. and Herzog, A.R. (1987). Interviewing Older Adults: The Accuracy of Factual Information, *Journal of Gerontology*, 42, 387-94.

Rogers, R. (1993). The Patient as a Consumer of Health Care. *In* S. Hinchliff, S. Norman and J. Schober (eds.) (1993), *Nursing Practice and Health Care.* London: Edward Arnold.

Rowntree, B.S. (1901). *Poverty: A Study of Town Life.* London: Macmillan.

Royal Commission on the Distribution of Income and Wealth (1978). *Report No.6 Lower Incomes.* London: HMSO.

Rush, M. (1981). *Parliamentary Government in Britain.* London: Pitman.

Rush, M. (1992). *Politics and Society: An Introduction to Political Sociology.* London: Prentice Hall.

Ruzek, S. (1986). Feminist Visions of Health: an international perspective. *In* J. Mitchell and A. Oakley (eds.) (1986), *What is Feminism?* Oxford: Basil Blackwell.

Ryan, M. (1994). Agency in Health Care: Lessons for Economists from Sociologists, *American Journal of Economics and Sociology*, 53 (2), 207-17.

Saltman, R.B. and von Otter, C. (eds.) (1995). *Implementing Planned Markets in Health Care: Balancing Social and Economic Responsibility.* Buckingham: Open University Press.

Saunders, P. (1995). Encouraging patients to take a part in their own care, *Nursing Times*, 91 (9), 42-43.

Saunders, P. and Harris, C. (1990). Privatization and the Consumer, *Sociology*, 24(1), 57-75.

Schumpter, J.A. (1976). *Capitalism, Socialism and Democracy.* London: George Allen and Unwin Ltd.

Scrivens, E. (1992). Choosing choice in social welfare. *In* N. Manning and R. Page (eds.) (1992), *Social Policy Review 4.* London: Social Policy Association.

Seaman, C.H.C. (1987). *Research Methods: Principles, Practice and Theory for Nursing.* Connecticut: Appleton and Lange.

Sefton Health (1995). *Continuing Health Care Policy Document.* Sefton: Sefton Health.

Shackley, P. and Ryan, M. (1994). What Is the Role of the Consumer in Health Care? *Journal of Social Policy*, 23, 517-41.

Sherman, H.J and Wood, J.L. (1979). *Sociology: Traditional and Radical Perspectives.* New York: Harper and Row.

Siltanen, J. (1994). *Locating Gender: Occupational Segregation, Wages and Domestic Responsibilities.* London: UCL Press.

Silverman, D. (1993). *Interpreting Qualitative Data: Methods for Analysing Talk, Text and Interaction.* London: Sage Publications.

Sinclair, I. (1990). Residential Care. *In* I. Sinclair, R. Parker, D. Leat and J. Williams (eds.) (1990), *The Kaleidoscope of Care: A Review of Research on Welfare Provision for Elderly People.* London: HMSO.

Sitzia, J. and Wood, N. (1997). Patient Satisfaction: A Review of Issues and Concepts, *Social Science and Medicine*, 45 (12), 1829-1843.

Skelcher, C. (1996). Public Service Consumerism: Some Questions of Strategy, *Community Development Journal*, 31, 66-72.

Smee, C.H. (1995). Self-governing Trusts and GP Fundholders: The British Experience. *In* R.B. Saltman and C. von Otter (eds.) (1995), *Implementing Planned Markets in Health Care: balancing social and economic responsibility.* Buckingham: Open University Press.

Social Services Committee (1990). *Community Care: Choice for Service Users.* London: HMSO.

Social Services Inspectorate (1991). *Assessment Systems and Community Care.* London: HMSO.

SPSS (1994). *SPSS Training: Introduction to Statistics.* Woking: SPSS (UK) Ltd.

Stacey, M. (1988). *The Sociology of Health and Healing.* London: Unwin Hyman.

Stewart, J. and Clarke, M. (1987). The Public Service Orientation and the Citizen, *Local Government Policy Making*, 14 (1), 34.

Stewart, M. and Roter, D. (1989). Introduction. *In* M. Stewart and D. Roter (eds.) (1989), *Communicating With Medical Patients.* Newbury Park: Sage Publications.

Strauss, A.L. (1987). *Qualitative Analysis for Social Scientists.* Cambridge: Cambridge University Press.

Street, R. (1991). Information-giving in Medical Consultations: the influence of Patients' Communicative Styles and Personal Characteristics, *Social Science and Medicine*, 32, 541-548.

Strull, W.M., Lo, B. and Charles, G. (1984). Do patients want to participate in medical decision making? *Journal of the American Medical Association*, 252 (21), 2990-2994.

Symonds, A. (1991). *The Patient As Consumer*. Swansea: University College of Swansea.

Szasz, T.S. and Hollender, M.H. (1956). A Contribution to the Philosophy of Medicine, *AMA Archives of Internal Medicine*, 97, 585-92.

Taylor, P. and Walker, A. (1995). Utilising Older Workers, *Employment Gazette*, April, 141-45.

Taylor, R. (1988). The Elderly as Members of Society: An Examination of Social Differences in an Elderly Population. *In* N. Wells and C. Freer (eds.) (1988), *The Ageing Population: Burden or Challenge?* London: Macmillan.

Taylor, R. and Ford, G. (1993). Inequalities in Old Age, *Ageing and Society*, 3, 183-208.

The Labour Party (1997). *New Labour: Because Britain Deserves Better*. London: The Labour Party.

Thompson, S.G., Pitts, J.S. and Schwantovsky, L. (1992). Preferences for involvement in medical decision-making: situational and demographic influence, *Patient Education and Counselling*, 22, 133-140.

Thomson, P. (1992). Public Sector Management in a Period of Radical Change: 1979-1992, *Public Money and Management*, September-July, 33-41.

Tierney, A. and Closs, J. (1993). Discharge Planning for Elderly Patients, *Nursing Standard*, 7, 52, 30-33.

Tillsley, C. (1995). Older Workers: Findings from the 1994 Labour Force Survey, *Employment Gazette*, April, 133-40.

Tinker, A. (1997). *Elderly People in Modern Society*. London: Longman.

Tinker, A., McCreadie, C., Wright, F. and Salvage, A.V. (1994). *The Care of Frail Elderly People in the United Kingdom*. London: HMSO.

Titmuss, R.M. (1969). The Culture of Medical Care and Consumer Behaviour. *In* F.N.L. Poynter (ed.) (1969), *Medicine and Culture*. London: Wellcome.

Touraine, A. (1981). *The Voice and the Eye. An Analysis of Social Movements*. Cambridge: Cambridge University Press.

Townsend, P. (1979). *Poverty in the UK: a study of household resources and standards of living*. Harmondsworth: Penguin.

Townsend, P. (1981). The Structured Dependency of the Elderly: A Creation of Social Policy in the Twentieth Century, *Ageing and Society*, 1, 5-28.

Townsend, P. (1986). Ageism and Social Policy. *In* C. Phillipson and A. Walker (eds.) (1986), *Ageing and Social Policy*. Aldershot: Gower.

Townsend, P. and Davidson, N. (1982). *Inequalities in Health*. Harmondsworth: Penguin.

Tritter, J. (1994). The Citizen's Charter: Opportunities for Users' Perspectives? *The Political Quarterly*, 65 (4), 397-414.

Turner, B.S. (1987). *Medical Power and Social Knowledge*. London: Sage.

Vaux, A. (1985). Variations in Social Support associated with Gender, Ethnicity and Age, *Journal of Social Issues*, 41 (1), 89-110.

Verba, S., Nie, N.H. and Kim, J. (1978). *Participation and Political Equality*. Cambridge: Cambridge University Press.

Vickridge, R. (1995). NHS Reforms and Community Care – means-tested health care masquerading as consumer choice? *Critical Social Policy*, 15 (1), 76-80.

Victor, C.R. (1989). Inequalities in Health in Later Life, *Age and Ageing*, 18, 387-91.

Victor, C.R. (1994). *Old Age in Modern Society*. 2nd ed. London: Chapman and Hall.

Victor, C.R. and Vetter, N.J. (1986). Poverty, Disability and Use of Services by the Elderly: Analysis of the 1980 General Household Survey, *Social Science and Medicine*, 22, 1087-91.

Victor, C.R. and Vetter, N.J. (1988). Preparing the elderly for discharge from hospital: a neglected aspect of patient care? *Age and Ageing*, 17, 155-163.

Walby, S. and Greenwell, J. (1994). Managing the National Health Service. *In* J. Clarke, A. Cochrane and E. McLoughlin (eds.) (1994), *Managing Social Policy*. London: Sage Publications.

Walker, A. (1980). The Social Creation of Poverty and Dependence in Old Age, *Journal of Social Policy*, 9, 49-75.

Walker, A. (1981). Towards a Political Economy of Old Age, *Ageing and Society*, 1, 73-94.

Walker, A. (1982). Dependency and Old Age, *Social Policy and Administration*, 16 (2), 115-35.

Walker, A. (1992). The Poor Relation: Poverty Among Older Women. *In* C. Glendinning and J. Millar (eds.) (1992), *Women and Poverty in Britain the 1990s*. London: Harvester Wheatsheaf.

Walker, A. (1993). A Cultural Revolution? Shifting the UK's Welfare Mix in the Care of Older People. *In* A. Evans and I. Svetlik (eds.) (1993), *Balancing Pluralism: New Welfare Mixes in Care for the Elderly*. Aldershot: Avebury.

Ward, D. and Mullender, A. (1993). Empowerment and Oppression: An Indissoluble Pairing for Contemporary Social Work, *In* J. Walmsley, J. Reynolds, P. Shakespeare and R. Woolfe (eds.) (1993), *Health, Welfare and Practice: Reflecting on Roles and Relationships*. London: Sage Publications.

Warnes, A.M. (1993). Being Old, Old People and the Burdens of Burden, *Ageing and Society*, 13, 297-338.

Waters, K.R. (1987). Discharge Planning: an exploratory study of the process of discharge planning on geriatric wards, *Journal of Advanced Nursing*, 12, 71-83.

Watkins, S. (1987). *Medicine and Labour: The Politics of a Profession*. London: Lawrence and Wishart.

Weinholtz, D., Kacer, B. and Rocklin, T. (1995). Salvaging Quantitative Research With Qualitative Data, *Qualitative Health Research*, 5 (3), 388-97.

Wells, N. (1992). Responses to changes in demography and patterns of disease. *In* E. Beck, S. Lonsdale, S. Newman and D. Patterson (eds.) (1992), *In the Best of Health?: The status and future of helath care in the UK*. London: Chapman and Hall.

Wells, N. and Freer, C. (1988). Conclusion. *In* N. Wells and C. Freer (eds.) (1988), *The Ageing Population: Burden or Challenge?* London: The Macmillan Press Ltd.

Wenger, C., Davies, R., Shahtahmasebi, S. and Scott, A. (1996). Social Isolation and Loneliness in Old Age: Review and Model Refinement, *Ageing and Society*, 16, 333-358.

Whitehead, M. (1987). *The Health Divide. Inequalities in Health in the 1980s*. London: The Health Education Authority.

Whitehead, M. (1994). Is it Fair? Evaluating the equity implications of the NHS reforms, *In* R. Robinson and J. Le Grand (eds.) (1994), *Evaluating the NHS Reforms*. London: King's Fund Institute.

Whitting, G., Moore, J. and Tilson, B. (1995). Employment Policies and Practices Towards Older Workers: An International Overview, *Employment Gazette*, April, 147-52.

Wilding, P. (1992). The British Welfare State: Thatcherism's enduring legacy, *Policy and Politics*, 20 (3), 201-212.

Wiles, R. (1993). Consumer Involvement in Outcomes Measurement – What Are the Barriers? *Public Health*, 4, 35-40.

Wilkinson, R. (1996). *Unhealthy Societies: The Afflictions of Inequality*. London: Routledge.

Williams, A. (1988). Priority setting in public and private health care, a guide through the methodological jungle, *Journal of Health Economics*, 7, 173-183.

Williams, A. (1997). The Rationing Debate. Rationing Health Care by Age: the case for, *British Medical Journal*, 314, 822-825.

Williams, B. (1994). Patient Satisfaction: A Valid Concept? *Social Science and Medicine*, 38, 509-16.

Williams, F. (1989). *Social Policy: A Critical Introduction: Issues of Race, Gender and Class*. Cambridge: Polity Press.

Williams, F. (1993). Gender, 'Race' and Class in British Welfare Policy. *In* A. Cochrane and J. Clarke (eds.) (1993), *Comparing Welfare States: Britain in International Context*. London: Sage Publications.

Williams, J. (1993). What is a profession? Experience versus Expertise, *In* J. Walmsley, J. Reynolds, P. Shakespeare and R. Woolfe (eds.) (1993), *Health, Welfare and Practice: Reflecting on Roles and Relationships*. London: Sage Publications.

Wilson, G. (1991). Models of Ageing and Their Relation to Policy Formation and Service Provision, *Policy and Politics*, 19, 37-47.

Wilson, G. (1993). Money and Independence in Old Age. *In* S. Arber and M. Evandrou (eds.) (1993), *Ageing, Independence and the Life Course*. London: Jessica Kingsley Publishers Ltd.

Wilson, G. (1994). Assembling their own care packages: payments for care by men and women in advanced old age, *Health and Social Care in the Community*, 2 (5), 283-291.

Winkler, F. (1987). Consumerism in Health Care: Beyond the Supermarket Model. *Policy and Politics*, 15, 1-8.

Winkler, F. (1990). Consumerism and Information. *In* L. Winn (ed.) (1990), *Power to the People: The Key to Responsive Services in Health and Social Care*. London: King's Fund Centre.

Wistow, G. (1995). Paying for Long-Term Care: The Shifting Boundary between Health and Social Care, *Community Care Management and Planning*, 3 (3), 82-89.

Wistow, G., Knapp, M., Hardy, B. and Allen, C. (1992). From Providing to Enabling: Local Authorities and the Mixed Economy of Social Care, *Public Administration*, 70, 25-45.

Wistow, G., Knapp, M., Hardy, B. and Allen, C. (1994). *Social Care in a Mixed Economy*. Buckingham: Open University Press.

Wistow, G., Knapp, M., Hardy, B., Forder, J., Kendall, J. and Manning, R. (1996). *Social Care Markets: Progress and Prospects*. Buckingham: Open University Press.

Wood, J. (1984). Patient Participation in General Practice. *In* R. Maxwell and N. Weaver (eds.) (1984), *Public Participation in Health*. London: King's Fund.

Yin, R.K. (1984). *Case Study Research: Design and Methods*. London: Sage Publications.

Young, K. (1991). Consumer-centred approaches in the Public/Voluntary/Personal Services, *Public Money and Management*, Summer, 33-39.

Young, R.F. and Olson, E.A. (1991). Health, Illness and Disability in Later Life: Concerns for Practitioners. *In* R.F. Young and E.A. Olson (eds.) (1991), *Health, Illness and Disability in Later Life: Practical Issues and Interventions*. London: Sage Publications.

Young, S. (1986). The nature of privatisation in Britain 1979-85, *West European Politics*, 9, 235-252.

*For Product Safety Concerns and Information please contact
our EU representative GPSR@taylorandfrancis.com Taylor & Francis
Verlag GmbH, Kaufingerstraße 24, 80331 München, Germany*